Second Edition

A Guide to
the SQL Standard

A user's guide to
the standard relational language SQL

C. J. Date

Codd and Date International

ADDISON-WESLEY PUBLISHING COMPANY

Reading, Massachusetts • Menlo Park, California • New York •
Don Mills, Ontario • Wokingham, England • Amsterdam • Bonn •
Sydney • Singapore • Tokyo • Madrid • San Juan

It is only fitting to dedicate this book to
the many people responsible, directly or indirectly,
for the rise of SQL to its present preeminent position—
the original SQL language designers in IBM,
the implementers of the IBM prototype System R
and the principal IBM products (DB2 and SQL/DS)
derived from that prototype,
and the ANSI and ISO SQL standards committees.
I hope this book does justice to their efforts.

Library of Congress Cataloging-in-Publication Data

Date, C. J.
  A guide to the SQL standard / C. J. Date.—2nd ed.
    p. cm.
  Bibliography: p.
  Includes index.
  ISBN 0-201-50209-7
  1. Data base management. 2. SQL (Computer program language)
I. Title.
QA76.9.D3D3695 1989
005.75′6—dc19   89-30694
                                                         CIP

ABCDEFGHIJ–DO–89

Preface to the First Edition

The purpose of this book is to describe the relational database language SQL. SQL has been adopted as an official standard in the United States by the American National Standards Institute (ANSI) and as an international standard by the International Standards Organization (ISO). Also, numerous SQL-based products are already available in the marketplace (nearly 100 of them at the last count), and several others are rumored to be in the pipeline. There can thus be absolutely no question that, at least from a commercial point of view, SQL represents an extremely important development in the database world—which is of course the principal justification for the present book.

Now, some readers may be aware that I have already discussed the SQL language at considerable length in several other books, including the following in particular:*

- *A Guide to INGRES* (Addison-Wesley, 1987)
- *A Guide to DB2* (Addison-Wesley, 2nd edition, 1988)
- *A Guide to SQL/DS* (Addison-Wesley, 1988)

Thus, I am very conscious that I may be accused of writing the same book over and over again "until I get it right." However, the treatment of SQL in the present book differs from that in those other books in a number of significant ways:

---

*The second and third of these were written with a coauthor, Colin White. Colin also has a related book in production, *A Guide to ORACLE,* due to be published by Addison-Wesley in the near future.

- The emphasis is on the official standard version of SQL instead of on one of the implemented dialects. The book should thus be relevant to *anyone* interested in the SQL language and SQL implementations—not just those from "the IBM world," which is where SQL originated, but also those with an interest in SQL implementations for, e.g., DEC, Data General, Honeywell, ICL, . . . and other environments.

- The emphasis in the standard on the use of SQL for *programmed* (as opposed to interactive) access to the database has many ramifications and repercussions on the way the book is structured and the way the material is presented. In some ways the discussions are almost the reverse of what they were in those other books; those books concentrated primarily on interactive SQL and discussed programming SQL at the end, almost as an afterthought. The present book, by contrast, necessarily deals almost exclusively with the use of SQL in application programs.

- The treatment is more thorough. All aspects of the language are discussed in detail. In the other books, by contrast, I was not aiming at any such completeness, and it was expedient to simplify and/or ignore certain aspects of the language.

- At the same time, the book is (I hope) more "user-friendly" than the official SQL standard, in that it includes a more tutorial treatment of the material. The official standard is not very easy to read—partly because it necessarily reflects the structure of the SQL language itself, which in some ways is very ill-structured (despite the fact that the "S" in SQL stands for "Structured"!), and partly also because it tends to present the language bottom up instead of top down.

- It follows from the previous two paragraphs that the book is intended both as a work of reference and as a tutorial guide; it includes both formal definitions and numerous worked examples. However, I must make it very clear that the book is not intended to replace the official standard document but to complement it.

- The book also includes a discussion of the differences between the standard version of SQL and the IBM version supported by the IBM product DB2, an examination of the official proposed extensions to the standard known as SQL2, an annotated SQL critique, an annotated bibliography, and other relevant items.

- Finally, the book also includes numerous comments on (and criticisms of) the standard. Such material is set off by "Comment" and "End of comment" delimiters, in order to be readily distinguishable from the body of the text.

The book consists of twelve chapters and a set of appendixes. The twelve chapters fall into three broad groups, as follows:

1. Introductory (Chapters 1–3)
2. The standard in detail (Chapters 4–11)
3. Proposed extensions (Chapter 12)

Most of the examples are based on the familiar suppliers-and-parts database (see Chapter 2). I make no apology for using this old warhorse still one more time; basing the examples on such a familiar database should (I hope) make it easy for the reader to relate to those examples, and should also facilitate comparisons between the standard version of SQL and specific vendor implementations—in particular, the implementations described in the books mentioned above (*A Guide to DB2, A Guide to INGRES,* and the rest). In some respects, in fact, the book can be seen as a complement to those other books.

The book is intended to be reasonably self-contained. The only background assumed of the reader is a general interest in the SQL language. All relevant terms and concepts are defined and explained as they are introduced.

ACKNOWLEDGMENTS

As usual, I am delighted to acknowledge my debt to the many people involved, directly or indirectly, in the production of this book. First, it is a pleasure to acknowledge my gratitude to Phil Shaw, the IBM representative to the ANSI Database Committee, for his patience and assistance with my numerous technical questions. Second, I am pleased to be able to thank my reviewers Randell Flint, Carol Joyce, Geoff Sharman, and Phil Shaw (again) for their many helpful comments on the manuscript. Third, I am deeply indebted to my long-suffering family and to numerous friends and colleagues for their support throughout this project. Last, I am (as always) grateful to my editor, Elydia Davis, and to the staff at Addison-Wesley for their assistance and their continually high standards of professionalism. It has been (as always) a pleasure to work with them.

Saratoga, California   C. J. Date

Preface to the Second Edition

Since the first edition of this book was published, several major events have occurred in the SQL world:

1. The original American (ANSI) SQL standard has been adopted as an international (ISO) standard and, in the United States, as a Federal Information Processing Standard (FIPS).

2. An *Integrity Enhancement Feature* (IEF) has been defined as a major extension to the original ANSI/ISO standard.

3. The ANSI and ISO standards committees have published a series of documents describing a voluminous set of proposals for future extensions to the standard.

4. The number of SQL implementations has grown by leaps and bounds (it has more than doubled in about two years).

5. In particular, IBM has produced several new releases of its DB2 and SQL/DS products (with very significant new SQL function), and has also introduced SQL products for the OS/2 and OS/400 environments.

6. Another standards committee, X/OPEN, has adopted a version of SQL as a standard for the UNIX environment.

7. Yet another version of SQL has been adopted by IBM as the database language component of its own Systems Application Architecture (SAA) standard.

All of these developments either have already had, or are likely soon to have, a significant effect on the existing standard. It therefore seems appropriate to upgrade this book to reflect these new developments; hence this new edition. Of course, I have also taken the opportunity to correct a few errors in the previous edition and to improve the presentation in many places.

ACKNOWLEDGMENTS

Once again, I am delighted to acknowledge my debt to the many people involved in the production of this book. In particular, I would like to thank three members of the ANSI/X3H2 committee—Lynn Francis of American Bankers Association, Carol Joyce of Relational Technology, and Phil Shaw of IBM—for their help with various technical and procedural questions. I would also like to acknowledge the many attendees at seminars and presentations (too numerous to mention individually) who have offered constructive comments on the first edition. In addition, of course, I remain indebted to everyone who helped with that first edition—my family, various friends and colleagues, and (last but not least) my editor, Elydia Davis, and the staff at Addison-Wesley.

Saratoga, California   C. J. Date

A NOTE ON EMBEDDED SQL

Most SQL application programs in existence today use the well-known "embedded SQL" feature, by which SQL statements can be incorporated directly into the source text of programs written in host languages such as COBOL and PL/I. Strictly speaking, however, that embedded SQL feature is not actually part of the official standard. Instead, the standard defines a mechanism by which host language programs can invoke SQL procedures written in a separate "module language" (see Chapters 3 and 6 of this book). The embedded SQL facility is described in a set of "annexes" (i.e., appendixes) to the official standard.

As this book was going to press, however, the American National Standards Institute (ANSI) approved the embedded SQL feature as a new (distinct) American National Standard, "Database Language Extended SQL." That new standard includes specifications for embedding SQL statements in programs written in any of the following languages: Ada, C, COBOL, FORTRAN, Pascal, and PL/I (note that Ada and C have been added to the original set; "ADA" and "C" are now included in the list of SQL key words). From a pragmatic point of view, this change is perhaps not very significant, except that henceforth embedded SQL *should* be regarded as part of "official ANSI SQL." The discussions of this book should be interpreted accordingly.

Contents

1

Why SQL Is Important

1.1 BACKGROUND

The name "SQL"—the official pronunciation is "ess-cue-ell," but most people usually pronounce it "sequel"—was originally an abbreviation for "Structured Query Language." The SQL language consists of a set of facilities for defining, manipulating, and controlling data in a relational database. In order to understand why the language has become so widespread and so generally important, it is helpful to have an appreciation of some of the major developments in database technology over the past eighteen or so years. We therefore begin by summarizing those developments.

1. In 1970, E. F. Codd, at that time a member of the IBM Research Laboratory in San Jose, California, published a now classic paper, "A Relational Model of Data for Large Shared Data Banks" (*Communications of the ACM*, Vol. 13, No. 6, June 1970), in which he laid down a set of abstract principles for database management: the so-called *relational model*. The entire field of relational database technology has its origins in that paper. Codd's ideas led directly to a great deal of experimentation and research in universities, industrial research laboratories, and similar establishments, and that activity in turn led to the numerous relational products now available in the marketplace. The many advantages of the relational approach are far too well known to need repeating here; see, e.g., any of the books *A*

1

Guide to DB2 (Addison-Wesley, 3rd edition, 1989) or *A Guide to INGRES* (Addison-Wesley, 1987) or *A Guide to SQL/DS* (Addison-Wesley, 1988) for a discussion of those advantages.

2. One particular aspect of the research just referred to was the design and prototype implementation of a variety of relational languages. A relational language is a language that realizes, in some concrete syntactic form, some or all of the features of the abstract relational model. Several such languages were created in the early and mid 1970s. One such language in particular was the "Structured English Query Language" (SEQUEL), defined by D. D. Chamberlin and others at the IBM San Jose Research Laboratory (1974) and first implemented in an IBM prototype called SEQUEL-XRM (1974–75).

3. Partly as a result of experience with SEQUEL-XRM, a revised version of SEQUEL called SEQUEL/2 was defined in 1976–77. (The name was subsequently changed to SQL for legal reasons.) Work began on another, more ambitious, IBM prototype called System R. System R, an implementation of a large subset of the SEQUEL/2 (or SQL) language, became operational in 1977 and was subsequently installed in a number of user sites, both internal IBM sites and also (under a set of joint study agreements) selected IBM customer sites. *Note:* A number of further changes were made to the SQL language during the lifetime of the System R project, partly in response to user suggestions; for instance, an EXISTS function was added to test whether some specified data existed in the database.

4. Thanks in large part to the success of System R, it became generally apparent in the late 1970s that sooner or later IBM would develop one or more commercial products based on the System R technology—specifically, products that implemented the SQL language. As a result, other vendors did not wait for IBM but began to construct their own SQL-based products. (In fact, at least one such product, namely ORACLE from Relational Software Inc.—subsequently renamed Oracle Corporation—was actually introduced to the market prior to IBM's own products.) Then, in 1981, IBM did announce a SQL product, namely SQL/DS, for the DOS/VSE environment. IBM then followed that announcement with one for a VM/CMS version of SQL/DS (1982), and another for an MVS product called DB2 that was broadly compatible with SQL/DS (1983).

5. Over the next several years, numerous other vendors also announced SQL-based products. Those announcements included both entirely new products such as DG/SQL (Data General Corporation, 1984) and SYBASE (Sybase Inc., 1986), and SQL interfaces to established products such as INGRES (Relational Technology Inc., 1981, 1985) and the IDM (Britton-Lee Inc., 1982, 1985). There are now (late 1988) nearly 100 products in the

marketplace that support some dialect of SQL, running on machines that range all the way from quite small micros to the largest mainframes. *SQL has become the de facto standard in the relational database world.*

6. SQL has also become an *official* standard. In 1982, the American National Standards Institute (ANSI) chartered its Database Committee (X3H2) to develop a proposal for a standard relational language. The X3H2 proposal, which was finally ratified by ANSI in 1986, consisted essentially of the IBM dialect of SQL, "warts and all" (except that a few—in this writer's opinion, far too few—minor IBM idiosyncrasies were removed). And in 1987, the ANSI standard was also accepted as an international standard by the International Standards Organization (ISO).

The foregoing is not the end of the story, of course. As explained in the preface to this book (second edition), various versions of SQL have subsequently been adopted as

- an X/OPEN standard (for UNIX systems)
- an SAA standard (for IBM systems)
- a Federal Information Processing Standard (for US Federal Government systems)

In this book we are concerned primarily with the ANSI/ISO version of SQL, which is the version that is usually meant when people refer to "the SQL standard." From this point forward, therefore, we will take the unqualified name "SQL" (also terms such as "standard SQL," "the standard," "the official standard," etc.) to refer to that version. When we need to refer to some specific dialect other than the ANSI/ISO version, we will always use an appropriately qualified name, such as "DB2 SQL" or "X/OPEN SQL" or "SAA SQL" (etc.).

In many ways, the existing standard is not particularly useful in itself; it has been characterized, perhaps a little unkindly, as "the intersection of existing implementations,"* and as such is severely deficient in a number of respects (see Section 1.2). Recognizing this fact, the ANSI and ISO committees are currently at work on a set of proposed extensions to the base standard. We will discuss some of those extensions in this book—but the reader is cautioned that they *are* only proposed extensions and are not (yet) part of the official standard, and hence are subject to possible change.

---

*More accurately, this description refers to "Level 1" of the standard (see Appendix C). But the comment does highlight a general criticism, which is that the SQL standard, at least in its present form, does seem more concerned with protecting existing vendor implementations than with establishing a truly solid foundation for the future.

Following on from the previous point: It is only fair to stress the fact that, while (as already stated) there are nearly 100 SQL implementations available today, it is virtually certain that no two of those implementations are precisely identical, and none of them is precisely identical to standard SQL! Even the IBM implementations in SQL/DS and DB2 are not 100 percent compatible with one another, and each of them differs from System R SQL and also from standard SQL on numerous points of detail—not all of them trivial, incidentally. (This state of affairs may possibly change with time, of course.) As explained above, we are primarily concerned in this book with standard SQL specifically (for the most part); however, we will also mention certain major deviations from the standard. In particular, we will indicate where IBM (in the shape of DB2, and sometimes SQL/DS) supports some significant feature that standard SQL does not, and vice versa (see Appendix E for a summary of such differences).

One final point of a historical nature: The original version of SQL was intended for standalone, interactive use. However, facilities were added later to allow the invocation of SQL operations from an application programming language such as COBOL or PL/I. By contrast, the SQL standard concentrates almost exclusively on those latter (application programming) facilities, presumably on the grounds that standardization is much more significant for portability of programs than it is for interactive interfaces. This emphasis is reflected in the structure of the present book, as will be seen.

1.2   IS A STANDARD DESIRABLE?

Before going any further, we should perhaps consider the question of whether a SQL standard is a good thing. On the one hand, the advantages are fairly obvious:

- *Reduced training costs:* Application developers can move from one environment to another without the need for expensive retraining.

- *Application portability:* Applications—in particular, applications developed by third-party software vendors—can run unchanged in a variety of different hardware and software environments. Applications can be developed in one environment (e.g., on a PC) and then run in another (e.g., on a large mainframe).*

---

*A word of caution is in order here. SQL is only a *database* language, not a complete programming language; thus, a typical application will involve, not only SQL statements, but also statements in some host language such as COBOL. The portability of such an application will therefore obviously depend on the portability of the host language as well as on that of SQL.

- *Application longevity:* Standard languages are assured of a reasonably long lifetime. Applications developed using such languages can therefore be assured of a reasonably long lifetime also.

- *Cross-system communication:* Different systems can more easily communicate with one another. In particular, different database management systems might be able to function as equal partners in a single distributed database system if they all support the same standard interface (a consideration that is becoming increasingly important in the commercial world, incidentally).

- *Customer choice:* If all systems support the same interface, customers can concentrate on the problem of choosing the implementation that best meets their own particular needs, without having to get involved in the additional complexity of choosing among different interfaces (possibly widely different interfaces).

On the other hand, there are some significant disadvantages also:

- *A standard can stifle creativity:* Implementers may effectively be prevented from providing "the best" (or a good) solution to some problem because the standard already prescribes some alternative, less satisfactory, solution to that same problem.

- *SQL in particular is very far from ideal as a relational language:* This criticism is elaborated in Appendix F. To quote from that appendix: ". . . it cannot be denied that SQL in its present form leaves rather a lot to be desired—even that, in some important respects, it fails to realize the full potential of the relational model." The basic problem (in this writer's opinion) is that, although there are well-established principles for the design of formal languages, there is little evidence that SQL was ever designed in accordance with any such principles. As a result, the language is filled with numerous restrictions, ad hoc constructs, and annoying special rules. These factors in turn make the language hard to define, describe, teach, learn, remember, apply, and implement.

- *Standard SQL especially is severely deficient in several respects:* In addition to the deficiencies mentioned under the previous point (i.e., deficiencies that are intrinsic to the original SQL language per se), standard SQL in particular suffers from certain additional deficiencies. Specifically, it fails to include any support at all for several functions that are clearly needed in practice (e.g., the DROP TABLE function), and it leaves as "implementation-defined" certain aspects that would be much better spelled out as part of the standard (e.g., the effect of certain operations on cursor position). As a result, it seems likely that every realistic implementation of the standard will necessarily include many implementation-defined extensions and variations, and hence that no two "standard" SQL implementations will ever be truly identical.

Despite these drawbacks, however, the fact is that the standard exists, vendors are scrambling to support it, and customers are demanding such support. Hence this book.

2

An Overview of SQL

2.1 INTRODUCTION

The aim of this chapter is to present a brief and very informal introduction to some of the major facilities of standard SQL, and thereby to pave the way for an understanding of the more formal and thorough treatment of the language in subsequent chapters. The chapter is loosely based on Chapter 1 ("Relational Database: An Overview") from the author's book *Relational Database: Selected Writings* (Addison-Wesley, 1986).

The function of the SQL language is to support the definition, manipulation, and control of data in a relational database. A *relational database* is simply a database that is perceived by the user as a collection of *tables*—where a table is *an unordered collection of rows* ("relation" is just a mathematical term for such a table). An example, the suppliers-and-parts database, is shown in Fig. 2.1. Tables S, P, and SP in that figure represent, respectively, suppliers, parts, and shipments of parts by suppliers. Note that each table can be thought of as a *file*, with the rows representing records and the columns fields. The SQL standard always uses the terms "row" and "column," however, never "record" and "field," and in this book we will therefore generally do likewise.

SQL "data manipulation" statements—i.e., SQL statements that perform data retrieval or updating functions—can be invoked either interactively or from within an application program. Fig. 2.2 illustrates both cases;

S	SNO	SNAME	STATUS	CITY
	S1	Smith	20	London
	S2	Jones	10	Paris
	S3	Blake	30	Paris
	S4	Clark	20	London
	S5	Adams	30	Athens

P	PNO	PNAME	COLOR	WEIGHT	CITY
	P1	Nut	Red	12	London
	P2	Bolt	Green	17	Paris
	P3	Screw	Blue	17	Rome
	P4	Screw	Red	14	London
	P5	Cam	Blue	12	Paris
	P6	Cog	Red	19	London

SP	SNO	PNO	QTY
	S1	P1	300
	S1	P2	200
	S1	P3	400
	S1	P4	200
	S1	P5	100
	S1	P6	100
	S2	P1	300
	S2	P2	400
	S3	P2	200
	S4	P2	200
	S4	P4	300
	S4	P5	400

Fig. 2.1 The suppliers-and-parts database (sample values)

it shows a data retrieval operation (SELECT in SQL) being used both (a) interactively and (b) from within a PL/I program. In general, interactive invocation means that the statement in question is executed from an interactive terminal and (in the case of retrieval) the result is displayed at that terminal. Invocation from within an application program means that the statement is executed as part of the process of executing that program and (in the case of retrieval) the result is fetched into an input area within that program (":SC" in Fig. 2.2(b)). *Note:* The syntactic style illustrated in Fig. 2.2 for invoking SQL from an application program is not the only one possible. See Chapter 3.

One further introductory remark: The reader will have noticed that we used qualified column names (S.SNO, S.CITY) in Fig. 2.2. SQL in fact allows qualifiers to be omitted in many contexts (including, in particular, the SELECT and WHERE clauses), provided no ambiguity can result from such omission. Thus, for example, the two SELECT clauses of Fig. 2.2

(a) *Interactive invocation:*

```
SELECT  S.CITY              Result:  CITY
FROM    S                            ------
WHERE   S.SNO = 'S4'                 London
```

(b) *Invocation from an application program (PL/I):*

```
EXEC SQL SELECT  S.CITY INTO :SC    Result:  SC
         FROM    S                           ------
         WHERE   S.SNO = 'S4' ;               London
```

Fig. 2.2 SQL retrieval example

could have been abbreviated to just "SELECT CITY" in each case. However, it is not wrong to include the qualifiers as we have done. In this book, for reasons of clarity and explicitness, we will generally use qualified names even when they are not strictly necessary—except, of course, in contexts where they are expressly prohibited. An example of a context in which qualified names are prohibited is the left-hand side of a SET clause assignment in an UPDATE statement (see Section 2.3).

2.2 DATA DEFINITION

Fig. 2.1, the suppliers-and-parts database, of course represents that database as it appears at some specific time. The corresponding database definition, or *schema*,* is shown in Fig. 2.3, which we explain (in outline) as follows:

- The clause AUTHORIZATION TED specifies that user TED is the creator of this schema.

- The three CREATE TABLE statements define three empty tables with the specified names and specified named columns (with specified data types).

```
CREATE SCHEMA AUTHORIZATION TED

CREATE TABLE S  ( SNO    CHAR(5)    NOT NULL,
                  SNAME  CHAR(20),
                  STATUS DECIMAL(3),
                  CITY   CHAR(15),
                  PRIMARY KEY ( SNO ) )

CREATE TABLE P  ( PNO    CHAR(6)    NOT NULL,
                  PNAME  CHAR(20),
                  COLOR  CHAR(6),
                  WEIGHT DECIMAL(3),
                  CITY   CHAR(15),
                  PRIMARY KEY ( PNO ) )

CREATE TABLE SP ( SNO    CHAR(5)    NOT NULL,
                  PNO    CHAR(6)    NOT NULL,
                  QTY    DECIMAL(5),
                  PRIMARY KEY ( SNO, PNO ),
                  FOREIGN KEY ( SNO ) REFERENCES S,
                  FOREIGN KEY ( PNO ) REFERENCES P )
```

Fig. 2.3 Schema definition example

---

*More accurately, a schema defines that piece of the database that is owned by some specific user. The complete database definition will typically consist of multiple schemas, not just one.

▪ Within table S, column SNO is defined to be the PRIMARY KEY (i.e.,
unique identifier); note that the primary key must be defined to be NOT
NULL. Similarly for column PNO in table P and the combination of
columns (SNO,PNO) in table SP.

▪ Within table SP, columns SNO and PNO are defined to be FOREIGN
KEYs, referencing tables S and P respectively. We defer an explanation
of foreign keys to Chapter 5.

Data can subsequently be entered into the tables via the SQL INSERT
statement, discussed in the next section. *Note:* We will be using this schema
as the basis for most of our examples throughout this book.

There are two kinds of tables that can be defined in a SQL schema: *base
tables* and *viewed tables* (usually referred to simply as *views*). The tables of
Fig. 2.3 are all base tables. A base table is a "real" table—i.e., a table that
physically exists, in the sense that there exist physical stored records, and
possibly physical access paths such as indexes, in one or more stored files,
that directly support that table in physical storage. By contrast, a view is a
"virtual" table—i.e., a table that does not exist in physical storage, but
looks to the user as if it did. Views are defined, in a manner to be explained
in Section 2.5, in terms of one or more underlying base tables.

Note: The foregoing paragraph should not be construed as meaning
that a base table is physically *stored* as a table—i.e., as a set of physically
adjacent stored records, with each record consisting simply of a direct copy
of a row of the base table. A base table is best thought of as an *abstraction*
of some set of stored data—an abstraction in which numerous storage-level
details (such as physical data location, physical ordering, stored value en-
codings, physical access paths, etc.) are concealed. Thus, there are typically
many differences between a base table and its storage representation. The
point is, however, that users can always *think* of base tables as "physically
existing," while not having to concern themselves with how those tables are
actually represented in storage. Views on the other hand do not "physically
exist" in this sense; views are merely a different way of looking at the data
in the base tables. Views are not represented by any separate, distinguishable, physically stored data of their own.

2.3 DATA MANIPULATION

There are four basic SQL data manipulation operations: SELECT,
INSERT, UPDATE, and DELETE. We have already given an example of
SELECT (two versions) in Fig. 2.2. Fig. 2.4 gives examples of the other
three operations—the so-called update operations.

```
INSERT                              Result: Specified row
INTO SP ( SNO, PNO, QTY )                   added to table SP
VALUES   ('S5','P1',1000 )

UPDATE S                            Result: STATUS doubled
SET    STATUS = 2 * S.STATUS                for suppliers in
WHERE  S.CITY = 'London'                    London (i.e., S1
                                            and S4)

DELETE                              Result: Rows deleted from
FROM   P                                    table P for parts
WHERE  P.WEIGHT > 15                        P2, P3, and P6
```

Fig. 2.4 Update examples

Note: The term "update" unfortunately has two meanings in SQL: It is used generically to refer to the three operations INSERT, UPDATE, and DELETE as a class, and also specifically to refer to the UPDATE operation per se. We will distinguish between the two meanings in this book by always using lower case when the generic meaning is intended and upper case when the specific meaning is intended.

Note that the UPDATE and DELETE operations of Fig. 2.4 operate on multiple rows each, not just on a single row. The same is true in general for INSERT operations (though the INSERT of Fig. 2.4 is actually single-row), and also for SELECT operations. In the case of SELECT, however, standard SQL does not permit a multiple-row SELECT operation to be executed directly (i.e., as a separate statement in its own right); instead, it is necessary to define a *cursor* having that SELECT operation as its "scope," and then to access the SELECTed rows one at a time by means of that cursor. For tutorial reasons, however, we defer discussion of cursors to Section 2.4, and assume for the time being that multiple-row SELECTs can indeed be executed directly. (Note that single-row SELECTs *can* be executed directly, as shown in Fig. 2.2.)

The SELECT operation has the general form "SELECT–FROM–WHERE," as illustrated in Fig. 2.5. (*Note:* The symbol "< >" in that figure stands for "not equals.") Observe that the result of the SELECT is another table (one that is derived from an existing table, not one that is stored in the database). Several points arise in connexion with this simple example:

- The result table is ordered in accordance with the ORDER BY clause. If DESC (descending) is not specified, ASC (ascending) order is assumed.

```
SELECT DISTINCT P.COLOR, P.CITY        Result:   COLOR    CITY
FROM    P                                        ------   ------
WHERE   P.WEIGHT > 10                              Red     London
AND     P.CITY <> 'Paris'                       ---Red-----London---
ORDER   BY P.COLOR DESC                          ---Red-----London---
                                                  Blue     Rome
```

(2nd and 3rd rows
eliminated if user
specifies DISTINCT)

Fig. 2.5   The basic "SELECT–FROM–WHERE"

- If the entire ORDER BY clause is omitted, the result appears in unspecified (implementation-defined) order.

- If the entire WHERE clause is omitted, all rows of the FROM table qualify.

- If DISTINCT is omitted, the result may contain duplicate rows (in the example, four rows will be returned if DISTINCT is omitted, two if it is included).

Join

One feature that, almost more than any other, distinguishes relational systems from nonrelational systems is the availability of the relational *join* operator. Loosely speaking, what this means is that it is possible to select data from two, three, four, . . . or any number of tables by means of a single SELECT operation. An example is given in Fig. 2.6 (the query is

```
     ---  ---  ---           ---        ------          ---  ------
SP   SNO  PNO  ...      S    SNO   ...   CITY           PNO  CITY
     ---  ---  ---           ---        ------          ---  ------
     S1   P1   ...           S1         London          P1   London
     S1   P2   ...    PLUS   S2         Paris     ==>    P2   London
      .    .    .            .           .               .    .
      .    .    .            .           .               .    .
      .    .    .                                         .    .
     S2   P1   ...                                       P1   Paris
      .    .    .                                         .    .

                      SELECT SP.PNO, S.CITY
                      FROM   SP, S
                      WHERE  SP.SNO = S.SNO
```

Fig. 2.6   Example involving join

"For each part supplied, retrieve part number and names of all cities in which there is located a supplier who supplies the part"). The term "join" arises from the fact that (in the example) tables SP and S are conceptually being *joined* on their common SNO column. Note that the references to columns S.SNO and SP.SNO in the WHERE clause *must* be qualified in this example, to avoid ambiguity.

Aggregate Functions

SQL provides a set of special builtin *aggregate functions:* COUNT, SUM, AVG, MAX, MIN, and COUNT (*) (the "*" refers to an entire row of the table concerned). Examples are given in Fig. 2.7. The last example also illustrates the GROUP BY clause, which is used to divide a table up (conceptually) into groups so that a function such as SUM can be applied to each individual group. Note, incidentally, that the first three examples are all single-row SELECTs.

		Result:
Number of suppliers:	`SELECT  COUNT(*)` `FROM    S`	5
Number of suppliers supplying parts:	`SELECT  COUNT ( DISTINCT SP.SNO )` `FROM    SP`	4

Total quantity of P2:	`SELECT  SUM ( SP.QTY )`
	`FROM    SP`
	`WHERE   SP.PNO = 'P2'`
		1000

		PNO	

Part number and total quantity for each part supplied:	`SELECT  PNO, SUM ( SP.QTY )`
	`FROM    SP`
	`GROUP   BY SP.PNO`
		P1
		P2
		P3
		P4
		P5
		P6
			600
			1000
			400
			500
			500
			100

Fig. 2.7 SQL aggregate function examples

2.4 CURSOR OPERATIONS

As mentioned in Section 2.3, multiple-row SELECT operations cannot be executed directly in standard SQL. The reason for this state of affairs is that the standard is primarily concerned with the use of SQL in conjunction with programming languages such as PL/I and COBOL, and such languages are generally not well equipped to deal with sets (consisting of multiple rows) as single operands. What is needed, therefore, is a mechanism for stepping through such a set and picking off the rows one by one; and *cursors* provide such a mechanism. A cursor is a SQL object that is associated (via an appropriate declaration) with a specific SELECT operation.* To access the rows corresponding to that SELECT, the user must:

(a) OPEN the cursor, which (conceptually) causes the SELECT to be executed, and hence identifies the corresponding set of rows;

(b) Use FETCH repeatedly on the opened cursor, which (on each execution) steps that cursor to the next row in the SELECTed set and retrieves that row; and finally

(c) CLOSE the cursor when all required rows have been processed.

Special forms of UPDATE and DELETE are also provided for updating or deleting the row on which the cursor is currently positioned. An example is given (in outline—many important details are omitted) in Fig. 2.8.

Note: As mentioned in Section 2.1, the SQL standard permits a variety of different methods for invoking SQL operations from an application program. Fig. 2.8 illustrates the commonest method, that of embedding SQL statements directly into the program source text. Embedded SQL statements must be prefixed with EXEC SQL, for ease of recognition. They

```
EXEC SQL DECLARE C1 CURSOR FOR
        SELECT SP.SNO, SP.QTY
        FROM   SP
        WHERE  SP.PNO = 'P2' ;

DECLARE X CHAR(5) ;
DECLARE Y FIXED DEC(5) ;
DECLARE Z FIXED DEC(3) ;

EXEC SQL OPEN C1 ;
DO for all rows accessible via cursor C1 ;
   EXEC SQL FETCH C1 INTO :X, :Y ;
   process X and Y ;
   EXEC SQL UPDATE SP
           SET    QTY = QTY + :Z
           WHERE  CURRENT OF C1 ;
END ;
EXEC SQL CLOSE C1 ;
```

Fig. 2.8 Example of the use of a cursor

---

*More accurately, with a specific "query expression." See Sections 7.2 and 10.1.

can include references to host language variables; such references must be prefixed with a colon (:), again for purposes of recognition. For more details, see Section 3.2 or Chapter 11. (In the interests of accuracy, however, we should mention that embedded SQL is strictly not part of the standard per se; rather, it is defined in an "annex" to the standard. This point notwithstanding, the fact remains that embedded SQL is—as suggested above—the form of interface most likely to be encountered in practice.)

2.5 VIEWS

Recall from Section 2.2 that a view (or "viewed table") is a *virtual* table—i.e., a table that does not "really exist" but looks to the user as if it did. Views are not directly supported by their own physically stored data; instead, their *definition* in terms of other tables (base tables and/or other views) is specified as part of the database definition. Fig. 2.9 shows the definition of a view called LS ("London suppliers").

```
CREATE VIEW LS ( SNO, SNAME, STATUS )
     AS SELECT S.SNO, S.SNAME, S.STATUS
        FROM    S
        WHERE   S.CITY = 'London'
```

Fig. 2.9 CREATE VIEW (example)

The view LS ("London suppliers") acts as a kind of *window*, through which the user can see the SNO, SNAME, and STATUS values (only) of rows in base table S for which the CITY value is London (only). The SELECT defining this view is *not* executed when the view is created but is merely remembered by the system in some way. But to the user it now appears as if a table called LS really does exist in the database. Fig. 2.10 shows an example of a retrieval against that table.

```
SELECT LS.SNO                  Result:  SNO
FROM    LS                              ---
WHERE   LS.STATUS < 50                  S1
                                        S4
```

Fig. 2.10 Retrieval against a view (example)

Operations against a view are handled (conceptually) by replacing references to the view by the view definition (i.e., by the SELECT operation that was remembered by the system). The system thus logically "merges"

the SELECT of Fig. 2.9 with the SELECT of Fig. 2.10 to give the modified
SELECT of Fig. 2.11.

```
                                        ---
   SELECT  S.SNO              Result:   SNO
   FROM    S                             ---
   WHERE   S.STATUS < 50                 S1
   AND     S.CITY = 'London'             S4
```

Fig. 2.11 Merged SELECT statement

The modified SELECT can now be executed in the normal way. In
other words, the original SELECT on the view is converted into an equivalent SELECT on the underlying base table. Update operations are handled
in a similar fashion; however, update operations on views are subject to a
number of restrictions, the details of which are beyond the scope of this
chapter. Simplifying matters somewhat, standard SQL allows a view to be
updated only if it represents a simple row-and-column subset of a single
underlying base table (for example, it is not a join). See Chapter 9 for more
details.

Two more examples of views (both nonupdatable) are shown in Fig.
2.12.

```
   CREATE  VIEW PQ ( PNO, SUMQTY )
       AS  SELECT SP.PNO, SUM ( SP.QTY )
           FROM    SP
           GROUP   BY SP.PNO

   CREATE  VIEW CITY_PAIRS ( SCITY, PCITY )
       AS  SELECT S.CITY, P.CITY
           FROM    S, SP, P
           WHERE   S.SNO = SP.SNO AND SP.PNO = P.PNO
```

Fig. 2.12 Additional view examples

2.6 DATA CONTROL

As mentioned in Section 2.1, SQL provides facilities for data control as
well as for data definition and data manipulation. The data control facilities
fall into three categories: (a) security, (b) integrity, and (c) recovery and
concurrency.

Security

There are two aspects to security in SQL, the view mechanism and the
GRANT operation. First, views can be used to hide sensitive data from

unauthorized users. Some examples of views that might be used in this way
are shown in Fig. 2.13. The first reveals information only for red parts; the
second reveals information only for parts that are supplied by the user of
the view; the third conceals supplier status information; and the fourth
gives average quantity per part, but no individual quantities. *Note:*
"SELECT *" is shorthand for a SELECT that names all columns of the
table—i.e., a SELECT that accesses the entire row (for all rows satisfying
the WHERE clause).

```
CREATE VIEW RED_PARTS AS
        SELECT * FROM P WHERE P.COLOR = 'Red'

CREATE VIEW MY_PARTS AS
        SELECT * FROM P WHERE P.PNO IN
                       ( SELECT SP.PNO FROM SP
                         WHERE  SP.SNO = USER )

CREATE VIEW STATUS_HIDDEN AS
        SELECT S.SNO, S.SNAME, S.CITY FROM S

CREATE VIEW AVG_QTYS ( PNO, AVGQTY ) AS
        SELECT SP.PNO, AVG ( SP.QTY ) FROM SP GROUP BY SP.PNO
```

Fig. 2.13 Using views to hide data (examples)

Second, the GRANT operation. To execute any SQL statement at all,
the user must hold the appropriate *privilege* for the combination of operation and operand concerned (otherwise the statement will be rejected). The
possible privileges are SELECT, UPDATE, DELETE, and INSERT (representing in each case the privilege to perform the indicated operation on
the table in question), also REFERENCES (see Chapters 4 and 5 for an
explanation of the REFERENCES privilege). In the case of UPDATE, the
privilege can be restricted to specific columns. Privileges are assigned as
follows:

- A user who creates a table is automatically granted all applicable privileges on that table, "with the grant option."

- Any user holding a privilege "with the grant option" can in turn grant
  that privilege to another user, and moreover can optionally pass the
  grant option on to that other user (so that that user in turn can go on
  to grant the privilege to a third party, and so on).

- Granting privileges is performed by means of the GRANT operation,
  which is specified as part of the database definition (i.e., in the
  schema).

Some examples of GRANT are shown in Fig. 2.14.

```
GRANT INSERT, DELETE, UPDATE ON SP TO JOE

GRANT SELECT ON SP TO ALICE WITH GRANT OPTION

GRANT UPDATE ( STATUS ) ON S TO JUDY

GRANT DELETE ON SP TO BONNIE, CLYDE
```

Fig. 2.14 GRANT examples

Integrity

The term "integrity" refers to the correctness of the data in the database. Standard SQL allows certain *database integrity constraints* to be defined (by means of appropriate specifications within the CREATE TABLE operation); any update that would violate any specified constraint is rejected, and the database remains unchanged. The possible constraints are as follows:

- NOT NULL: Can be specified for any column. Any attempt to introduce a null into such a column is rejected.

- CHECK: Can be specified for any column or combination of columns within a specified table. Any attempt to introduce a row into that table that violates the specified CHECK constraint is rejected.

- UNIQUE: Can be specified for any column or combination of columns within a specified table, provided NOT NULL is also specified for every column involved. Any attempt to introduce a row having the same value in the specified column or column combination as some existing row will be rejected.

- PRIMARY KEY: A special case of UNIQUE. See Chapter 5.

- FOREIGN KEY: Again, see Chapter 5.

- REFERENCES: An alternative way of specifying a foreign key. Once again, see Chapter 5.

For completeness, two further integrity features should also be mentioned here, data type checking and "the check option." First, SQL will reject any attempt to violate data type specifications—e.g., an attempt to insert a character string value into a column defined as DECIMAL. Second, SQL also supports the clause WITH CHECK OPTION on CREATE VIEW. For details of the check option, the reader is referred to Chapter 9.

Recovery and Concurrency

Standard SQL includes support for the transaction concept. A tutorial on transaction management and the associated concepts of recovery and concurrency can be found in the author's book *An Introduction to Database Systems: Volume I* (4th edition, Addison-Wesley, 1985). We defer detailed discussion of the SQL features for transaction management to Chapters 3 and 6; what follows is only a very brief sketch.

- A transaction is a sequence of operations that is guaranteed to be atomic for recovery and concurrency purposes. Every transaction terminates by executing either COMMIT WORK (normal termination) or ROLLBACK WORK (abnormal termination).

- Database updates made by a given transaction T1 are not visible to any distinct transaction T2 until and unless T1 executes COMMIT WORK. COMMIT WORK causes all updates made by the transaction to become visible to other transactions; such updates are guaranteed never to be canceled. If the transaction executes ROLLBACK WORK instead, all updates made by the transaction are canceled.

- The interleaved execution of a set of concurrent transactions is required to be *serializable*, in the sense that it must produce the same result as executing those same transactions one at a time in some (unspecified) serial order.

2.7 SOME DIFFERENCES FROM DB2

Readers familiar with DB2 or some other existing SQL implementation will have noticed a number of differences between SQL as described in this chapter and SQL as currently implemented. We sketch some of those differences below. *Note:* Most of the features identified below (for brevity) as features of DB2 have direct counterparts in many other SQL products.

1. In DB2, both data manipulation operations such as SELECT and data definition operations such as CREATE TABLE (and also a number of other operations that do not appear in standard SQL at all) can all be invoked both interactively and from within a program. In standard SQL, by contrast:

(a) Only data manipulation operations can be invoked both interactively and from within a program;

(b) Data definition operations can be invoked only in the context of a "schema"—i.e., as part of the database definition; and while the standard does not specify how the database definition is entered into the system (see the next point below), it does seem as if the database definition interface is something distinct from both a conventional interactive interface and a conventional programming interface.*

2. Following on from the previous point: The concept of a schema as such does not exist at all in DB2. DB2 SQL was always intended to be highly *dynamic*—all operations are available in all contexts (or at least all contexts that make sense), and hence it is possible, e.g., to create a new base table interactively at any time. By contrast, the schema concept seems to be rather static—though (as indicated above) the mechanism for making the schema known to the system (i.e., the "schema language processor") is not specified in the standard, and hence the possibility of a dynamic, DB2-like technique is not totally ruled out.

3. DB2 supports several additional definitional operations—ALTER TABLE, DROP TABLE, and DROP VIEW (also a number of more physically oriented operations, such as CREATE/DROP INDEX and CREATE/DROP TABLESPACE).

4. DB2 allows direct interactive execution of a multiple-row SELECT without using a cursor.

5. A DB2 cursor declaration requires a FOR UPDATE clause if an UPDATE . . . WHERE CURRENT operation will be executed using that cursor.

6. Interleaved executions in DB2 are not guaranteed to be serializable unless the RR ("repeatable read") option is specified on the BIND command for all transactions. *Note:* BIND is a command to the DB2 SQL compiler, not a DB2 SQL statement. It is not specified within the application program.

7. DB2 supports a REVOKE operation to remove a previously granted privilege. DB2 also supports a large number of additional privileges, over and above those supported by standard SQL.

8. DB2 does not support UNIQUE on CREATE TABLE (though it does support PRIMARY KEY and FOREIGN KEY specifications). DB2 also does not support the CHECK clause.

---

*The separation of definitional and manipulative operations in the standard was deliberate: It allowed the committee to avoid certain language definition problems that arise from the possibility of interleaving the two kinds of operation against the same table. However, it is easy to lose sight of this rationale—especially as there is no mention of it in the official standard document—and the separation per se is unfortunate, to say the least.

9. DB2 includes a set of system tables called the *catalog*, which (in effect) contains the database definition or schema. Ordinary SQL SELECT statements can be used to interrogate the catalog.

Comments:

We offer the following opinions on the foregoing differences (having regard always for the presumed fact that the main objective of the standard is *program portability*). The comments are keyed to paragraphs 1–9 above.

1. The DB2 approach is preferable. The ability to perform all operations in all contexts that make sense is desirable (though perhaps not very important for program portability per se).

2. Same as 1.

3. Support for ALTER TABLE, DROP TABLE (etc.) is desirable.

4. The ability to perform an interactive multiple-row SELECT without using a cursor is desirable.

5. The FOR UPDATE clause is a blemish in DB2; X3H2 did right to abolish it (but see the comment on "positioned UPDATE" in Section 7.3).

6. It is slightly unfortunate that the DB2 "RR" option is specified outside the program, since it can affect program logic (not a major point). Otherwise, no comment.

7. Support for REVOKE is desirable.

8. DB2's support for PRIMARY KEYs (and FOREIGN KEYs) is superior to that of the standard; however, support for UNIQUE specifications is desirable also. Support for the CHECK clause is also needed.

9. While it is difficult to see how the X3H2 committee could have specified a standard catalog structure, the fact is that *generalized* application programs, at least, do frequently need to read and interpret catalog information, precisely because of their generalized nature. (An example of such a generalized application is IBM's own Query Management Facility QMF, which is an ad hoc query and report-writing frontend subsystem for both DB2 and SQL/DS.) The lack of a standard catalog structure is likely to impose severe limitations on the portability of such applications.

End of comments.

Preliminaries

3.1 BASIC DATA OBJECTS

1. The SQL standard starts with an undefined notion, the notion of *environment* (that is, exactly what it is that constitutes an environment for any given implementation is left for that implementation to specify). Each environment is defined to include just a single *database* (in other words, every application program operates on just one database). The database for a given environment is defined to be the aggregate of all data defined by all *schemas* in that environment. Each schema in turn consists of a set of base table definitions, a set of view definitions, and a set of privilege definitions (GRANT operations). Privileges are discussed in Section 3.3; base tables and views are discussed below.

2. The data in the database is perceived by the user as a collection of *named tables*, no two of which have the same name. Each named table is either a *base table* or a *viewed table* (view for short). A base table is a "real" table—i.e., it is a named, autonomous table (where "autonomous" means "not defined in terms of any other table(s)"). A view is a "virtual" table—i.e., it is a named, derived table (where "derived" means "not autonomous"). Base tables and views are created by CREATE TABLE and CREATE VIEW operations, respectively; the standard does not specify any means for destroying them. *Note:* The result of evaluating a *query expres-*

sion (see Chapter 10 later) is also a derived table (like a view), but one that is unnamed. Such a table exists (conceptually) only during the execution of the statement that causes evaluation of that query expression.

3. A table consists of a row of *column headings*, together with zero or more rows of *data values* (different numbers of data rows at different times, in general). For a given table:

- The column heading row specifies one or more named columns (giving, among other things, a data type for each such column). Within a given table, no two columns can have the same name.

- Each data row contains exactly one value for each of the columns specified in the column heading row. Furthermore, all the values in a given column are of the same data type, namely the data type specified for that column in the column heading row. *Note:* The term "data row" is usually abbreviated to just "row."

  Comment: We follow the SQL standard here in using the unqualified term "value" to refer to what would more accurately be called a *scalar* value (i.e., an individual number or character string; see paragraph 4 below). The problem with the unqualified "value" usage is that it usurps a very general term and gives it a very special meaning, thereby making it difficult to talk about more general, nonscalar values—for example, the value of a query expression. In this book we will usually use the term "scalar" or "scalar value" for the construct, in order to emphasize the fact that the value in question *is* a scalar. *End of comment.*

  Two points arise in connexion with the foregoing definition.

- Note that there is no mention of *row ordering*. The rows of a table are considered to be unordered, top to bottom. It is possible, as we saw in Section 2.3, to *impose* an order on those rows when they are retrieved in response to a query, but such an ordering should be regarded as nothing more than a convenience for the user—it is not part of the notion of "table" per se.

- In contrast to the first point, the columns of a table *are* considered to be ordered, left to right. For example, in table S (see Fig. 2.1 in Chapter 2), column SNO is the first column, column SNAME is the second column, and so on. *Note:* Actually there are very few situations in which that left-to-right ordering is significant, and even those can be avoided with a little discipline. Such avoidance is generally to be recommended in practice, for reasons outlined in Appendix F (Section F.8).

The number of rows in a given table is called the *cardinality* of that table. The number of columns is called the *degree*.

4. Scalar values are of two fundamental types, character strings (strings for short) and numbers. *Note:* Specific data types are discussed in Chapter 4. Also, note that host variables and parameters are also considered to represent scalar values, and hence that the following remarks apply to such variables and parameters also. See Section 3.2.

- A character string is a sequence of one or more characters. Any two strings can be compared with one another; such comparisons are performed in accordance with the implementation-defined character collating sequence. If two strings of different lengths are to be compared, the shorter is conceptually padded at the right with space characters to make it the same length as the longer before the comparison is done.

- A number is either *exact* or *approximate*.

  - An exact number has a precision (p) and a scale (q), where $p >= q >= 0$ (and $p > 0$). Such a number consists of p significant digits and has a value equal to

$$n* (10 ** (-q))$$

    where n is the integer value of the p significant digits (and where ** stands for exponentiation; note, however, that standard SQL does not support such an operator).

  - An approximate number has a precision (p), where $p > 0$. Such a number consists of a signed mantissa (m) of p significant digits and a signed exponent (e), and has a value approximately equal to

$$m* (10 ** e)$$

  Any two numbers can be compared with one another; such comparisons are performed algebraically.

- Any string can be assigned to an object of string type. The source string is conceptually truncated on the right or padded on the right with space characters (as necessary) to make it the same length as the target object before the assignment is performed.

- Any number, exact or approximate, can be assigned to an object of approximate numeric type. Only an exact number can be assigned to an object of exact numeric type. In either case, the source number is conceptually converted to the precision (and scale, if applicable) of the target object before the assignment is performed.

- Note that numbers and strings cannot be compared with each other, nor can a number be assigned to an object of string type, nor can a string be assigned to an object of numeric type.

5. The *null value* (null for short) is a special scalar that can appear as a column value in a base table or derived table but not as a host variable or parameter value (at least, not directly; see Section 6.3). Null is intended to mean "information missing" (e.g., "value unknown" or "value does not apply"). The representation of nulls is implementation-defined; however, it must be such that the system can distinguish nulls from all "known" (i.e., nonnull) values. Nulls are treated by arithmetic and scalar comparison operators as follows:

- Let A and B be objects of numeric type. If A is null, then each of the expressions $+A$ and $-A$ evaluates to null. If A is null or B is null or both, then each of the expressions

  ```
  A + B      A - B      A * B      A / B
  ```

  evaluates to null.

- Let A and B be comparable objects. If A is null or B is null or both, then (in the context of a WHERE or HAVING clause) each of the expressions

  ```
  A = B      A <> B      A < B      A > B      A <= B      A >= B
  ```

  evaluates to the *unknown* truth-value (i.e., not to *true* and not to *false*). The unknown truth-value behaves as defined by the following truth tables (T = true, F = false, ? = unknown):

  ```
  AND | T ? F          OR  | T ? F          NOT|
  ----+------          ----+------          ---+---
   T  | T ? F           T  | T T T           T | F
   ?  | ? ? F           ?  | T ? ?           ? | ?
   F  | F F F           F  | T ? F           F | T
  ```

  Two special operators, IS NULL and IS NOT NULL, are provided for testing to see whether a given scalar value is or is not null. See Chapter 10.

- The previous point notwithstanding, two nulls *are* considered to be equal to each other (equivalently, to be duplicates of each other) for purposes of duplicate elimination (DISTINCT) and grouping (GROUP BY) and ordering (ORDER BY). Note too that if a column is defined to be UNIQUE, it must also be defined to be NOT NULL (see Chapter 4).

Comments:

1. To repeat a statement made earlier: The representation of nulls must be such that the system can distinguish them from all nonnull values. As already explained, however, it does *not* follow that if A is null, the comparison (e.g.) "A < > 3" evaluates to *true*. For this reason, it is somewhat misleading to state (as the standard does) that null is a *value*; it would be better to regard it as a *placeholder* for a value, a value that is currently unknown. For this reason also, we prefer the unadorned term "null" to the term "null value."

2. In fact, it is the opinion of this writer that nulls (at least, nulls as defined in SQL) are a mistake and should never have been included in the standard at all. It is certainly incontestable that SQL-style nulls display very strange and inconsistent behavior and can be a rich source of error and confusion (as can be seen already from the remarks above concerning WHERE and HAVING and UNIQUE and DISTINCT and GROUP BY and ORDER BY). It may well be preferable in practice to represent missing information by a "default" value—i.e., an ordinary nonnull value such as spaces or − 1 (minus one). See Chapter 4 for a discussion of default values. An extensive discussion of the problems caused by SQL-style nulls can be found in the author's book *Relational Database: Selected Writings* (Addison-Wesley, 1986).

End of comments.

3.2 MODULES, PROCEDURES, AND EMBEDDED SQL

1. In attempting to define a standard application programming version of SQL, the ANSI X3H2 committee was faced with a major (though nontechnical) problem: ANSI standard versions of languages such as COBOL and PL/I are already defined, and ANSI committees (e.g., X3J4, in the case of COBOL) already exist to protect those standard definitions. Extending each of those standard languages separately to include the required SQL function would involve an enormous amount of work—work, moreover, that generally would have little to do with database technology per se—and would delay the appearance of a SQL standard by many years. Consequently, X3H2 proposed the so-called *module language* approach.

2. The module language consists essentially of a small language for expressing SQL data manipulation operations in pure SQL syntactic form. A procedure in the module language consists basically of a set of parameter declarations and a single SQL statement formulated in terms of those parameters. For example:

```
PROCEDURE DELETE_PART
            SQLCODE
            PNO_PARAM CHAR(6) ;
   DELETE FROM P WHERE P.PNO = PNO_PARAM ;
```

Note the (required) SQLCODE parameter, which is used to pass a return code back to the program that invokes the procedure. A SQLCODE value of zero means that the statement executed successfully and no exceptional conditions occurred; a value of $+100$ means that no rows were found to satisfy the request; a negative value means that some error occurred.

The procedure shown above could be invoked from a PL/I program as follows:

```
DCL RETCODE FIXED BINARY(15) ;
DCL PNO_ARG CHAR(6) ;
DCL DELETE_PART ENTRY ( FIXED BINARY(15), CHAR(6) ) ;
   .......
PNO_ARG = 'P6' ;                 /* for example              */
CALL DELETE_PART ( RETCODE, PNO_ARG ) ;
IF RETCODE = 0 THEN ... ;   /* delete operation succeeded    */
               ELSE ... ;   /* some exception occurred       */
```

Note (for readers who may be unfamiliar with PL/I): "DCL" is just a standard PL/I abbreviation for DECLARE; an "ENTRY" declaration is just a definition of an external entry point or procedure.

The module language thus provides the ability for programs written in host languages such as PL/I, COBOL, etc., to execute SQL data manipulation operations without requiring any change to the syntax or semantics of those languages. All that is required is

(a) the ability on the part of the host to invoke procedures that are written in a different language and are separately compiled, together with

(b) a defined correspondence between host and module language data types for argument-passing purposes.

In other words, the relationship between the host language and standard SQL is analogous to (actually identical to) that between two host languages: The host language program calls a separately compiled program (i.e., external procedure) that happens to be written in SQL, instead of in the host language under consideration or in some other host language.

3. The X3H2 committee did not necessarily intend (or even primarily intend) that users actually code direct calls to the module language as shown in the example above. Instead, the normal method of operation is to embed SQL statements directly into the text of the host language program, as illustrated by Figs. 2.2 and 2.8 in Chapter 2. An embedded SQL example corresponding to the direct call example above might appear as shown below.

Note: The example is incomplete; the SQLCODE and PNO declarations need to be nested within an "embedded SQL declare section," delimited by the statements "EXEC SQL BEGIN DECLARE SECTION;" and "EXEC SQL END DECLARE SECTION;" (see Chapter 11).

```
DCL SQLCODE FIXED BINARY(15) ;
DCL PNO CHAR(6) ;
.......
PNO = 'P6' ;                          /* for example                */
EXEC SQL DELETE FROM P WHERE P.PNO = :PNO ;
IF SQLCODE = 0 THEN ... ;   /* delete operation succeeded  */
              ELSE ... ;   /* some exception occurred      */
```

Note that no explicit definition of the procedure DELETE_PART is now needed.

However, "embedded SQL" is not truly a part of the SQL standard as such. Instead, the embedded SQL code shown above is defined to be a mere syntactic shorthand for the direct call version (including explicit procedure definition) shown earlier. An embedded SQL implementation must provide some kind of preprocessor whose effect is (logically) to convert an embedded SQL program into an equivalent direct call version.

The X3H2 SQL specification includes a set of "annexes" or appendixes (not part of the standard per se) defining embedded versions of SQL for COBOL, FORTRAN, Pascal, and PL/I. We defer our description of the details of embedding SQL into such languages to Chapter 11.

4. Note that the module language approach does not preclude the possibility of eventually extending the host languages to provide native SQL support. However, the SQL standard does not explicitly propose any such native support, for the reasons outlined earlier.

5. We give another example of the use of the module language to illustrate the point that, in general, parameters also serve as the mechanism by which values can be returned to the invoking program. Of course, this point has already been illustrated by the DELETE example above for the special case of the SQLCODE parameter.

Procedure:

```
PROCEDURE  GET_WEIGHT
               SQLCODE
               PNO_PARAM    CHAR(6)
               WEIGHT_PARAM DECIMAL(3) ;
     SELECT  P.WEIGHT
     INTO    WEIGHT_PARAM
     FROM    P
     WHERE   P.PNO = PNO_PARAM ;
```

Possible invocation from PL/I:

```
DCL RETCODE    FIXED BINARY(15) ;
DCL PNO_ARG    CHAR(6) ;
DCL WEIGHT_ARG DECIMAL(3) ;
DCL GET_WEIGHT ENTRY ( FIXED BINARY(15),
                       CHAR(6), DECIMAL(3) ) ;
  .......
PNO_ARG = 'P6' ;                  /* for example          */
CALL GET_WEIGHT ( RETCODE, PNO_ARG, WEIGHT_ARG ) ;
IF RETCODE = 0 THEN ... ;  /* WEIGHT_ARG = retrieved value */
               ELSE ... ;  /* some exception occurred      */
```

Embedded SQL version (again omitting the necessary BEGIN and END DECLARE SECTION statements):

```
DCL SQLCODE FIXED BINARY(15) ;
DCL PNO     CHAR(6) ;
DCL WEIGHT  DECIMAL(3) ;
  .......
PNO = 'P6' ;                      /* for example          */
EXEC SQL SELECT P.WEIGHT
         INTO   :WEIGHT
         FROM   P
         WHERE  P.PNO = :PNO ;
IF SQLCODE = 0 THEN ... ;  /* WEIGHT = retrieved value    */
               ELSE ... ;  /* some exception occurred     */
```

3.3   SECURITY, INTEGRITY, AND TRANSACTION PROCESSING

Security

1. The SQL standard includes the concept of an *authorization identifier*, which can informally be thought of as the name by which some user is known to the system. We will generally use the term "user" instead of "authorization identifier," for brevity; note, however, that the standard does not include any formal concept of "user" as such. Each schema has an associated authorization identifier; the user designated by that authorization identifier is the "owner" of all tables and views created in that schema. No two schemas in the environment can have the same authorization identifier.

2. To perform a given operation on a given object, the user must hold the necessary *privilege* for that combination of operation and object. The objects to which such privileges apply are base tables and views; the corresponding operations are CREATE, SELECT, INSERT, UPDATE, and DELETE.

- To create a base table T2, no special privileges are needed *unless* table T2 includes a foreign key referencing some base table T1, in which case the REFERENCES privilege is needed on all columns of T1 referenced by that foreign key. See Chapter 5 for further discussion of the REFERENCES privilege.

- To create a view V, the SELECT privilege is needed on every table mentioned in the definition of V.

- To perform a SELECT or INSERT or UPDATE or DELETE operation on table T, the SELECT or INSERT or UPDATE or DELETE privilege (as applicable) is needed on table T. The SELECT privilege is also needed for all other tables mentioned in the operation (e.g., in the WHERE clause, if any). In the case of UPDATE, the UPDATE privilege is needed on every column of table T mentioned as an assignment target in the SET clause of the UPDATE.

No special privileges are needed to create a schema.

3. The owner of a base table holds all privileges on that base table. The owner of a view holds all privileges on that view that "make sense":

- If the view is updatable (see Chapter 9) and the owner holds the INSERT and/or the UPDATE and/or the DELETE privilege on the underlying table, then the owner holds those same privileges on the view. (In the case of UPDATE, of course, the owner holds the privilege only on columns of the view that correspond to columns for which he or she holds the privilege on the underlying table.)

- Otherwise the owner holds just the SELECT privilege on the view.

4. The owner of an object can grant privileges on that object to other users by means of the GRANT operation (specified in the schema). Also, if user A grants some privilege P to user B, then user A has the option of granting that privilege P to user B "with the grant option" (via the clause WITH GRANT OPTION in the GRANT operation). Granting a privilege with the grant option means that the recipient of the privilege can in turn grant that same privilege—with or without the grant option—to some further user. No user can grant a privilege not held by that user.

5. Each module also has an associated authorization identifier (i.e., user). The user represented by that authorization identifier must hold all necessary privileges for all SQL statements contained in that module. Note that a single module (possibly even a single SQL statement) can refer to tables from multiple schemas.

6. Tables (base tables and views) are identified by a two-part name of the form U.T, where "U" is a user name (authorization identifier) and "T" is a simple (i.e., unqualified) identifier. Tables defined in different schemas can have the same unqualified name; thus, e.g., the names U1.T and U2.T (where U1 and U2 are two distinct user names) identify two distinct tables.

7. A reference to a table in a SQL statement can optionally omit the "U." portion of the name (indeed, this is the normal case). Omitting the "U." portion is equivalent to specifying the authorization identifier of the schema or module in which the reference appears.

Integrity

1. The definition of a base table can optionally include certain *integrity constraints*. Any update operation that would violate any specified constraint will be rejected; the database remains unchanged, and SQLCODE is set to an implementation-defined negative value. The standard supports the following integrity constraints:

- NOT NULL: Can be specified for any column of the table. Any attempt to introduce a null into such a column will be rejected. If NOT NULL is not specified for a given column, then that column is allowed to contain nulls.

- CHECK: Can be specified for any column or combination of columns of the table. Any attempt to introduce a row into the table that violates the specified CHECK constraint is rejected. The constraint must be of such a form that it can be checked for a given row by examining just that row in isolation—i.e., it is not necessary to examine any other row of the table, nor any row of any other table.

- UNIQUE: Can be specified for any column or combination of columns of the table. Every such column, or every column in such combination of columns, must also be specified to be NOT NULL. Any attempt to introduce a row into the table having the same value in the specified column or column combination as some existing row will be rejected. If UNIQUE is not specified for a given column (combination), then that column (combination) is allowed to contain duplicate values.

- PRIMARY KEY: Can be specified at most once for a given table. PRIMARY KEY implies UNIQUE. For more details, see Chapter 5.

- FOREIGN KEY: Again, for more details, see Chapter 5.

- REFERENCES: An alternative syntax for specifying certain foreign key constraints. Once again, for details see Chapter 5.

  Comment: It would be desirable to support a much wider range of integrity constraints. See Chapter 12. *End of comment.*

2. The definition of an updatable view (see Section 9.4) can optionally include the clause WITH CHECK OPTION. Any attempt to insert a row into such a view, or update a row in such a view, such that the newly inserted or updated record does not satisfy the "search condition" that defines the

view (see Chapter 9) will be rejected; the database remains unchanged, and SQLCODE is set to an implementation-defined negative value. Note that if view W is an updatable view derived from updatable view V, and WITH CHECK OPTION is specified for view V, that check option does *not* apply to updates performed via view W—i.e., the check option does not inherit.

Comments:

1. In DB2, the check option can be specified only if the view is updatable *and* the view definition does not involve a subquery (see Chapter 10 for a discussion of subqueries). This anomaly is avoided in the standard because views that involve a subquery are defined to be nonupdatable. However, the standard does still suffer from another DB2 anomaly—a legacy from earlier releases—namely, that the check option is not inheritable. (This was a problem with the first two releases of DB2 but was corrected in Version 1.3.)

2. In any case, the check option is really rather a strange feature of the language altogether. Integrity constraints belong more properly with the base data, not with views. Further discussion of this point (and of the check option in particular) can be found in the author's book *An Introduction to Database Systems: Volume I* (4th edition, Addison-Wesley, 1985).

End of comments.

Transaction Processing

1. A transaction is a sequence of SQL (and possibly other) operations that is guaranteed to be atomic for the purposes of recovery and concurrency control.

2. If a program invokes a SQL operation and no transaction is currently active for that program, then one is automatically initiated. Each subsequent invocation of a SQL operation by the same program is considered to be part of that same transaction, until the transaction terminates. Transactions thus cannot be nested.

3. A transaction terminates by executing either a COMMIT WORK operation (normal or successful termination) or a ROLLBACK WORK operation (abnormal or unsuccessful termination). Successful termination is called "termination with commit"; unsuccessful termination is called "termination with rollback."

4. The standard does not specify what should happen if a transaction fails to terminate with either an explicit COMMIT WORK or an explicit

ROLLBACK WORK (e.g., if it simply returns control to the operating system, or if a system crash occurs).

5. Database updates made by a given transaction T1 do not become visible to any distinct transaction T2 until and unless transaction T1 terminates with commit. Termination with commit causes all updates made by the transaction to become visible to other transactions; such updates are guaranteed never to be canceled. Termination with rollback causes all updates made by the transaction to be canceled; such updates will never become visible to other transactions at all.

6. The interleaved execution of a set of concurrent transactions is guaranteed to be *serializable*, in the sense that it will produce the same effect as some (unspecified) serial execution of those same transactions. *Note:* A serial execution is an execution in which the transactions are executed one at a time, each one completing before the next one starts.

3.4   BASIC LANGUAGE ELEMENTS

Characters

The most primitive language elements are the individual characters of the underlying character set. Those characters are used to construct higher-level (nonprimitive) language elements and also character string data values. The character set consists of the upper case letters A, B, . . ., Z, the lower case letters a, b, . . ., z, the digits 0, 1, 2, . . ., 9, a newline marker,* and a set of other characters, called special characters. The special characters must include at least all of the following—

%   _   ,   (   )   <   >   .   :   =   +   -   *   /

—plus a space character. The complete character set, and the collating sequence for that character set, are both implementation-defined.

Literals

Literals (also called constants, though "constant" is not an official standard term) are of two types, character string (string for short) and numeric. A *string* literal consists of a sequence of characters enclosed in single quotes; within such a literal, the single quote character itself is represented by two immediately consecutive single quotes. Examples:

---

*The newline marker is optional. The implementation is free to mark "end of line" in some way other than by means of a distinguished character, if it chooses.

```
'XYZ'   '123 Main Street'   'PIG'   '01234'   'honey don''t'
```

Numeric literals in turn are of two types, exact and approximate. An *exact numeric* literal consists of an optionally signed decimal number, with or without a decimal point. Examples:

```
4     7.5     12.00     0.001     -4.75
```

An *approximate numeric* literal consists of an optionally signed decimal number with or without a decimal point—in other words, an exact numeric literal—followed by the letter E and an optionally signed decimal integer. Examples:

```
1E0     4E3     -95.7E46     +364E-5     0.7E1
```

A literal is considered to have the obvious data type and length, precision, or precision and scale (according to the data type), as indicated by the literal format. Literals are also considered to have the NOT NULL property.

Tokens

Tokens represent lexical units in the language. A token is either a delimiter or a nondelimiter. A *delimiter* is either a string literal or one of the following special symbols:

```
,   (   )   <   >   .   :   =   +   -   *   /   <>   <=   >=
```

A *nondelimiter* is a numeric literal, an identifier, or a key word. An *identifier* is a string of not more than 18 characters, of which the first must be an upper case letter; the rest can be any combination of upper case letters, digits, and the underscore character (_), except that adjacent underscores are not allowed. The following are all identifiers:

    authorization identifiers
    unqualified table names
    unqualified column names
    range variable names (or "correlation names"—see Section 10.5)
    cursor names
    module names
    procedure names
    parameter names

A *key word* is a name that has some prescribed meaning within the SQL language itself. Key words are reserved (i.e., no key word can be used as an identifier). The key words are as follows:

ALL	DELETE	INTO	REFERENCES
AND	DESC	IS	ROLLBACK
ANY	DISTINCT	KEY	SCHEMA
AS	DOUBLE	LANGUAGE	SECTION
ASC	END	LIKE	SELECT
AUTHORIZATION	ESCAPE	MAX	SET
AVG	EXEC	MIN	SMALLINT
BEGIN	EXISTS	MODULE	SOME
BETWEEN	FETCH	NOT	SQL
BY	FLOAT	NULL	SQLCODE
CHAR	FOR	NUMERIC	SQLERROR
CHARACTER	FOREIGN	OF	SUM
CHECK	FORTRAN	ON	TABLE
CLOSE	FOUND	OPEN	TO
COBOL	FROM	OPTION	UNION
COMMIT	GO	OR	UNIQUE
CONTINUE	GOTO	ORDER	UPDATE
COUNT	GRANT	PASCAL	USER
CREATE	GROUP	PLI	VALUES
CURRENT	HAVING	PRECISION	VIEW
CURSOR	IN	PRIMARY	WHENEVER
DEC	INDICATOR	PRIVILEGES	WHERE
DECIMAL	INSERT	PROCEDURE	WITH
DECLARE	INT	PUBLIC	WORK
DEFAULT	INTEGER	REAL	

Any token can optionally be followed by any number of *separators*, where a separator is a space, a newline marker, or a comment. Every nondelimiter token *must* be followed by either a separator or a delimiter token. A *comment* consists of two consecutive hyphens (--), followed by any sequence of characters excluding a newline marker, followed by a newline marker. *Note:* The syntax notation introduced in the next section generally ignores separators entirely.

No token is allowed to include any space characters—except (of course) a character string literal, where embedded space characters are both allowed and significant.

Uniqueness of Names

For convenience, we summarize below the rules regarding uniqueness of names:

1. Within a given "environment" (see Section 3.1), no two schemas have the same owner (authorization ID).
2. Within a given schema, no two tables (base tables and/or views) have the same unqualified name.
3. Within a given table (base table or view), no two columns have the same unqualified name.

3.5 NOTATION

The syntax of SQL language elements is specified in this book by means of a variant of the well-known BNF notation. Our variant is defined as follows:

- Special characters and material in upper case must be written exactly as shown. Material in lower case represents a syntactic category that is the subject of another production rule,* and hence must (eventually) be replaced by specific values chosen by the user.

- Vertical bars "|" are used to separate alternatives.

- Square brackets "[" and "]" are used to indicate that the material enclosed in those brackets is optional; i.e., it consists of a set of one or more items (separated by vertical bars) from which at most one is to be chosen.

- Braces "{" and "}" are used to indicate that the material enclosed in those braces consists of a set of several items (separated by vertical bars) from which exactly one is to be chosen.

By way of example, we show a set of production rules for the syntactic category "numeric literal" (defined informally in the previous section).

```
numeric-literal
    ::=    exact-numeric-literal
       | approximate-numeric-literal

exact-numeric-literal
    ::=    [ + | - ] { integer [ . [ integer ] ] | . integer }

approximate-numeric-literal
    ::=    exact-numeric-literal   E   signed-integer

signed-integer
    ::=    [ + | - ] integer
```

The category "integer" is not further defined; i.e., it is a *terminal category* with respect to this simple example. (Note, incidentally, that although the production rules shown in this example include numerous embedded spaces for readability reasons, a numeric literal is a token—see Section 3.4—and thus in fact must *not* include any such spaces.)

So far our BNF notation is essentially the same as that used in the SQL standard documentation. However, we introduce two further simplifying conventions of our own, as follows:

---

*In this book, however, some of the production rules at the lowest level of detail, such as the rule that defines the construction of an identifier, are not shown in explicit BNF style but are merely described informally in the text.

- If "xyz" is a syntactic category, then "xyz-commalist" is a syntactic category consisting of a list of one or more "xyz"'s in which each pair of adjacent "xyz"'s is separated by a comma.

- If "xyz" is a syntactic category, then "xyz-list" is a syntactic category consisting of a list of one or more "xyz"'s in which each pair of adjacent "xyz"'s is separated by at least one separator (normally a space).

These two rules have the net effect of reducing the overall length and/or number of production rules required. Here is an example to illustrate their use (the first few production rules for "schema" from Chapter 4):

```
schema
    ::=     CREATE SCHEMA
            AUTHORIZATION user
            [ schema-element-list ]

schema-element
    ::=     base-table-definition
          | view-definition
          | grant-operation

base-table-definition
    ::=     CREATE TABLE base-table
                ( base-table-element-commalist )

base-table-element
    ::=     column-definition
          | table-constraint-definition
```

And so on.

Comment: For reasons of clarity and explicitness, we deliberately do not always use the same names for syntactic categories as the SQL standard does. The SQL standard terms are often not particularly apt. For example, the standard uses the name "table definition" to refer to what we have called a "base table definition" above, which tends to obscure the (important) fact that a *view* is also a defined table, and hence that a "view definition" ought to be just a special case of a "table definition." To pursue this latter point a moment longer: In fact, SQL is generally ambivalent as to the meaning of the term "table"; sometimes it means either a base table or a view, sometimes it means a base table explicitly. In this book we will generally use "table" to mean *any* kind of table, and "base table" when we mean a base table specifically. *End of comment.*

4

Data Definition:
The Schema
Definition Language

4.1 SYNTAX

In this chapter we consider database definition in some detail. Recall from
Chapter 2 that a database is defined by one or more *schemas*, created by
means of the *schema definition language*. The following is a syntax for that
language. (The syntax as shown is accurate so far as it goes, but several
details are deliberately omitted for now.)

```
schema
    ::=    CREATE SCHEMA
           AUTHORIZATION user
         [ schema-element-list ]

schema-element
    ::=    base-table-definition
         | view-definition
         | grant-operation

base-table-definition
    ::=    CREATE TABLE base-table
               ( base-table-element-commalist )
```

```
base-table-element
    ::=    column-definition
         | table-constraint-definition

column-definition
    ::=    column  data-type
         [ NOT NULL ]
         [ DEFAULT ( literal | USER | NULL ) ]

table-constraint-definition
    ::=    candidate-key-definition
         | primary-key-definition
         | foreign-key-definition
         | check-condition

candidate-key-definition
    ::=    UNIQUE ( column-commalist )

primary-key-definition
    ::=    ... See Chapter 5.

foreign-key-definition
    ::=    ... See Chapter 5.

check-condition
    ::=    CHECK ( search-condition )

search-condition
    ::=    ... See Section 10.6.

view definition
    ::=    ... See Chapter 9.

grant-operation
    ::=    ... See Section 4.4.
```

As the syntax indicates, a schema consists of a CREATE SCHEMA clause, an AUTHORIZATION clause, and zero or more CREATE TABLE operations and/or view definitions and/or grant operations. The AUTHORIZATION clause identifies the owner of any base tables and/or views defined in this schema, also the grantor of any privileges granted by any grant operations in this schema. We defer discussion of views to Chapter 9; base tables and privileges are discussed in Sections 4.2–4.4 of the present chapter (except that certain important aspects of base tables, namely primary and foreign keys, are deferred to Chapter 5).

Comment: The expression "CREATE SCHEMA" is slightly confusing. It would have been more consistent to call the operation (e.g.) "CREATE DATABASE" (by analogy with CREATE TABLE and CREATE VIEW). Otherwise why not (e.g.) CREATE TABLE DEFINITION and CREATE VIEW DEFINITION? By the same token, "schema definition language" should really be just "schema language" (by analogy with "module language"). *End of comment.*

We remind the reader that schema definition operations are not part of the module language and cannot be invoked from a conventional application program.

4.2   BASE TABLES

We now discuss the CREATE TABLE operation in detail. CREATE TABLE is used to create new (empty) base tables. The syntax is

```
CREATE TABLE base-table ( base-table-element-commalist )
```

where "base table" is the unqualified name for the newly created base table,* and each base table element is either a column definition or a (base) table constraint definition. Column definitions are discussed below; constraints are discussed in the next section. The fully qualified name of the new base table is U.T, where U is the authorization identifier specified in the AUTHORIZATION clause of the schema that includes the CREATE TABLE operation, and T is the identifier specified in that operation.

Each column definition, in turn, takes the form

```
column  data-type  [ NOT NULL ]  [ default-definition ]
```

where "column" is the unqualified name for the column in question, "data type" specifies the column data type, NOT NULL is as explained in Chapter 3 (Section 3.3), and "default definition" is explained below. The column can be referenced in SQL data manipulation operations by the name T.C, where T is the qualified or unqualified name of the base table that contains the column, and C is the identifier specified in the column definition.†

The optional "default definition" takes the form

```
DEFAULT { NULL | literal | USER }
```

For example:

```
CREATE TABLE S
     ( SNO    CHAR(5)     NOT NULL,
       SNAME  CHAR(20)    DEFAULT '???',
       STATUS DECIMAL(3)  NOT NULL DEFAULT 0,
       CITY   CHAR(15)    DEFAULT '  ',
       .....                )
```

---

*Actually the name can be qualified, but if it is, then the qualifier *must* be the authorization identifier specified in the schema AUTHORIZATION clause.

†It can also be referenced by the name R.C., where R is the name of a range variable (or "correlation variable") that ranges over T. See Section 10.5.

The purpose of the DEFAULT clause is to specify the value to be entered in the indicated position if the user does not supply a value on INSERT. "DEFAULT NULL" means that null is the default (NOT NULL must not apply if DEFAULT NULL is specified); "DEFAULT literal" means that the specified literal is the default (the specified literal must be of a data type that can legitimately be assigned to the relevant column); "DEFAULT USER" means that the value of USER (see Section 4.3) is the default. If no explicit default clause is specified, then:

(a) If NOT NULL applies to the column in question, then the column does not have a default value (i.e., a value is required for that column on INSERT);

(b) If NOT NULL does not apply to the column in question, then DEFAULT NULL is assumed.

Comment: As suggested in Section 3.1, user-defined default values ("DEFAULT literal") allow the user to avoid some of the difficulties associated with SQL-style nulls. *End of comment.*

Data Types

Standard SQL supports the following data types:

```
CHARACTER [ ( length ) ]
NUMERIC [ ( precision [, scale ] ) ]
DECIMAL [ ( precision [, scale ] ) ]
INTEGER
SMALLINT
FLOAT [ ( precision ) ]
DOUBLE PRECISION
REAL
```

Notes:

1. CHARACTER, DECIMAL, and INTEGER can be abbreviated to CHAR, DEC, and INT, respectively. SMALLINT *cannot* be "deabbreviated" to SMALLINTEGER. Note also that there is no SINGLE PRECISION.

2. NUMERIC, DECIMAL, INTEGER, and SMALLINT are exact numeric data types. FLOAT, DOUBLE PRECISION, and REAL are approximate numeric data types.

3. "Length," "precision," and "scale" are all unsigned nonnegative decimal integers (greater than zero in the case of "length" and "precision"). For a given NUMERIC or DECIMAL column, the value of "precision" must be greater than or equal to the value of "scale." The default values for

"length," "scale," and "precision" are 1, 0, and implementation-defined, respectively.

4. INTEGER and SMALLINT have implementation-defined precision $p1$ and $p2$, respectively (with a scale of 0 in both cases), such that $p1 >= p2$.

5. The actual precision and scale for NUMERIC are the "precision" and "scale" specified. The actual precision for DECIMAL must be greater than or equal to the "precision" specified; the actual scale must be the "scale" specified.

6. The actual precision for FLOAT must be greater than or equal to the "precision" specified. DOUBLE PRECISION and REAL have implementation-defined precision $p1$ and $p2$, respectively, such that $p1 > p2$.

> *Comment:* The only data types provided are basically fixed length strings and fixed and floating point decimal numbers. The reason for limiting the data types to just these few was presumably that they are the only ones that are common to all major host languages;* but it is pity that the committee did not see fit to include other commonly required types, such as dates, times, money values, binary numbers, bit strings, boolean values, varying strings, etc. As for the specific types that are included, they seem a trifle confusing, to say the least. *End of comment.*

4.3 CONSTRAINTS

We turn our attention now to (base) table constraints. A table constraint is one of the following:

- a primary key definition
- a foreign key definition
- a candidate key definition
- a check condition

---

*This statement is an oversimplification. The only data type that is truly common to all host languages is probably fixed length character strings. Thus, for example, if a SQL table includes a column defined as DECIMAL(5,3), then that column can be accessed from a PL/I program without any problem, because PL/I includes a precisely analogous data type. It *can* also be accessed from a FORTRAN program, but here there may well be problems, because FORTRAN does not include a precisely analogous data type; thus those DECIMAL(5,3) values will have to be converted to (e.g.) REAL values, with possible conversion errors.

Primary and foreign key definitions are a big topic in their own right, and we defer them to Chapter 5; the other two cases are discussed in the present section. First, candidate keys. Loosely speaking, a *candidate key* is just a unique identifier for a table. A candidate key definition thus takes the form

```
UNIQUE ( column-commalist )
```

where each "column" is the unqualified name of a column of the base table in question. The identified column or combination of columns constitutes a candidate key for that table (note that a given base table can have any number of candidate keys). Every column that participates in any candidate key definition must be explicitly specified to be NOT NULL.* See Section 3.3 for further discussion.

Note: If the specified candidate key consists of just a single column— i.e., if the candidate key definition is of the form

```
UNIQUE ( column-X )
```

—then the fact that it *is* a candidate key can alternatively be specified as part of the definition of the column in question (instead of via a separate UNIQUE clause), as follows:

```
column-X data-type-X NOT NULL UNIQUE
```

Note that in this format, the UNIQUE specification is regarded as an extension of, and subordinate to, the (required) NOT NULL specification. However, specifying uniqueness as part of a column definition in this manner is defined to be merely a shorthand for the version shown earlier (using a separate UNIQUE clause).

The second kind of constraint to be discussed in this section is the check condition, specified by means of a CHECK clause. The CHECK clause takes the general form

```
CHECK ( search-condition )
```

The purpose of a CHECK clause is to specify a condition—i.e., an integrity constraint—that must be satisfied by all rows in the base table in question at all times. Here is an example:

---

*This is a SQL requirement, not a requirement of the underlying relational model.

```
CREATE TABLE S
     ( SNO    ...,
       SNAME  ...,
       STATUS ...,
       CITY   ...,
       CHECK ( S.STATUS BETWEEN 10 AND 100 ),
       CHECK ( S.CITY IN ('Athens','London','Madrid','Oslo',
                          'Paris','Rome') ),
       CHECK ( S.CITY <> 'London' OR S.STATUS = 20 ) )
```

The first of these CHECK clauses states that values of S.STATUS must lie in a prescribed range; the second states that values of S.CITY must be drawn from a prescribed list; the third states that, if the value of S.CITY is London, then the value of S.STATUS must be 20. Any attempt to violate any of these constraints (via an INSERT or UPDATE operation) will be rejected.

Note: Search conditions in general are discussed in Chapter 10 (Section 10.6). Search conditions in a CHECK clause, in particular, are required to be of a certain limited form known technically as a *restriction predicate*. A restriction predicate is a condition that can be evaluated for a given row by examining just that row in isolation—it is not necessary to examine any other row, from this table or any other, in order to determine whether the condition is *true* for the row under consideration. In SQL terms, this requirement means that the condition must not include any subqueries or aggregate functions, and the only table that can be referenced (explicitly or implicitly) in the condition is the particular table in question (i.e., the table that is the subject of the CREATE TABLE statement itself).

If a CHECK clause refers to just one column of the table (as in the first two examples above), then it can optionally be specified as part of the definition of that column instead of at the table level. For example:

```
CREATE TABLE S
     ( SNO    ... ,
       SNAME  ... ,
       STATUS ... CHECK ( S.STATUS BETWEEN 10 AND 100 ) ,
       CITY   ... CHECK ( S.CITY IN ('Athens','London',
                                     'Madrid','Oslo',
                                     'Paris','Rome') ) ,
       CHECK ( S.CITY <> 'London' OR S.STATUS = 20 ) )
```

Note, however, that the third CHECK clause here *must* be specified at the table level, because it refers to two distinct columns.

Comment: Note that the familiar NOT NULL specification at the column level can be regarded as a shorthand for a CHECK clause. For example, the column definition

```
STATUS DECIMAL(3) NOT NULL
```

(part of the definition of base table S) is really just shorthand for

```
STATUS DECIMAL(3) CHECK ( S.STATUS IS NOT NULL )
```

Furthermore, this CHECK clause could be specified either at the individual column level or at the overall table level.

Such syntactic redundancy (i.e., the provision of many alternative ways of saying the same thing) is typical of the SQL standard, as we shall see. In this writer's opinion, however, such redundancy does not serve any genuinely useful purpose; rather, it merely complicates the language and makes life more difficult for both the user and the implementer. *End of comment.*

4.4   PRIVILEGES

As explained in Chapter 3, in order to perform a given operation on a given object, the user must hold the necessary *privilege* for that combination of operation and object. To repeat some details from that chapter: The objects to which such privileges apply are base tables and views; the corresponding operations are CREATE, SELECT, INSERT, UPDATE, and DELETE.

- To create a base table T2, no special privileges are needed (unless table T2 includes a foreign key referencing some base table T1, in which case the REFERENCES privilege is needed on all columns of T1 referenced by that foreign key; we defer detailed discussion of the REFERENCES privilege to Chapter 5).

- To create a view V, the SELECT privilege is needed on every table mentioned in the definition of V.

- To perform a SELECT or INSERT or UPDATE or DELETE operation on table T (base table or view), the SELECT or INSERT or UPDATE or DELETE privilege (as applicable) is needed on table T. The SELECT privilege is also needed for all other tables mentioned in the operation (e.g., in the WHERE clause, if any). In the case of UPDATE, the UPDATE privilege is needed on every column of table T mentioned as an assignment target in the SET clause of the UPDATE.

No special privileges are needed to create a schema.

If T is a table (base table or view) and O is an operation that can validly be performed on T, then user U1 holds the privilege to perform O on T if and only if either

(a) U1 is the owner of T, or

(b) U1 has been explicitly granted that privilege by another user U2, where U2 holds that privilege "with the grant option" (see below).

Finally (to state the obvious): User U can perform operation O on table T if and only if U holds the privilege to perform O on T.

GRANT

Privileges are explicitly granted by means of the GRANT operation, with syntax:

```
GRANT privileges ON table TO grantee-commalist
                 [ WITH GRANT OPTION ]
```

where:

(a) "Privileges" is either ALL [PRIVILEGES] or a commalist of specific operations (SELECT and/or INSERT and/or UPDATE and/or DELETE and/or REFERENCES—possibly with a parenthesized commalist of unqualified column names, in the case of UPDATE and REFERENCES);

(b) The subject of the ON clause is a qualified or unqualified table name (identifying either a base table or a view); and

(c) Each "grantee" is either an authorization identifier or the special key word PUBLIC.

For some examples, see Fig. 2.14 in Section 2.6.

Omitting the parenthesized commalist of column names in the case of UPDATE (and REFERENCES) is equivalent to including such a commalist that specifies all columns in the table. ALL is shorthand for all privileges held by the grantor (with or without the grant option) on the table. PRIVILEGES is just noise. PUBLIC is shorthand for all users (i.e., all authorization identifiers). *Note:* If privilege P has been granted to PUBLIC, then user U automatically enjoys privilege P even if user U was not known to the system at the time the grant was made.

The user issuing the GRANT operation (i.e., the user identified by the AUTHORIZATION clause for the containing schema) must either

(a) be the owner of the table on which the privileges are being granted (i.e., that table must be created in the same schema), or

(b) have been granted those privileges by some other user "with the grant option" (see below).

No user can grant a privilege not held by that user.

The Grant Option

If user A is allowed to grant some privilege P to user B, then (by definition) user A is allowed to grant that privilege P to user B "with the grant option" (by means of the clause WITH GRANT OPTION in the GRANT operation). Granting a privilege with the grant option means that the recipient of the privilege can in turn grant that same privilege—with or without the grant option—to some further user (and so on, recursively).

USER

USER is a reserved word that designates what might be called a *system variable* (or zero-argument scalar builtin function). The value of USER is a character string representing the authorization identifier specified in the AUTHORIZATION clause of the module that contains the SQL statement that causes the USER reference to be invoked. Consider the following example (which is based on one given earlier in Chapter 2, Section 2.6, Fig. 2.13):

Schema:

```
CREATE SCHEMA
AUTHORIZATION TED
   ...
CREATE VIEW MY_PARTS AS
       SELECT * FROM P WHERE P.PNO IN
                      ( SELECT SP.PNO FROM SP
                        WHERE   SP.SNO = USER )
   ...
GRANT ALL ON MY_PARTS TO PUBLIC
```

Module:

```
MODULE M2
AUTHORIZATION S2
   ...
SELECT *
FROM   MY_PARTS ;
```

When the SELECT operation in module M2 is executed, it will retrieve just part rows for parts supplied by supplier S2.

In practice USER is very likely to be used in conjunction with GRANTs to PUBLIC, as the example suggests.

5

Data Definition:
Primary and
Foreign Keys

5.1 PRIMARY KEYS

A primary key definition is a particular case of a base table constraint (see Chapter 4). Its syntax is

```
PRIMARY KEY ( column-commalist )
```

where each "column" is the unqualified name of a column of the base table in question. The identified column or combination of columns constitutes the *primary key* (i.e., principal unique identifier) for the base table whose definition contains the primary key definition. For example:

```
CREATE TABLE S
     ( SNO    CHAR(5)     NOT NULL,
       SNAME  CHAR(20)    DEFAULT '???',
       STATUS DECIMAL(3) NOT NULL DEFAULT 0,
       CITY   CHAR(15)    DEFAULT '   ',
       PRIMARY KEY ( SNO ) )
```

In general, the specification

```
PRIMARY KEY ( column-commalist )
```

is semantically identical to the specification

```
UNIQUE ( column-commalist )
```

(see Section 4.3), except that:

(a) A given CREATE TABLE statement can include at most one PRIMARY KEY clause (it can additionally have one or more UNIQUE clauses, if the table in question has one or more additional candidate keys); and

(b) The primary key receives special treatment in any corresponding foreign key definitions (see Section 5.2 below).

Recall that any column mentioned in a UNIQUE clause (and hence in a PRIMARY KEY clause also) must be explicitly specified to be NOT NULL.

> *Comment:* The PRIMARY KEY clause has to be optional for compatibility with the past, but it is strongly recommended that every CREATE TABLE statement include such a clause in practice. Primary keys are required by the relational model. *End of comment.*

> *Note:* If a primary key is single-column, as in the example above, it can be specified as part of the definition of the column in question instead of via a separate PRIMARY KEY clause. For example:

```
CREATE TABLE S
     ( SNO     CHAR(5)     NOT NULL  PRIMARY KEY,
       SNAME   CHAR(20)    DEFAULT '???',
       STATUS  DECIMAL(3)  NOT NULL DEFAULT 0,
       CITY    CHAR(15)    DEFAULT '   ' )
```

Note that in this format, the PRIMARY KEY specification is regarded as an extension of, and subordinate to, the (required) NOT NULL specification. However, specifying PRIMARY KEY as part of a column definition in this manner is defined to be merely a shorthand for the version shown earlier (using a separate PRIMARY KEY clause).

5.2 FOREIGN KEYS

> *Comment:* The foreign key concept as originally defined in the relational model is essentially straightforward. However, the standard SQL support for that concept unfortunately introduces a considerable degree of unnecessary complexity. In what follows, we explain the basic ideas first, then get into the specifics of SQL per se afterwards. *End of comment.*

1. In the relational model, a *foreign key* is a column (or combination of columns) in one base table T2 whose values are required to match values of the primary key in some base table T1 (speaking a trifle loosely). For example, in the suppliers-and-parts database, column SP.SNO of table SP is a foreign key matching the primary key S.SNO of table S; every supplier number value appearing in column SP.SNO must also appear in column S.SNO (for otherwise the database would not be consistent). Likewise, column SP.PNO of table SP is a foreign key matching the primary key P.PNO of table P; every part number value appearing in column SP.PNO must also appear in column P.PNO.

Note, incidentally, that the converse is *not* a requirement—that is, a primary key value can exist without a matching foreign key value. For example, given the suppliers-and-parts sample data of Fig. 2.1, supplier S5 currently does not supply any parts, and hence the value S5 occurs in column S.SNO but not in column SP.SNO.

2. The two base tables T1 and T2 in our loose definition of "foreign key" do not necessarily have to be distinct. That is, a table might include a foreign key whose values are required to match values of the primary key of that same table. An example might be a table

```
CHILDOF ( CHILD, MOTHER )
```

where each MOTHER is in turn a CHILD of some other MOTHER (etc.). Here CHILD is the primary key and MOTHER is a foreign key matching CHILD (i.e., the MOTHER value in a given row must be equal to the CHILD value in some other row).

The foregoing example is actually just a special case of a more general situation, namely the situation in which there is a cycle of tables T1, T2, T3, ... , T*n*, such that T1 includes a foreign key referencing T2, T2 includes a foreign key referencing T3, and so on, ... , and T*n* includes a foreign key referencing T1.

3. The CHILDOF example also serves to illustrate another point—namely, that foreign keys (unlike primary keys) must sometimes be allowed to accept nulls. In the case at hand, there will presumably be at least one row in the CHILDOF table for which the MOTHER is unknown. (In the standard, in fact, a cycle involving multiple tables *must* have nulls permitted for at least one of the foreign keys, for otherwise there would be no way to insert the first row into the cycle.) Note, however, that foreign keys must sometimes be allowed to accept nulls even in cases where there is no cycle involved.

4. A given foreign key value represents a *reference* from the row(s) containing it to the row containing the matching primary key value. For that

reason, the problem of ensuring that every foreign key value does in fact match a value of the corresponding primary key is known as the *referential integrity* problem. The table containing the foreign key is called the *referencing table;* the table containing the corresponding primary key is called the *referenced table*. The integrity constraint is called a *referential constraint.*

5. Turning now to SQL specifically: A given CREATE TABLE statement can include any number of foreign key definitions. The syntax is:

```
FOREIGN KEY ( column-commalist )
          REFERENCES base-table [ ( column-commalist ) ]
```

The first "column commalist" identifies the column or combination of columns that constitute the foreign key (each column must be identified by its *un*qualified name). The "base table" in the REFERENCES clause identifies the referenced table. The second, optional "column commalist" must be identical to the "column commalist" in a candidate key definition (i.e., UNIQUE or PRIMARY KEY specification) in the definition of the referenced table (again, each column must be identified by its unqualified name). Omitting that second column commalist is equivalent to specifying a column commalist that is identical to that in the PRIMARY KEY specification for the referenced table (the referenced table must possess a defined primary key in this case). Here is an example:

```
CREATE TABLE SP
      ( SNO     CHAR(5)     NOT NULL,
        PNO     CHAR(6)     NOT NULL,
        QTY     DECIMAL(5)  NOT NULL DEFAULT 0 )
        PRIMARY KEY ( SNO, PNO ),
        FOREIGN KEY ( SNO ) REFERENCES S,
        FOREIGN KEY ( PNO ) REFERENCES P )
```

The first of the two FOREIGN KEY clauses here states that column SP.SNO is a foreign key matching the primary key of table S (note that the definition of table S must include an appropriate PRIMARY KEY specification for this FOREIGN KEY specification to be legal). The second FOREIGN KEY clause is analogous.

Note 1: It so happens in our example that each of the two foreign keys is a component of the primary key of the containing table. However, this is *not* a requirement. In fact, *any column* (or combination of columns) can be a foreign key. For example, column CITY of table S might be a foreign key, if the database included another table representing cities.

Note 2: If a foreign key is single-column, as in both examples above, the REFERENCES specification can be included in the column definition instead of being made part of a separate FOREIGN KEY clause. For example:

```
CREATE TABLE SP
     ( SNO     CHAR(5)     NOT NULL  REFERENCES S,
       PNO     CHAR(6)     NOT NULL  REFERENCES P,
       QTY     DECIMAL(5)  NOT NULL  DEFAULT 0  )
       PRIMARY KEY ( SNO, PNO ) )
```

However, REFERENCES specifications that are part of an individual column-definition are defined to be merely a shorthand for corresponding table-level FOREIGN KEY specifications as shown earlier.

Note 3: Observe that the standard permits a foreign key to match *any candidate key* in the referenced table, not necessarily just the primary key specifically.

> *Comment:* In this writer's opinion, the ability to have a foreign key that matches a candidate key that is not the primary key is a good example of "spurious generality": The extra degree of freedom does not actually provide any extra functionality, it only leads to extra complexity. We recommend *very strongly* that users not "take advantage" of this option, but instead insist that foreign keys always match primary keys specifically. *End of comment.*

Note 4: A foreign key and its matching candidate key must contain the same number of columns, n say; the ith column of the foreign key corresponds to the ith column of the matching candidate key ($i = 1$ to n), and the data types of corresponding columns must be identical.

Note 5: The standard apparently permits the definition of a foreign key for which the referenced table does not yet exist (this feature is necessary in order to deal with cycles). However, the definition is not considered to be "valid" (and the containing table presumably cannot be used) until the referenced table has been created.

> *Comment:* There are some language definition problems in this area. It is not clear that the standard really does support the definition of cycles as claimed. See also the comment regarding the REFERENCES privilege at the end of this section. *End of comment.*

7. Let T2.FK be a foreign key and let T1.CK be the matching candidate key. Let T2.FK and T1.CK consist of n columns each. So far as the standard is concerned, the referential constraint between T2.FK and T1.CK is considered to be satisfied if and only if every row *t2* of table T2 is such that *either:*

(a) Some component column of T2.FK contains a null in row *t2* (if nulls are allowed for that component of T2.FK), *or*

(b) There exists a row *t1* in T1 with *t1*.CK equal to *t2*.FK (i.e., every com-

ponent of the *t2*.FK value is equal to the corresponding component of
the *t1*.CK value).

Comment: It is very unfortunate that the standard permits composite
(multiple-column) foreign key values to be partly null, and moreover
considers such values to be legal *even if the nonnull components do not
make sense*. For example, suppose an EMPLOYEE table has a foreign
key (DIVNO,DEPTNO), meaning division number and department
number. Then the foreign key value (DIV99,null) is considered to be
legal, even if there is no division DIV99. In order to avoid such sole-
cisms, we recommend—again *very strongly*—that users not "take ad-
vantage" of this capability, but instead insist that every foreign key
value be either wholly nonnull (i.e., all components nonnull) or wholly
null (i.e., all components null), and not a mixture. *End of comment*.

8. In order to maintain the referential constraint between T2.FK and
T1.CK, the system will simply reject any (update) operation that would
violate it. The operations that will be rejected are:

- An INSERT on table T2 or an UPDATE on T2.FK that would introduce a (wholly nonnull) value for T2.FK that does not exist as a value
  of T1.CK.

- A DELETE on table T1 or an UPDATE on T1.CK that would leave
  "dangling references" in table T2 (i.e., rows in table T2 that do not
  reference any row in T1).

  Comments: It would be very desirable to be able to specify that the
  system perform some compensating action—e.g., "cascade delete"—
  instead of merely rejecting the update. Such a capability has recently
  been introduced into the IBM products DB2 and SQL/DS, incidentally.
  End of comment.

9. To specify that T2.FK in table T2 is a foreign key referencing T1.CK
in table T1, the creator of table T2 must hold the REFERENCES privilege
on every component column of T1.CK. The creator of table T1 automatically holds the REFERENCES privilege on every column of table T1, and
can grant that privilege (on a column-by-column basis, if desired) to other
users. Syntax:

```
GRANT REFERENCES [ ( column-commalist ) ]
      ON base-table
      TO grantee-commalist
   [ WITH GRANT OPTION ]
```

Each "column" in the optional "column commalist" is identified by its
unqualified name. Omitting the "column commalist" is equivalent to specifying all columns of the table identified in the ON clause.

Comment: The standard does allegedly support cycles of referential constraints. However, it appears to follow from the foregoing that cycles *cannot* be supported, at least if the tables involved do not all have the same owner. Suppose, for example, that we wish to create a cycle involving two tables T1 and T2, with distinct owners U1 and U2; in other words, U1.T1 and U2.T2 are each to include a foreign key referencing the other. Then T1 cannot be created until U1 holds the REFERENCES privilege on T2, and U1 cannot be granted that privilege by U2 until U2 has created T2, and U2 cannot create T2 until U2 holds the REFERENCES privilege on T1, etc., etc. *End of comment.*

6

Data Manipulation:
The Module Language

6.1 SYNTAX

SQL data manipulation statements are specified in a host-language-independent manner by means of *modules* and *procedures*, which are written in the *module language*. The syntax of that language is as follows:

```
module-definition
    ::=    MODULE [ module ]
           LANGUAGE { COBOL | FORTRAN | PASCAL | PLI }
           AUTHORIZATION user
       [ cursor-definition-list ]
           procedure-definition-list

cursor-definition
    ::=    ... See Chapter 7.

procedure-definition
    ::=    PROCEDURE procedure
           parameter-definition-list ;
           manipulative-statement ;

parameter-definition
    ::=    parameter  data-type  |  SQLCODE
```

```
manipulative-statement
     ::=    close-statement
          | commit-statement
          | delete-statement-positioned
          | delete-statement-searched
          | fetch-statement
          | insert-statement
          | open-statement
          | rollback-statement
          | select-statement
          | update-statement-positioned
          | update-statement-searched
```

As the syntax indicates, a module consists of a MODULE clause (optionally specifying a module name), a LANGUAGE clause specifying the host language from which procedures in the module will be invoked, an AUTHORIZATION clause, zero or more cursor definitions, and one or more procedures. The user whose authorization identifier is specified in the AUTHORIZATION clause must hold all necessary privileges for all manipulative statements specified in all procedures in the module. Cursor definitions are explained in Chapter 7; procedures are discussed in the next section.

A given application program can have at most one associated SQL module. The mechanism for establishing the association between the two is left unspecified.

6.2 PROCEDURES, PARAMETERS, AND MANIPULATIVE STATEMENTS

A procedure consists of a PROCEDURE clause (specifying a name for the procedure), a list of parameter definitions (of which exactly one must specify the special parameter SQLCODE), and a single data manipulation statement. Procedure names must be unique within their containing module.

Parameters

Each parameter definition in a procedure (other than SQLCODE) consists of a parameter name and a data type. Parameters are used to represent:

(a) "Targets" (i.e., host program variables into which scalar values are to be retrieved). In this capacity, a parameter can appear only as the operand of an INTO clause in a FETCH or SELECT statement.

(b) Scalar values that are passed from the host program. In this capacity, a parameter can appear in a SQL data manipulation statement anywhere a literal can appear—i.e., as an element within any of the following (more precisely, as an element within an arithmetic expression within any of the following, if the parameter in question is numeric):

- A SELECT clause (representing a value to be retrieved) in any expression that includes such a clause (e.g., in a query expression—see Chapter 10);
- A WHERE or HAVING clause (representing a value to be compared) in a SELECT, INSERT, UPDATE, or DELETE statement or in a cursor definition;
- A SET clause in an UPDATE statement (representing a value to be used to update the database);
- A VALUES clause in an INSERT statement (representing a value to be inserted).

Note: For some reason the standard does not permit operational expressions in the last of these four cases. Thus, for example, if PARAM is numeric, then the expression PARAM is legal in a VALUES clause but the expression PARAM + 1 is not.

If procedure P includes a data manipulation statement S, and statement S includes a reference to column C, and the unqualified name of C is the same as the name of some parameter defined in P, then the reference to C *must* be qualified. For example:

```
PROCEDURE GET_PART
   SQLCODE
   PNO ... ;

SELECT * FROM P WHERE P.PNO = PNO ;
```

Here "P.PNO" is a reference to the PNO column of table P, "PNO" (unqualified) is a reference to the PNO parameter.

SQLCODE

The argument corresponding to the SQLCODE parameter is used to receive a return code (r, say) indicating what happened when the manipulative statement (S, say) was executed. Values of r are defined as follows:

1. If S executed successfully, then:
   a. If S was any of the following:
      - a FETCH for which there was no next row
      - a SELECT or INSERT . . . SELECT for which no rows were found
      - a "searched" UPDATE for which there were no rows to update

- a "searched" DELETE for which there were no rows to delete then r is set to $+100$.

    b. Otherwise, r is set to 0.

2. If S did not execute successfully, then r is set to an implementation-defined negative value.

Parameter Data Types

The purpose of specifying the data type for a parameter is to inform the implementation of the data type it can expect for the corresponding argument from the host language. The range of data types that can be specified therefore depends on the range of data types supported by the host language in question; not all data types can be specified for all host languages. The following table indicates which ones are valid for which hosts.

	SQLCODE	other parameters
COBOL	COMP PIC S9 (*pc*)	CHARACTER or NUMERIC
FORTRAN	INTEGER	CHARACTER or INTEGER or REAL or DOUBLE PRECISION
Pascal	INTEGER	CHARACTER or INTEGER or REAL
PL/I	FIXED BIN (*pp*)	CHARACTER or DECIMAL or FLOAT
Note: The values *pc* and *pp* must be greater than or equal to 4 and 15, respectively.		

Note 1: "SQLCODE" in the table refers to the host argument that corresponds to the SQLCODE parameter; the data types shown in that column are host data types. The data types in the "other parameters" column are SQL standard data types.

Note 2: Actually, the official standard document contains several contradictions concerning legal parameter data types. For example, in the case of PL/I, in one place it states that the only parameter data types supported are CHARACTER, DECIMAL, and FLOAT (as shown in the table), in another it states that INTEGER is permitted also (though apparently SMALLINT is not). Similar remarks apply to COBOL (but not FORTRAN or Pascal). The table gives the most restrictive interpretation in each case. The reader is referred to the standard document itself for further details.

Manipulative Statements

The SQL data manipulation statements fall into three categories:

1. Cursor operations:
   OPEN
   FETCH
   UPDATE ... CURRENT (positioned UPDATE)
   DELETE ... CURRENT (positioned DELETE)
   CLOSE

2. Noncursor operations:
   SELECT
   INSERT
   UPDATE (searched UPDATE)
   DELETE (searched DELETE)

3. Transaction termination operations:
   COMMIT
   ROLLBACK

Cursor operations and noncursor operations are discussed in Chapters 7 and 8, respectively. COMMIT and ROLLBACK are discussed at the end of the present chapter, in Section 6.4 (for want of a more appropriate place). *Note:* All data manipulation statements are guaranteed to be *atomic*, in the sense that if an error occurs during the execution of such a statement, the effect on the database is as if the statement had never been executed at all.

6.3 INDICATOR PARAMETERS

Nulls require special treatment in the module language (as indeed they do almost everywhere). Consider the following example of a procedure that contains a SELECT statement:

```
PROCEDURE GET_WEIGHT
   SQLCODE
   PNO_PARAM    CHAR(6)
   WEIGHT_PARAM DECIMAL(3) ;

SELECT P.WEIGHT
INTO   WEIGHT_PARAM
FROM   P
WHERE  P.PNO = PNO_PARAM ;
```

Suppose there is a chance that the value of WEIGHT might be null for some part (which in fact is the case, since NOT NULL was not specified for column WEIGHT in the schema of Fig. 2.3). The SELECT statement shown above will fail if the WEIGHT selected is null: SQLCODE will be set to a negative value, and the target parameter WEIGHT_PARAM will be left in an implementation-defined state. In general, if it is possible that a value to be retrieved might be null, the programmer should specify an *indicator parameter* in addition to the normal target parameter for that value, as we now illustrate:

```
PROCEDURE GET_WEIGHT
   SQLCODE
   PNO_PARAM    CHAR(6)
   WEIGHT_PARAM DECIMAL(3)
   WEIGHT_INDIC DECIMAL(5) ;

SELECT P.WEIGHT
INTO   WEIGHT_PARAM INDICATOR WEIGHT_INDIC
FROM   P
WHERE  P.PNO = PNO_PARAM ;
```

If the value to be retrieved is null and an indicator parameter has been specified, then that indicator parameter will be set to −1 (minus one); if the value to be retrieved is nonnull, the indicator parameter will be set to zero.* Indicator parameters are specified as shown—i.e., following the corresponding ordinary target parameter, and optionally separated from that ordinary parameter by the key word INDICATOR. They must be of data type "exact numeric" (the precise data type is implementation-defined).

The foregoing example shows the use of an indicator parameter in conjunction with a target parameter. Indicator parameters can also be used with ordinary parameters (i.e., parameters that are merely used to supply values). For example, the statement

```
UPDATE P
SET    WEIGHT = WEIGHT_PARAM INDICATOR WEIGHT_INDIC
WHERE  P.CITY = 'London'
```

will set the weight for all London parts to null if the value of WEIGHT_INDIC is negative (any negative value, not necessarily just −1). So also of course will the statement

```
UPDATE P
SET    WEIGHT = NULL
WHERE  P.CITY = 'London'
```

Note: Indicator parameters can also be used in a WHERE clause but probably should not be. For example, even if the value of WEIGHT_INDIC is negative, the following statement will *not* retrieve part numbers for parts where the weight is null. (*Exercise for the reader:* What will it do?)

---

*A slight oversimplification. If the value to be retrieved is nonnull and is a character string of length $n1$, and if the data type of the target parameter is CHARACTER($n2$), and if $n1 > n2$, then the result is truncated by dropping the rightmost $n1–n2$ characters and the indicator parameter is set to $n1$.

```
SELECT  P.PNO
INTO    PNO_PARAM
FROM    P
WHERE   P.WEIGHT = WEIGHT_PARAM  INDICATOR  WEIGHT_INDIC
```

The correct way to retrieve part numbers where the weight is null is:

```
SELECT  P.PNO
INTO    PNO_PARAM
FROM    P
WHERE   P.WEIGHT IS NULL
```

See Chapter 10 for further discussion of "IS NULL."

6.4 COMMIT AND ROLLBACK

COMMIT

The COMMIT operation takes the form

```
COMMIT WORK
```

The current transaction is terminated (normal termination). All updates made by the transaction are committed. All open cursors are closed.

ROLLBACK

The ROLLBACK operation takes the form

```
ROLLBACK WORK
```

The current transaction is terminated (abnormal termination). All updates made by the transaction are canceled. All open cursors are closed.

7

Data Manipulation: Cursor Operations

7.1 INTRODUCTION

The general idea of cursor-based access to the database was explained in Chapter 2, Section 2.4; refer back to that section if you need to refresh your memory regarding the general idea. In this chapter we consider the cursor operations in some detail. Those operations are as follows (to repeat from Section 6.2):

OPEN

FETCH

UPDATE . . . CURRENT (positioned UPDATE)

DELETE . . . CURRENT (positioned DELETE)

CLOSE

Section 7.2 explains what exactly a cursor is and what is involved in defining a cursor. Section 7.3 then discusses the five cursor operations in detail. *Note:* For tutorial reasons, we make a number of simplifying assumptions throughout this chapter, namely as follows:

- First, we assume that all tables are base tables. The special considerations that apply to views are deferred to Chapter 9.

- Second, we assume that the user holds all the privileges necessary to perform the operations in question.

- Third, we ignore the possibility of errors (for the most part). In particular, we ignore the possibility that any integrity violations might occur; i.e., we assume that no attempt is made to introduce a null into a column for which nulls are not allowed, or to introduce a row that violates a primary or foreign key constraint, or to enter a value into a column that is of the wrong data type (etc., etc.).

- Last, we do not attempt to explain query expressions (see the subsection "Cursor Definition" in the next section) in full generality. That explanation is deferred to Chapter 10.

7.2 CURSORS

A cursor consists essentially of a kind of *pointer* that can be used to run through an ordered collection of rows, pointing to each of the rows in that collection in turn and thus providing addressability to those rows one at a time. If cursor X is pointing to row R, it is said to be *positioned on* row R. Row R can then be updated or deleted via the "positioned" form of the UPDATE and DELETE operations (UPDATE/DELETE . . . WHERE CURRENT OF X).*

Each cursor has an associated *query*, specified as part of the operation that defines the cursor. The query can be parameterized. For example:

```
DECLARE X CURSOR
    FOR SELECT SP.SNO, SP.QTY
        FROM   SP
        WHERE  SP.PNO = PNO_PARAM
        ORDER  BY SP.SNO
```

This DECLARE defines a cursor called X, with associated query as defined by the expression "SELECT . . . PNO_PARAM" (where PNO_PARAM is a parameter). That query is not executed at this time; DECLARE CURSOR is a purely declarative operation. The query *is* (effectively) executed when cursor X is opened (see Section 7.3); if the query is parameterized, arguments corresponding to those parameters must be speci-

---

*In other words, for a positioned UPDATE or DELETE, the cursor must be in the "on state"; i.e., it must be positioned on some row. (This remark of course assumes that updates are permitted through the cursor in the first place; see later in this section.)

fied to the procedure that performs the OPEN. The collection of rows resulting from the execution of the query is now associated with the cursor, and remains so until the cursor is closed again (again, see Section 7.3). Furthermore, that collection of rows is *ordered* (see the discussion of ORDER BY at the end of the present section).

Note: If the query is parameterized, the values of the corresponding arguments are conceptually fixed at OPEN time; i.e., changing the values of those arguments after the cursor has been opened (and while it remains open) has no effect on the collection of rows accessible via the cursor.

While it is open, therefore, a cursor designates a certain ordered collection of rows. It also designates a certain specific *position* with respect to that ordering. The possible positions are as follows:

- *on* some specific row ("on" state)
- *before* some specific row ("before" state)
- *after* the last row ("after last" state)

OPEN positions the cursor before the first row. FETCH positions the cursor on the next row or (if there is no next row) after the last row. If the cursor is on or before some row and that row is deleted, the cursor is positioned before the next row or (if there is no next row) after the last row. Note that the cursor can be "before the first row" or "after the last row" even in the special case where the collection of rows is empty.

> *Comment:* The foregoing paragraph covers all cursor position changes that are specified by the standard. Others are possible, but are either not mentioned by the standard at all or at best are left as "implementation-defined." See Appendix F. *End of comment.*

All cursors are in the closed state at the beginning of the transaction and are forced into the closed state (if open) at transaction termination. Between transaction initiation and transaction termination, however, the same cursor can be opened and closed any number of times (possibly with different parameter values, and therefore different associated collections of rows, on different occasions).

Cursor Definition

Recall from Chapter 6 that cursors are defined as part of a module specification (prior to any procedures that might use those cursors). For each cursor definition in a given module, there must be exactly one procedure in that module whose function is to OPEN the cursor in question. The syntax for a cursor definition is:

```
DECLARE cursor CURSOR FOR query-expression
                       [ order-by-clause ]
```

An example has already been given at the beginning of this section. For details of "query expression," see Chapter 10; in this chapter we will generally assume that it is just a SELECT-expression (without however attempting to give a formal definition of that term), plus an optional ORDER BY clause. The purpose of the query expression is to define the collection of rows that will be accessible via the cursor when the cursor is opened. That collection of rows will be updatable via the cursor (i.e., "the cursor will be updatable," to use an inaccurate but common expression) if and only if all three of (a), (b), and (c) below apply:

(a) The query expression does not involve UNION—in other words, it is in fact a "query *specification*" (see Section 10.2); *and*

(b) That query specification would define an updatable view if it appeared in the context of a view definition (see Section 9.4); *and*

(c) The cursor definition does not include ORDER BY.

When the cursor is opened (and not before), the SELECT-expression is evaluated to yield a table of (in general) multiple rows. The ORDER BY clause specifies an ordering for those rows; if no such clause is specified, the ordering of rows is implementation-defined. Here is an example of a procedure to open a cursor (see Section 7.3 for more details):

```
PROCEDURE OPENX
   SQLCODE
   PNO_PARAM CHAR(6) ;
   OPEN X ;
```

Note that any parameter mentioned in the definition of a given cursor must be defined in the procedure that opens that cursor.

The ORDER BY Clause

The ORDER BY clause is defined as follows:

```
order-by-clause
   ::=   ORDER BY ordering-specification-commalist

ordering-specification
   ::=   { integer | column-reference } [ ASC | DESC ]
```

A column reference is just a qualified or unqualified column name. The left-to-right sequence of ordering specifications in the ORDER BY clause corresponds to major-to-minor ordering in accordance with familiar convention. Usually each such specification consists of a column name (identifying a column of the result table, i.e., the table represented by the

SELECT-expression), with an optional qualifier and an optional specification of ASC or DESC (ASC means ascending order and DESC means descending order; ASC is the default). Alternatively, an ordering specification can consist of an unsigned integer, as in the following example:

```
DECLARE Y CURSOR
      FOR SELECT SP.PNO, AVG ( SP.QTY )
          FROM    SP
          GROUP   BY SP.PNO
          ORDER   BY 2
```

The integer refers to the ordinal (left-to-right) position of the column in the result table. This feature makes it possible to order a result on the basis of a result column that is derived from something other than a simple named column, and hence does not possess a name of its own. In the example, the "2" refers to the column of averages. *Note:* Ordering specifications *must* be integers, not names, if the cursor definition involves a UNION. See Chapter 10.

Note that (as already indicated) each ordering specification must identify a column of the *result table*. Thus, for example, the following is *** *ILLEGAL* ***:

```
DECLARE Z CURSOR
      FOR SELECT S.SNO
          FROM    S
          ORDER   BY S.CITY
```

7.3 CURSOR-BASED MANIPULATION STATEMENTS

OPEN

The OPEN statement takes the form

```
OPEN cursor
```

where "cursor" identifies a cursor (X, say). Cursor X must currently be in the closed state. The query expression in the definition of X is evaluated, using current values for any parameters referenced in that query expression, to yield a collection of rows. That collection is ordered as explained at the end of Section 7.2. Cursor X is placed in the open state and is positioned before the first row of that ordered collection.

Example:

```
OPEN X
```

FETCH

The FETCH statement takes the form

```
FETCH cursor INTO target-commalist
```

where "cursor" identifies a cursor (X, say), and each target has the form

```
parameter [ [ INDICATOR ] parameter ]
```

(i.e., each consists of a target parameter with an optional associated indicator parameter—see Section 6.3). The target commalist must contain exactly one target for each expression in the SELECT clause in the definition of cursor X. The target identified by the ith entry in the commalist of targets corresponds to the ith expression in the SELECT clause in the definition of cursor X.

Cursor X must currently be open. If there is no next row in the ordered collection of rows currently associated with X (with respect to the current position of X in that ordering), nothing is retrieved; otherwise, cursor X is positioned on the next row, values are retrieved from that row, and assignments are made to targets in accordance with the specifications in the INTO clause.

Note that FETCH is logically a "fetch next" operation. Note also that "fetch next" is the *only* cursor movement operation; it is not possible to move the cursor (e.g.) "forward three positions" or "backward two positions" or "direct to the nth row," etc.

Example:

```
FETCH X INTO SNO_PARAM, QTY_PARAM INDICATOR QTY_INDIC
```

UPDATE (positioned)

The positioned UPDATE statement takes the form

```
UPDATE table
SET    assignment-commalist
WHERE  CURRENT OF cursor
```

where "table" identifies a table (T, say) and "cursor" identifies a cursor (X, say), and each assignment has the form

```
column = { scalar-expression | NULL }
```

The "column" on the left-hand side of each such assignment must be the *un*qualified name of a column of table T. Cursor X must currently be open, must be "updatable," and must be positioned on a row of table T. For each assignment in the SET clause, the result of evaluating the scalar expression, or null if NULL is specified, is assigned to the indicated column within the row that cursor X is currently positioned on. Any reference to a column of table T in the scalar expression is taken to mean the value in that column within the row on which cursor X is currently positioned before any of the assignments have been performed.

Note: The syntax of "scalar expression" is given in Chapter 10 (Section 10.3). As explained in Chapter 3, its general purpose is to designate some scalar value. In the particular context under discussion, such an expression must not include any references to any of the aggregate builtin functions (COUNT, SUM, AVG, etc.).

Example:

```
UPDATE SP
SET    QTY = SP.QTY + INCR_PARAM
WHERE  CURRENT OF X
```

Comment: The standard does not specify what happens if the positioned UPDATE changes the position of the updated row with respect to the ordering associated with the cursor. In the example, for instance, what happens if SP rows happen to be ordered by ascending QTY values? *End of comment.*

DELETE (positioned)

The positioned DELETE statement takes the form

```
DELETE
FROM    table
WHERE   CURRENT OF cursor
```

where "table" identifies a table (T, say) and "cursor" identifies a cursor (X, say). Cursor X must currently be open, must be "updatable," and must be positioned on a row of table T. That row is deleted.

Example:

```
DELETE
FROM    SP
WHERE   CURRENT OF X
```

Cursor X will now be positioned before the row immediately following the row just deleted, or after the last row if no such immediately following row exists.

CLOSE

The CLOSE statement takes the form

```
CLOSE cursor
```

where "cursor" identifies a cursor (X, say). Cursor X (which must currently be open) is placed in the closed state.

Example:

```
CLOSE X
```

7.4   A COMPREHENSIVE EXAMPLE

We conclude with a somewhat contrived, but comprehensive, example (Fig. 7.1) which shows how many of the ideas introduced in this chapter (and in earlier chapters) fit together. The host program (which is written in PL/I) accepts four input values: a part number (GIVENPNO), a city name (GIVENCIT), a status increment (GIVENINC), and a status level (GIVENLVL). The program scans all suppliers of the part identified by GIVENPNO. For each such supplier, if the supplier city is GIVENCIT, then the status is increased by GIVENINC; otherwise, if the status is less than GIVENLVL, the supplier is deleted, together with all shipments for that supplier. In all cases, supplier information is listed on the printer, with an indication of how that particular supplier was handled by the program.

Note 1: We ignore throughout the possibility that some value to be retrieved might be null. This simplification is introduced purely to reduce the size of the example.

Note 2: Some of the statements illustrated have not yet been discussed in detail. Specifically, the UPDATE and DELETE statements are of the "searched" variety, not the "positioned" variety. A general description of such statements can be found in Chapter 2; Chapter 8 gives the details.

Note 3: Observe that the UPDATE and DELETE statements to update/ delete the current S row (see the procedures UPDATE_PROC and DELETE_S_PROC) do have to be of the searched variety, not of the positioned variety, even though cursor Z is in fact positioned on precisely the row we wish to update/delete. The reason is that cursor Z is not "updatable"—i.e., the definition of cursor Z is such as to prohibit updates through Z (because it involves a subquery). See Section 7.2.

Note 4: Observe also that we must delete shipment rows *before* we delete the corresponding supplier row. The reason, of course, is that if we attempted to delete the supplier first, and the supplier in question in fact did have some corresponding shipments, the DELETE would fail (because of the foreign key constraint from shipments to suppliers). We remark in passing that careful locking protocols need to be followed here in order to prevent some concurrent transaction from (e.g.) inserting another shipment for the current supplier between our two DELETEs. Unfortunately, the standard does not include any explicit locking facilities.

Note 5: We use bbbbbbb to represent a string of seven blanks (Fig. 7.1, line 15 of the procedural code).

```
PLIEX: PROC OPTIONS (MAIN) ;

        /* program input */

        DCL GIVENPNO        CHAR(6) ;
        DCL GIVENCIT        CHAR(15) ;
        DCL GIVENINC        DECIMAL(3) ;
        DCL GIVENLVL        DECIMAL(3) ;

        /* targets for "FETCH SUPPLIER" */

        DCL SNO             CHAR(5) ;
        DCL SNAME           CHAR(20) ;
        DCL STATUS          DECIMAL(3) ;
        DCL CITY            CHAR(15) ;

        /* housekeeping variables */

        DCL DISP            CHAR(7) ;
        DCL MORE_SUPPLIERS  BIT(1) ;

        /* SQL return code variable */

        DCL RETCODE         FIXED BINARY(15) ;

        /* SQL entry point declarations, in alphabetical order */

        DCL CLOSE_PROC      ENTRY ( FIXED BINARY(15) ) ;
        DCL COMMIT_PROC     ENTRY ( FIXED BINARY(15) ) ;
        DCL DELETE_S_PROC   ENTRY ( FIXED BINARY(15), CHAR(5) ) ;
        DCL DELETE_SP_PROC  ENTRY ( FIXED BINARY(15), CHAR(5) ) ;
        DCL FETCH_PROC      ENTRY ( FIXED BINARY(15), CHAR(5),
                                                      CHAR(20),
                                                      DECIMAL(3),
                                                      CHAR(15) ) ;
        DCL OPEN_PROC       ENTRY ( FIXED BINARY(15), CHAR(6) ) ;
        DCL ROLLBACK_PROC   ENTRY ( FIXED BINARY(15) ) ;
        DCL UPDATE_PROC     ENTRY ( FIXED BINARY(15), CHAR(5),
                                                      DECIMAL(3) ) ;

        /* database exception handler */

        ON CONDITION ( DBEXCEPTION )
        BEGIN ;
           PUT SKIP LIST ( RETCODE ) ;
           CALL ROLLBACK_PROC ( RETCODE ) ;
           PUT SKIP LIST ( RETCODE ) ;
           GO TO QUIT ;
        END ;
```

Fig. 7.1 A comprehensive example (part 1 of 3)

```
/* main program logic */

GET LIST ( GIVENPNO, GIVENCIT, GIVENINC, GIVENLVL ) ;
CALL OPEN_PROC ( RETCODE, GIVENPNO ) ;
IF NOT ( RETCODE = 0 )
THEN SIGNAL CONDITION ( DBEXCEPTION ) ;
MORE_SUPPLIERS = '1'B ;
DO WHILE ( MORE_SUPPLIERS ) ;
   CALL FETCH_PROC ( RETCODE, SNO, SNAME, STATUS, CITY ) ;
   SELECT ;            /* a PL/I SELECT, not a SQL SELECT */
   WHEN ( RETCODE = 100 )
      MORE_SUPPLIERS = '0'B ;
   WHEN NOT ( RETCODE = 100 | RETCODE = 0 )
      SIGNAL CONDITION ( DBEXCEPTION ) ;
   WHEN ( RETCODE = 0 )
      DO ;
         DISP = 'bbbbbbb' ;
         IF CITY = GIVENCIT
         THEN
            DO ;
               CALL UPDATE_PROC ( RETCODE, SNO, GIVENINC ) ;
               IF NOT ( RETCODE = 0 )
               THEN SIGNAL CONDITION ( DBEXCEPTION ) ;
               DISP = 'UPDATED' ;
            END ;
         ELSE
            IF STATUS < GIVENLVL
            THEN
               DO ;
                  CALL DELETE_SP_PROC ( RETCODE, SNO ) ;
                  IF NOT ( RETCODE = 0 | RETCODE = 100 )
                  THEN SIGNAL CONDITION ( DBEXCEPTION ) ;
                  CALL DELETE_S_PROC ( RETCODE, SNO ) ;
                  IF NOT ( RETCODE = 0 )
                  THEN SIGNAL CONDITION ( DBEXCEPTION ) ;
                  DISP = 'DELETED' ;
               END ;
            PUT SKIP LIST
               ( SNO, SNAME, STATUS, CITY, DISP ) ;
      END ;    /* WHEN ( RETCODE = 0 ) ... */
   END ;    /* PL/I SELECT */
END ;    /* DO WHILE */
CALL CLOSE_PROC ( RETCODE ) ;
CALL COMMIT_PROC ( RETCODE ) ;
QUIT:   RETURN ;
END ;    /* PLIEX */
```

Fig. 7.1 A comprehensive example (part 2 of 3)

```
MODULE SQLEXMOD LANGUAGE PLI AUTHORIZATION CJDATE

        DECLARE Z CURSOR FOR
            SELECT S.SNO, S.SNAME, S.STATUS, S.CITY
            FROM    S
            WHERE   S.SNO IN
                  ( SELECT SP.SNO
                    FROM    SP
                    WHERE   SP.PNO = PNO )        -- PNO is a parameter

PROCEDURE CLOSE_PROC
        SQLCODE ;
        CLOSE Z ;

PROCEDURE COMMIT_PROC
        SQLCODE ;
        COMMIT WORK ;

PROCEDURE DELETE_S_PROC
        SQLCODE
        SNO CHAR(5) ;
        DELETE FROM S WHERE S.SNO = SNO ;      -- "searched DELETE"

PROCEDURE DELETE_SP_PROC
        SQLCODE
        SNO CHAR(5) ;
        DELETE FROM SP WHERE SP.SNO = SNO ;   -- "searched DELETE"

PROCEDURE FETCH_PROC
        SQLCODE
        SNO     CHAR(5)
        SNAME   CHAR(20)
        STATUS  DECIMAL(3)
        CITY    CHAR(20) ;
        FETCH Z INTO SNO, SNAME, STATUS, CITY ;

PROCEDURE OPEN_PROC
        SQLCODE
        PNO CHAR(6) ;
        OPEN Z ;

PROCEDURE ROLLBACK_PROC
        SQLCODE ;
        ROLLBACK WORK ;

PROCEDURE UPDATE_PROC
        SQLCODE
        SNO       CHAR(5)
        GIVENINC DECIMAL(3) ;
        UPDATE S
        SET     STATUS = S.STATUS + GIVENINC
        WHERE   S.SNO = SNO ;                     -- "searched UPDATE"
```

Fig. 7.1 A comprehensive example (part 3 of 3)

8

Data Manipulation: Noncursor Operations

8.1 INTRODUCTION

The noncursor manipulative operations are as follows:

SELECT
INSERT
UPDATE (searched)
DELETE (searched)

As in Chapter 7, we make a number of assumptions (basically the same ones as in that chapter) in order to simplify the presentation:

- All tables are base tables.
- The user holds all necessary privileges.
- No errors occur.

We also continue to defer a full explanation of query expressions and related matters to Chapter 10.

8.2   SELECT

First, a word of caution to readers who might already have some knowledge
of the SQL language: The noncursor SELECT operation in standard SQL
is *not* the fully general (set-level) SELECT operation they are probably familiar with. Instead, it is what is sometimes called the *singleton SELECT*,
i.e., a SELECT that retrieves *at most one row*. For example:

```
SELECT  P.WEIGHT, P.COLOR
INTO    WEIGHT_PARAM, COLOR_PARAM
FROM    P
WHERE   P.PNO = 'P4'
```

It is an error if the table that results from evaluating the SELECT–FROM–
WHERE contains more than one row. Here are some more (valid) examples
(i.e., examples that do retrieve at most one row):

```
SELECT  *
INTO    SNO_PARAM, SNAME_PARAM, STATUS_PARAM, CITY_PARAM
FROM    S
WHERE   S.SNO = 'S1'

SELECT  AVG ( SP.QTY )
INTO    AVG_QTY_PARAM
FROM    SP

SELECT  MAX ( SP.QTY ) - MIN ( SP.QTY )
INTO    ARITH_PARAM
FROM    SP
WHERE   SP.PNO = 'P4'
```

The general syntax is:

```
SELECT [ ALL | DISTINCT ] selection
       INTO  target-commalist  table-expression
```

where:

(a) If neither DISTINCT nor ALL is specified, ALL is assumed.

(b) Let T1 be the table resulting from evaluation of the specified table expression; let T2 be the table that is derived from T1 by evaluating the
specified "selection" against T1; and let T3 be the table that is derived
from T2 by eliminating redundant duplicate rows from T2 if
DISTINCT is specified, or a table that is identical to T2 otherwise.
Table T3 should contain at most one row.

(c) If table T3 contains one row, that row is retrieved. If table T3 contains
no rows, a "not found" exception occurs (SQLCODE is set to +100).
If table T3 contains more than one row, an error occurs (SQLCODE is
set to a negative value).

(d) "Selection" is either a commalist of scalar expressions (each typically
but not necessarily involving one or more columns of T) or a single

asterisk ("*"). The asterisk is shorthand for a commalist specifying all columns of table T1, in their left-to-right order within that table. (In other words, table T2 is identical to table T1 in the "*" case.)

(e) The INTO clause is exactly as for FETCH (see Section 7.3).

(f) The table expression consists of a FROM clause and an optional WHERE clause. *Note:* In general, a table expression can also include a GROUP BY clause and/or a HAVING clause (see Section 10.5), but those clauses are not permitted in this particular context.

Comments:

1. The SQL standard uses the term "table expression" to refer to a construct of the form

```
    FROM ...
[ WHERE ... ]
[ GROUP BY ... ]
[ HAVING ... ]
```

Calling this construct a table expression is misleading, however, because it suggests that such an expression is the *only* construct in the language that represents a table value. In fact, *any query expression is table-valued* (this fact follows from the well known *closure* property of the relational model, and is very important). In particular, a "SELECT-expression" is table-valued.* A SELECT-expression is just a special case of a query expression; it consists of a SELECT clause followed by a table expression (in the above—deprecated—sense of that term). In other words, the entire SELECT statement is basically just a SELECT-expression, and as such it is of course table-valued.

2. Note that "selection" consists *either* of a commalist of scalar expressions *or* of a single asterisk, not a mixture. Thus, e.g., the following is *** *ILLEGAL* ***:

```
SELECT *, ( SP.QTY / 12 )
INTO    ...
FROM    SP
WHERE   SP.SNO = 'S1'
AND     SP.PNO = 'P1'
```

It is legal in DB2 (as it should be).

3. Note too that the asterisk cannot be qualified. Thus, e.g., the following is also ***ILLEGAL***:

---

*Remember from Chapter 7 that the term "SELECT-expression" is not (and will not be) formally defined. We use it merely as an informal term whose meaning we take to be intuitively obvious. We adopt this approach simply in order to avoid having to delve into the full complexity of query expressions too early in the book.

```
SELECT  S.*, SP.QTY
INTO    ...
FROM    S, SP
WHERE   S.SNO = 'S1'
AND     SP.SNO = 'S1'
AND     SP.PNO = 'P1'
```

It is legal in DB2 (as it should be).

End of comments.

Note: A SELECT clause* is not allowed to include the key word DISTINCT more than once (regardless of whether the clause appears in a SELECT statement or in any other context). Thus, e.g., the following is legal:

```
SELECT DISTINCT SP.PNO ...
```

and so is this:

```
SELECT SP.PNO, SUM ( DISTINCT SP.QTY ) ...
```

but the following is ***ILLEGAL ***:

```
SELECT DISTINCT SP.PNO, SUM ( DISTINCT SP.QTY ) ...
```

and so is this:

```
SELECT SUM ( DISTINCT SP.QTY ), AVG ( DISTINCT SP.QTY ) ...
```

8.3 INSERT

The INSERT statement is used to add new rows to a table. Two examples are given below; the first inserts a single row, the second inserts multiple rows. For the second example we assume that we have an additional table called TEMP, with columns SNO and CITY (where the data types of columns TEMP.SNO and TEMP.CITY are compatible with the data types of columns S.SNO and S.CITY, respectively).

---

*More accurately, a *query specification* or a *subquery* (excluding any nested subqueries in both cases). For example, the following is also *** *ILLEGAL* ***:

```
SELECT SUM ( DISTINCT ... )
...
HAVING AVG ( DISTINCT ... ) ...
```

See Chapter 10 for an explanation of query specifications and subqueries.

```
INSERT
INTO    S ( SNO, CITY, SNAME )
VALUES  ( SNO_PARAM, NULL, SNAME_PARAM )

INSERT
INTO    TEMP ( SNO, CITY )
        SELECT S.SNO, S.CITY
        FROM   S
        WHERE  S.STATUS > STATUS_PARAM
```

The general syntax is:

```
INSERT INTO table [ ( column-commalist ) ] source
```

where "table" identifies the target table, the optional "column commalist" identifies some or all of the columns of that table (by their *unqualified* column names), and "source" is explained below. Omitting the parenthesized commalist of column names is equivalent to specifying all of the columns of the target table, in their left-to-right order within that table.

The "source" in an INSERT statement is either a *query specification* (loosely, a SELECT-expression; see Chapter 10 for details), or a VALUES clause of the form

```
VALUES ( insert-atom-commalist )
```

where each "insert atom," in turn, is either an explicit null (represented by the key word NULL), the "system variable" USER (see Section 4.4), or a parameter (with an optional indicator parameter).

Explanation:

1. If an INSERT statement contains an explicit commalist of column names that omits one or more columns of the target table T, then any row inserted into T by that statement will have the appropriate default value (possibly null) in each such omitted column position. It is an error if a column is omitted and that column has no default value.

2. If the INSERT statement includes a VALUES clause, then a single row is inserted into the target table. The *i*th atom in the VALUES clause is inserted into the column position identified by the *i*th entry in the (explicit or implicit) commalist of column names in the INTO clause.

3. If the INSERT statement includes a query specification, then multiple rows are inserted into the target table (in general). The query specification is evaluated to yield an intermediate result table R. Each row of R in turn is then treated as if the scalar values in that row were specified as the atoms in a VALUES clause in the single-row version of the INSERT statement.

Comments:

We draw the reader's attention to two restrictions (both of them hang-overs from IBM SQL):

  1. First, observe that (as mentioned in Section 6.2) operational expressions such as PARAM + 1 are not allowed in a VALUES clause.
  2. If the INSERT statement includes a query specification, the target table T of the INSERT must not be referenced in any FROM clause within that query specification (at any level of nesting). Thus, for example, the following is *** *ILLEGAL* *** :

```
INSERT
INTO    T
        SELECT *
        FROM    T
```

(even if table T permits duplicate rows).

End of comments.

8.4 SEARCHED UPDATE

The searched UPDATE statement is used to update rows in a table without using a cursor. The update is multiple-row (in general); i.e., the statement updates zero, one, two, . . ., or any number of rows in a single operation. Here is an example (a variation on an example from Chapter 2):

```
UPDATE S
SET     STATUS = 2 * S.STATUS
WHERE   S.CITY = CITY_PARAM
```

The general syntax is:

```
UPDATE table
  SET       assignment-commalist
[ WHERE   search-condition ]
```

where "table" identifies the target table, the commalist of assignments is exactly as for a positioned UPDATE (see Section 7.3), and "search condition" identifies the rows of the target table that are to be updated. (Search conditions are discussed in detail in Chapter 10.) Omitting the WHERE clause means that the UPDATE is to be applied to all rows of the target table.

  The UPDATE is conceptually performed as if a hidden cursor (H, say) were used to run through the rows to be updated and a corresponding positioned UPDATE . . . WHERE CURRENT OF H were applied to each such row in turn.

Comment: The searched UPDATE operation suffers from a restriction similar to the second of the two restrictions mentioned under INSERT in the previous section, namely as follows: If the UPDATE statement includes a WHERE clause, then the target table T of the UPDATE must not be referenced in any FROM clause within that WHERE clause (at any level of nesting—see Chapter 10). Thus, for example, the following UPDATE is *** *ILLEGAL* *** :

```
UPDATE S
SET     CITY = CITY_PARAM
WHERE   S.STATUS <
        ( SELECT AVG ( S.STATUS )
          FROM    S )
```

This restriction is another hangover from IBM SQL. *End of comment.*

8.5 SEARCHED DELETE

The searched DELETE statement is used to delete rows in a table without using a cursor. The delete is multiple-row (in general); i.e., the statement deletes zero, one, two, . . ., or any number of rows in a single operation. Here is an example (a variation on an example from Chapter 2):

```
DELETE
FROM    P
WHERE   P.WEIGHT > WEIGHT_PARAM
```

The general syntax is:

```
  DELETE
  FROM    table
[ WHERE   search-condition ]
```

where "table" identifies the target table and "search condition" identifies the rows of the target table that are to be deleted. (Once again, search conditions are discussed in detail in Chapter 10.) Omitting the WHERE clause means that the DELETE is to be applied to all rows of the target table.

The DELETE is conceptually performed as if a hidden cursor (H, say) were used to run through the rows to be deleted and a corresponding positioned DELETE . . . WHERE CURRENT OF H were applied to each such row in turn.

Comment: The searched DELETE operation suffers from a restriction similar to the restriction mentioned under UPDATE in the previous section, namely as follows: If the DELETE statement includes a WHERE clause, then the target table T of the DELETE must not be referenced in any FROM clause within that WHERE clause (at any level of

nesting—see Chapter 10). Thus, e.g., the following **DELETE** is
*** *ILLEGAL* ***:

```
DELETE
FROM    S
WHERE   S.STATUS <
        ( SELECT AVG ( S.STATUS )
          FROM    S )
```

Again, this restriction is a hangover from IBM SQL. *End of comment.*

9

Views

9.1 INTRODUCTION

Throughout Chapters 7 and 8 we deliberately assumed for simplicity that all tables were base tables. We now turn our attention to the special considerations that apply to views (or "viewed tables," to use the official standard term). Recall from Chapter 2 that a view is a *virtual* table—i.e., a table that does not exist in its own right, but looks to the user as if it did. By contrast, a base table is a *real* table, in the sense that, for each row of such a table, there really is some stored counterpart of that row in physical storage.

Views are not supported by their own, physically separate, distinguishable stored data. All that happens when a view is defined is that the view's definition in terms of other tables (base tables and/or other views) is remembered by the system in some way (actually by storing it in the *system catalog*—but the concept of a catalog is outside the scope of the SQL standard per se). Here is an example:

```
CREATE VIEW GOODSUPPS ( SNO, STATUS, CITY )
     AS   SELECT S.SNO, S.STATUS, S.CITY
          FROM    S
          WHERE   S.STATUS > 15
```

Note the similarity to the definition of a cursor: Like a cursor definition, a view definition includes a SELECT-expression that defines a certain scope;* and as with a cursor definition, that SELECT-expression is *not* evaluated at the time of definition. Instead, it is merely remembered under the specified view name. *To the user, however, it is as if there really were a table in the database with the specified name.* In the example, it is as if there really were a table called GOODSUPPS, with rows and columns as shown in the unshaded portions (only) of Fig. 9.1.

Here is an example of a SELECT operation involving GOODSUPPS:

```
SELECT *
FROM    GOODSUPPS
WHERE   GOODSUPPS.CITY <> 'London'
```

The system will translate this SELECT into an equivalent operation on the underlying base table (or base tables, plural—see Section 9.2). The translation is done by "merging" the SELECT issued by the user with the SELECT that was saved in the catalog; in effect, by replacing references to the view by the view definition. In the example, the resultant operation is

```
SELECT S.SNO, S.STATUS, S.CITY
FROM    S
WHERE   S.CITY <> 'London'
AND     S.STATUS > 15
```

Note: The SELECT in this example (against view GOODSUPPS) is multiple-row and hence cannot be executed as a SELECT *statement*, at least so far as the standard is concerned. Rather, it must be included as a component within a query expression or query specification or other more complex language construct (e.g., within the definition of a cursor). See Chapter 10 for details. For simplicity, however, it is convenient to assume that multiple-row SELECTs *can* be executed directly, and for tutorial reasons we will make that assumption throughout most of the remainder of this chapter.

GOODSUPPS	SNO	SNAME	STATUS	CITY
	S1	Smith	20	London
	S2	Jones	10	Paris
	S3	Blake	30	Paris
	S4	Clark	20	London
	S5	Adams	30	Athens

Fig. 9.1 GOODSUPPS as a view of base table S (unshaded portions)

---

*Note, however, that view definitions appear within a schema, whereas cursor definitions appear within a module. As a consequence, a view definition, unlike a cursor definition, cannot include any references to parameters.

The translation process just illustrated also applies to update operations. For example, the operation

```
UPDATE  GOODSUPPS
SET     CITY = 'New York'
WHERE   GOODSUPPS.CITY = 'Paris'
```

is translated to

```
UPDATE  S
SET     CITY = 'New York'
WHERE   S.CITY = 'Paris'
AND     S.STATUS > 15
```

INSERT and DELETE operations are handled in the same general way. For example, the INSERT operation

```
INSERT
INTO    GOODSUPPS ( SNO, STATUS, CITY )
VALUES ( 'S6', 25, 'Madrid' )
```

translates to:

```
INSERT
INTO    S ( SNO, STATUS, CITY )
VALUES ( 'S6', 25, 'Madrid' )
```

(note, therefore, that SNAME will be set to the applicable default value in the inserted row). Likewise, the DELETE operation

```
DELETE
FROM    GOODSUPPS
WHERE   GOODSUPPS.CITY = 'New York'
```

translates to:

```
DELETE
FROM    S
WHERE   S.CITY = 'New York'
AND     S.STATUS > 15
```

Comment: Strictly speaking, the explanations of this section, to the effect that references to a view *V* are processed by (conceptually) replacing them by the definition of *V*, should be regarded as somewhat speculative. The official SQL standard does not actually specify how views are processed at all! The only guidance the standard gives is a rule stating that the value of a view *V* is "the table that would result if the [definition of *V*] were executed," together with a statement to the effect that whether or not *V* is materialized is implementation-defined. However, many of the numerous restrictions to which views are subject (see Sections 9.3 and 9.4) clearly stem from the likelihood that operations on views are indeed implemented by the merging process described above. *End of comment.*

9.2   VIEW DEFINITION

The general syntax of CREATE VIEW is

```
CREATE VIEW view [ ( column-commalist ) ]
    AS   query-specification
    [ WITH CHECK OPTION ]
```

where "view" is the unqualified name for the newly created view,* the optional "column commalist" lists the unqualified names of the columns of the view, the query specification is a SELECT-expression that defines the scope of the view (loosely speaking—see Chapter 10 for details), and the WITH CHECK OPTION clause is explained in Section 9.4. See Example 1 below for a discussion of when the commalist of column names can be omitted. The fully qualified name of the view is U.V, where U is the authorization identifier specified in the AUTHORIZATION clause of the schema that includes the CREATE VIEW operation, and V is the identifier specified (as "view") in that operation.

As explained in Section 9.1, the query specification in CREATE VIEW cannot include any parameter references.

Here are some examples:

```
1. CREATE VIEW REDPARTS ( PNO, PNAME, WT, CITY )
       AS SELECT P.PNO, P.PNAME, P.WEIGHT, P.CITY
          FROM   P
          WHERE  P.COLOR = 'Red'
```

The effect of this statement is to create a new view called REDPARTS, with four columns called PNO, PNAME, WT, and CITY, corresponding respectively to the four columns PNO, PNAME, WEIGHT, and CITY of the underlying base table P. For the sake of the example, we have specified the names of the columns of the newly created view explicitly, even though there is an obvious set of names (PNO, PNAME, WEIGHT, CITY) that can be inherited from the underlying table. In general, explicit specification of column names is required only if some column of the view is derived from something other than a simple column of (one of) the FROM table(s), and/or two of the view columns would otherwise have the same name. Note that in these latter two cases explicit names must be specified for *all* view columns, even if some of those columns have an obvious inherited name.

```
2. CREATE VIEW LREDPARTS
       AS SELECT REDPARTS.PNO, REDPARTS.WT
          FROM   REDPARTS
          WHERE  REDPARTS.CITY = 'London'
```

---

*Actually the name can be qualified, but if it is, then the qualifier *must* be the authorization identifier specified in the schema AUTHORIZATION clause.

It is perfectly possible to define a view in terms of other views, as this example illustrates. The column names for LREDPARTS are PNO and WT (inherited from REDPARTS).

```
3. CREATE VIEW CITYPAIRS ( SCITY, PCITY )
       AS SELECT S.CITY, P.CITY
          FROM   S, SP, P
          WHERE  S.SNO = SP.SNO
          AND    SP.PNO = P.PNO
```

The meaning of this view is that a pair of city names (x,y) will appear in the view if and only if a supplier located in city x supplies a part stored in city y. For example, supplier S1 supplies part P1; supplier S1 is located in London and part P1 is stored in London; and so the pair (London,London) appears in the view. Notice that the definition of this view involves a join (actually a "3-way join"), so that this is an example of a view that is derived from multiple underlying tables. Note also that the inherited names for the columns of the view are both CITY, and hence that new column names *must* be specified explicitly, as shown.

```
4. CREATE VIEW PQ ( PNO, TOTQTY )
       AS SELECT SP.PNO, SUM ( SP.QTY )
          FROM   SP
          GROUP  BY SP.PNO
```

In this example, there is no name that can be inherited for the "total quantity" column, since that column is derived from an aggregate builtin function; hence (again) new column names must be specified explicitly, as shown. Notice that, although this view is derived from a single underlying base table, it is not just a simple row-and-column subset of that base table (unlike the views REDPARTS and GOODSUPPS shown earlier). It might be regarded instead as a kind of statistical summary or compression of that underlying table.

9.3 RETRIEVAL OPERATIONS

We have already explained in outline (in Section 9.1) how retrieval operations on a view are translated into equivalent operations on the underlying base table(s). In many cases that translation process is quite straightforward and works perfectly well, without any surprises for the user. Sometimes, however, such surprises can occur. In particular, problems can arise in connexion with what are called "grouped views." View PQ (Example 4 from the previous section) is an example of a grouped view. In general, any view whose definition directly includes a GROUP BY clause (or a HAVING clause—see Chapter 10) is a grouped view. A view of a grouped view (i.e., a view whose definition directly contains a FROM clause that references a grouped view) is also considered to be a grouped view—and so on, to any number of levels.

Grouped views are subject to numerous restrictions. First, a FROM clause that includes a reference to a grouped view (in whatever context) is not allowed to reference any other table; in other words, a grouped view cannot be joined to any other table. Furthermore, a FROM clause that references a grouped view is not allowed to have an associated WHERE clause, GROUP BY clause, or HAVING clause. The following discussion represents a sketch of the reasoning behind such restrictions. Consider the following example.

View definition (legal):

```
CREATE VIEW PQ ( PNO, TOTQTY )
    AS SELECT SP.PNO, SUM ( SP.QTY )
       FROM    SP
       GROUP   BY SP.PNO
```

(a repeat of Example 4 from Section 9.2).

Attempted query:

```
SELECT  PQ.PNO
FROM    PQ
WHERE   PQ.TOTQTY > 500                    [*** ILLEGAL ***]
```

If we apply the simple translation process described in Section 9.1 to combine this expression with the view definition remembered by the system, we obtain something like the following:

```
SELECT  SP.PNO
FROM    SP
WHERE   SUM ( SP.QTY ) > 500               [*** ILLEGAL ***]
GROUP   BY SP.PNO
```

And this is not a valid SELECT-expression. Predicates in a WHERE clause are not allowed to refer to builtin functions such as SUM. What the original expression should be converted to is something more along the following lines:

```
SELECT  SP.PNO
FROM    SP
GROUP   BY SP.PNO
HAVING  SUM ( SP.QTY ) > 500
```

However, SQL is not capable of performing such a translation.

Here is another example of a situation in which the translation does not work (again using the "statistical summary" view PQ). The attempted query is:

```
SELECT  AVG ( PQ.TOTQTY )
FROM    PQ
```

"Translated" form:

```
SELECT  AVG ( SUM ( SP.QTY ) )           [*** ILLEGAL ***]
FROM    SP
GROUP   BY SP.PNO
```

Again this is illegal. SQL does not allow aggregate functions to be nested in this fashion.

> *Comment:* The foregoing examples do not exhaust the possibilities. Similar unpleasant surprises can occur if the view definition involves DISTINCT, or a column that is derived from an operational expression such as A + B, or a column that is derived from an aggregate function (even without GROUP BY). Furthermore, it is not easy to characterize the complete set of such "surprises" precisely. The best that can be formulated by way of a general principle seems to be: *The translated form of the original query must always be a legal SQL SELECT-expression.* The whole area of views (the retrieval aspect in particular) is one of the ugliest parts of the SQL language. *End of comment.*

9.4 UPDATE OPERATIONS

A given view may or may not be updatable. We demonstrate this point by means of the two views GOODSUPPS and CITYPAIRS from Sections 9.1 and 9.2, respectively. For convenience we repeat their definitions below:

```
CREATE VIEW GOODSUPPS ( SNO, STATUS, CITY )
    AS SELECT S.SNO, S.STATUS, S.CITY
       FROM  S
       WHERE S.STATUS > 15

CREATE VIEW CITYPAIRS ( SCITY, PCITY )
    AS SELECT S.CITY, P.CITY
       FROM   S, SP, P
       WHERE  S.SNO = SP.SNO
       AND    SP.PNO = P.PNO
```

Of these two views, GOODSUPPS is logically updatable, while CITYPAIRS is logically not. It is instructive to examine why this is so. In the case of GOODSUPPS:

(a) We can INSERT a new row into the view—say the row (S6,40,Rome)—by actually inserting the corresponding row (S6,ddd,40,Rome) into the underlying base table (where "ddd" is the appropriate default value for S.SNAME).

(b) We can DELETE an existing row from the view—say the row (S1,20,London)—by actually deleting the corresponding row (S1,Smith,20,London) from the underlying base table.

(c) We can UPDATE an existing value in the view—say the CITY value for supplier S1 (namely London), to change it to Rome—by actually making that change to the corresponding value in the underlying base table.

Now consider the view CITYPAIRS. As explained in Section 9.2, one of the rows in that view is the row (London,London). Suppose it were possible to DELETE that row. What would such a DELETE signify?—i.e., what updates (DELETEs or otherwise) on the underlying data would such a DELETE correspond to? The only possible answer has to be "We don't know"; there is simply no way (in general) that we can go down to the underlying base tables and make an appropriate set of updates there. In fact, such an "appropriate set of updates" does not even exist; there is *no* set of updates that could be applied to the underlying data (in general) that would have precisely the effect of removing the specified row from the view while leaving everything else in the view unchanged. In other words, *the original DELETE is an intrinsically unsupportable operation*. Similar arguments can be made to show that (in general) INSERT and UPDATE operations are also intrinsically not supportable on this view.

Thus we see that some views are inherently updatable, whereas others are inherently not. *Note the word "inherently" here*. It is not just a question of some systems being able to support certain updates while others cannot. *No* system can consistently support updates on a view such as CITYPAIRS unaided (by "unaided" we mean "without help from some human user").

For further discussion of which views are theoretically updatable and which not, the reader is referred to the author's book *Relational Database: Selected Writings* (Addison-Wesley, 1986). Here, however, we are not concerned so much with what is theoretically possible, but rather with what SQL will allow, which is a very different thing. In SQL, a view is updatable if and only if all of the following conditions (a)–(f) below apply to the view definition (i.e., to the SELECT-expression that defines the view):

(a) It does not include the key word DISTINCT.

(b) Every item in the SELECT clause consists of a simple reference to a column of the underlying table (i.e., it is not a constant, nor an operational expression such as COL + 1, nor a reference to a function such as AVG).

(c) The FROM clause identifies exactly one table, and that table in turn is updatable.

(d) The WHERE clause does not include a subquery.

(e) There is no GROUP BY clause.

(f) There is no HAVING clause.

Finally (to state the obvious): The operations INSERT, UPDATE, and DELETE can be applied to a SQL view only if that view is updatable as defined above.

Comments:

These restrictions are *extremely* restrictive. They are also logically unnecessary, in some cases. DB2 SQL is a little less restrictive (though not much); in DB2, rules (b) and (d) above are relaxed slightly, as follows.

(b) In DB2, if a column of the view is derived from a builtin function, then the view is not updatable. If it is derived from a constant or an operational expression such as COL + 1, then INSERT operations are not allowed, and UPDATE operations are not allowed on that column. However, DELETE operations are allowed, and so are UPDATE operations on other columns.

(d) In DB2, if the WHERE clause includes a subquery *and the FROM clause in that subquery refers to the base table on which the view is defined*, then the view is not updatable.

The basic problem (with both standard SQL and DB2 SQL) is that the language is very ad hoc: It is full of instances of lack of orthogonality, and it fails to take proper account of the fundamental semantics of primary and foreign keys. (See Appendix F for a discussion of these points, also Chapter 12 for an explanation of the term "orthogonality.")

End of comments.

The Check Option

Finally, we return to the GOODSUPPS view once again, in order to discuss one last issue. As explained at the beginning of this section, that view is updatable. But consider the following UPDATE:

```
UPDATE  GOODSUPPS
SET     STATUS = 0
WHERE   GOODSUPPS.SNO = 'S1'
```

Should this UPDATE be accepted? If it is, it will have the effect of removing supplier S1 from the view, since the S1 row will no longer satisfy the view-defining condition ("S.STATUS > 15"). Likewise, the INSERT operation

```
INSERT
INTO    GOODSUPPS ( SNO, STATUS, CITY )
VALUES ( 'S8', 7, 'Stockholm' )
```

(if accepted) will create a new supplier row, but that row will instantly vanish from the view. The check option (mentioned in Section 9.2) is designed to deal with such situations. If the clause

WITH CHECK OPTION

is included in the definition of a view, then all INSERTs and UPDATEs against that view will be checked to ensure that the newly INSERTed or UPDATEd row does indeed satisfy the view-defining condition. If it does not, then the operation will be rejected.

The check option can be specified only if the view is updatable.

Comments:

1. The standard and DB2 are different here. In DB2, the check option can be specified only if the view is updatable *and* its definition does not include a subquery. (The standard avoids this problem by stating that a view whose definition includes a subquery is not updatable anyway.) In DB2 also, if the view is such that UPDATEs are legal on certain columns only (and INSERTs are not allowed at all), then the check option applies only to UPDATEs on those columns.

2. Note that (as mentioned in Section 3.3) the check option is not inheritable. That is, if the definition of view V includes WITH CHECK OPTION, and view W is defined in terms of view V, then updates to view V via view W are not checked against the check option for view V. This state of affairs, ironically, is another hangover from DB2—"ironically," because the problem has subsequently been fixed in DB2 (i.e., in DB2 the check option on view V *is* now automatically inherited by all updatable views W that are defined in terms of view V).

End of comments.

10

Common Language Constructs

10.1 QUERY EXPRESSIONS

In this chapter (finally) we explain a number of important SQL constructs, such as "search condition," that have been heavily referenced in previous chapters but have not yet been properly defined. The constructs in question appear in a variety of different contexts within the language. We start with the construct "query expression," since in many ways that construct can be regarded as being at the top of the syntax tree. Here is the BNF definition:

```
query-expression
    ::=    query-term
        |  query-expression UNION [ ALL ] query-term

query-term
    ::=    query-specification | ( query-expression )
```

The construct "query expression" appears only within a cursor definition (note, therefore, that UNION—with or without ALL—is not allowed in a SELECT statement or in INSERT . . . SELECT or in a view definition). As the grammar indicates, a query expression is basically just a query specification, or a collection of two or more query specifications connected together by UNIONs—except that the grammar considers UNION to be a purely binary operation, so that (e.g.) a query expression involving the three query specifications x, y, and z must be written as

```
x UNION (y UNION z)
```

or as

```
(x UNION y) UNION z,
```

not just as *x* UNION *y* UNION *z*. The apparently excessive parentheses are required because of the possibility that some of the UNIONs might involve ALL (see below) and some not. For example, the expressions

```
x UNION ALL (y UNION z)
```

and

```
(x UNION ALL y) UNION z
```

are not equivalent, in general.

> *Comment:* We follow the SQL standard in using the terms "query expression" and "query specification," though they are not very descriptive of the constructs they refer to. Terms along the lines of "UNION-expression" and "SELECT-expression" might have been more satisfactory. *End of comment.*

Let A and B be two tables, resulting (in general) from two query specifications. Assume for the moment that the query expression

```
A UNION [ ALL ] B
```

is legal (see below). Then the value of that expression is a table containing a row for every row that appears in table A or in table B or in both. Redundant duplicate rows are retained if and only if the key word ALL is specified. Here is an example:

```
SELECT P.PNO FROM P WHERE P.WEIGHT > 16
UNION
SELECT SP.PNO FROM SP WHERE SP.SNO = 'S2'
```

The value of this expression is the set of part numbers (P1,P2,P3,P6)—i.e., duplicates are eliminated. If ALL had been specified, the value would have been (P1,P2,P2,P3,P6)—i.e., duplicates would have been retained. Note the difference between UNION and SELECT with regard to duplicate elimination: With SELECT, the user can specify ALL or DISTINCT, and ALL is the default; with UNION, the user can specify only ALL explicitly (omitting the specification is like specifying "DISTINCT"), and "DISTINCT" (by omission) is the default.

To return to the question of legality: The query expression

```
A UNION [ ALL ] B
```

is *legal* only if, for all *i*, the *i*th column of A and the *i*th column of B have exactly the same description—that is, they have exactly the same data type and exactly the same length (or precision, or precision and scale, as applicable). Note therefore that, e.g., CHAR(4) is not the same as CHAR(5), and DECIMAL(5,2) is not the same as NUMERIC(5,2) or as DECIMAL(6,2). Also, if NOT NULL applies to either column, then it must apply to both.

> *Comment:* These very tight restrictions are another unfortunate hangover from IBM SQL. They make the UNION operation almost impossible to use in practice. *End of comment.*

As indicated earlier, the construct "query expression" appears only within the definition of a cursor. Its purpose is to define the query that is associated with the cursor, and hence the set of rows that can be processed via that cursor when the cursor is opened.

> *Note:* A systematic set of definitions for the various SQL constructs that return a table (query expressions, query specifications, etc., etc.) ought really to include an appropriate set of *name inheritance rules*, specifying the names of the columns of the result tables (see Appendix F, Section F.5). The standard includes only a patchy approximation to such rules. For example, in the case of the expression

```
SELECT A, B, C
FROM    ...
   ...
```

the standard does state (obviously enough) that the result column names are A, B, and C. However, for the expression "*x* UNION *y*" (where *x* and *y* are arbitrary query specifications), it simply states that the result columns are unnamed! The reader is referred to the official standard document for more information; we omit the details here.

10.2   QUERY SPECIFICATIONS

A query specification appears as a component of a query expression. It also appears in the multiple-row format of the INSERT statement (i.e., INSERT . . . SELECT—see Chapter 8) and in a view definition (see Chapter 9). It is identical syntactically to a SELECT statement, except that a SELECT statement includes an INTO clause. However, it differs semantically from a SELECT statement in that its value is a table of multiple rows (in general), whereas a SELECT statement must return at most one row (at least in standard SQL). Here is the syntax:

```
query specification
    ::=   SELECT [ ALL | DISTINCT ] selection
                                     table-expression
```

where ALL, DISTINCT, and "selection" are exactly as in a SELECT statement—see Section 8.2—and "table expression" is defined in Section 10.5. *Note:* As explained in Section 8.2, the construct "selection" is basically a commalist of "scalar expressions." Scalar expressions are defined in Section 10.3.

Here is a fairly complex example of a query specification:

```
SELECT P.PNO, 'Weight in grams =', P.WEIGHT * 454, P.COLOR,
           'Max shipped quantity =', MAX ( SP.QTY )
FROM    P, SP
WHERE   P.PNO = SP.PNO
AND     ( P.COLOR = 'Red' OR P.COLOR = 'Blue')
AND     SP.QTY > 200
GROUP   BY P.PNO, P.WEIGHT, P.COLOR
HAVING  SUM ( SP.QTY ) > 350
```

This example is discussed in detail in Section 10.5.

Note: A query specification cannot contain the key word DISTINCT more than once at a given level of nesting. See the note on this point at the end of Section 8.2.

10.3   SCALAR EXPRESSIONS

Scalar expressions appear in many contexts. They are used to represent individual scalar (i.e., string or numeric) values. Their general syntax is as follows:

```
scalar-expression
    ::=    term
       |   scalar-expression ( + | - ) term

term
    ::=    factor
       |   term ( * | / ) factor

factor
    ::=    [ + | - ] primary

primary
    ::=    atom
       |   column-reference
       |   function-reference
       |   ( scalar-expression )
```

As the BNF shows, a scalar expression is basically an arithmetic expression involving a collection of "primaries"—where a primary is an atom or a column reference or a function reference. The expression can involve the operators prefix + and −, infix +, −, *, and /, and parentheses to force a desired order of evaluation. *Note:* The arithmetic operators cannot be applied to a primary of type character string.

Functions are discussed in the next section. The other "primary" objects, namely atoms and column references, are discussed below.

```
atom
    ::=     parameter-reference
          | literal
          | USER

parameter-reference
    ::=     parameter [ [ INDICATOR ] parameter ]
```

An atom is a parameter reference (discussed in Chapter 6) or a literal (discussed in Chapter 3) or the system variable USER (discussed in Chapter 4).

```
column-reference
    ::=     [ column-qualifier . ] column
```

A column reference is a (possibly qualified) column name.

Comments:

1. Observe that NULL is *not* an atom; thus, e.g., it is not possible to SELECT NULL.

2. Observe also that a SELECT-expression is not a scalar expression, even if it does in fact return a scalar value. Thus, e.g., it is not possible (within a single UPDATE statement) to UPDATE some value by replacing it by a value retrieved from somewhere else in the database.

3. The SQL standard includes rules for the data type, precision, etc., (though not the "NOT NULL"-ness or otherwise) of the result of a scalar expression. In many cases, however, all that the rules say is "implementation-defined"—an unfortunate state of affairs, given the criticality of such matters in certain contexts (see, e.g., the discussion of UNION in Section 10.1). We do not bother to spell out the rules in detail here.

End of comments.

10.4 FUNCTIONS

Standard SQL provides a set of five builtin aggregate functions: COUNT, SUM, AVG, MAX, and MIN.* Apart from the special case of

---

*EXISTS (see Section 10.9) can also be considered as a function; however, EXISTS differs from the functions discussed in the present section in that (a) its argument is specified in a different syntactic style (actually in a more logical style), and (b) it returns a truth value, not a number or a string, and truth values are not a SQL data type.

COUNT(*)—see later—each of these functions operates on a certain "aggregate," namely the collection of scalar values in one column of some table (usually a *derived* table, i.e., a table constructed in some way from the given base tables), and produces a single scalar value, defined as follows, as its result:

COUNT   number of scalars in the column

SUM   sum of the scalars in the column

AVG   average of the scalars in the column

MAX   largest scalar in the column

MIN   smallest scalar in the column

A function reference is a special case of a scalar expression. The syntax is as follows:

```
function-reference
    ::=    COUNT(*)
         | distinct-function-reference
         | all-function-reference

distinct-function-reference
    ::=    { AVG | MAX | MIN | SUM | COUNT }
                 ( DISTINCT column-reference )

all-function-reference
    ::=    { AVG | MAX | MIN | SUM }
                 ( [ ALL ] scalar-expression )
```

Notes:

1. For SUM and AVG the argument must be of type numeric.

2. In general, as the grammar indicates, the argument may optionally be preceded by the key word DISTINCT, to indicate that redundant duplicate values are to be eliminated before the function is applied. The alternative to DISTINCT is ALL; ALL is assumed if nothing is specified.

3. For COUNT, DISTINCT *must* be specified; the special function COUNT(*)—DISTINCT not allowed—is provided to count all rows in a table without any duplicate elimination.

4. If DISTINCT is specified, then (again as indicated in the BNF) the argument must consist of just a simple column reference; if DISTINCT is not specified, the argument can consist of an operational expression such as P.WEIGHT * 454.

5. Regardless of whether DISTINCT is specified, the argument cannot in turn involve any function references—i.e., function references cannot be nested.

6. Any nulls in the argument are always eliminated before the function is

applied, regardless of whether DISTINCT is specified, *except* for the case of COUNT(*), where nulls are handled just like nonnull values.

7. If the argument happens to be an empty set, COUNT returns a value of zero; the other functions all return null.

8. For details regarding the data type (etc.) of the result of a function reference, the reader is referred to the official standard document.

> *Comment:* All the various special rules and restrictions regarding such matters as the interaction between DISTINCT and the function argument (etc.) are once again hangovers from DB2 SQL. Note also, incidentally, that there is actually no point in specifying DISTINCT with MAX or MIN, since it can have no effect. *End of comment.*

We give a number of examples of the use of functions. Each of the following examples could form the basis of a singleton SELECT statement or could be nested within some more complex expression, such as a query expression (see Section 10.1). *Note:* If a function reference appears within a SELECT clause and the SELECT-expression does not include a GROUP BY clause, then the SELECT clause must consist of function references *only.* For example, the following is ***ILLEGAL***:

```
SELECT SP.PNO, AVG ( SP.QTY )
FROM    SP
```

Example 1: Get the total number of suppliers.

```
SELECT COUNT(*)
FROM    S
```

Result: 5 (i.e., a table consisting of a single unnamed column and a single row, containing the single value 5).

Example 2: Get the total number of suppliers currently supplying parts.

```
SELECT COUNT ( DISTINCT SP.SNO )
FROM    SP
```

Result: 4.

Example 3: Get the number of shipments for part P2.

```
SELECT COUNT(*)
FROM    SP
WHERE   SP.PNO = 'P2'
```

Result: 4. Note that the table to which COUNT(*) is applied in this example is a *derived* table, namely the table represented by the expression

```
SP WHERE SP.PNO = 'P2'
```

(a row subset of table SP).

Example 4: Get the total quantity of part P2 supplied.

```
SELECT SUM ( SP.QTY )
FROM   SP
WHERE  SP.PNO = 'P2'
```

Result: 1000.

Example 5: Get supplier numbers for suppliers with status value less than the current maximum status value in the S table.

```
SELECT S.SNO
FROM   S
WHERE  S.STATUS <
       ( SELECT MAX ( S.STATUS )
         FROM   S )
```

Result: A table of one column (with column name SNO) containing the values S1, S2, and S4. Note the use of a subquery in this example.

Example 6: Get supplier numbers for suppliers whose status is greater than or equal to the average for their particular city.

```
SELECT SX.SNO
FROM   S SX
WHERE  SX.STATUS >=
       ( SELECT AVG ( SY.STATUS )
         FROM   S SY
         WHERE  SY.CITY = SX.CITY )
```

Result: A table of one column (with column name SNO) containing the values S1, S3, S4, and S5. *Note:* This example illustrates both the use of a function in a "correlated subquery" and the use of "range variables" (SX and SY). See Sections 10.8 and 10.5 (Example 7), respectively, for explanations of these concepts.

10.5   TABLE EXPRESSIONS

A table expression* is an expression of the form

```
  from-clause
[ where-clause ]
[ group-by-clause ]
[ having-clause ]
```

---

*See the comments in Section 8.2 on why "table expression" is not a very good term for this construct.

Table expressions are used in SELECT statements and in query specifications (also in subqueries, which can be regarded as a special case of a query specification—see Section 10.8). The various clauses that go to make up a table expression have the following syntax:

```
from-clause
    ::=    FROM table-reference-commalist

table-reference
    ::=    table [ range-variable ]
```

Here "table" is a (qualified or unqualified) table name, identifying either a base table or a view. See Example 7 later in this section for an explanation of the optional "range variable."

```
where-clause
    ::=    WHERE search-condition
```

Search conditions are discussed in detail in the next section.

```
group-by-clause
    ::=    GROUP BY column-reference-commalist
```

As explained in Section 10.3, a column reference is just a qualified or unqualified column name.

```
having-clause
    ::=    HAVING search-condition
```

Again, search conditions are discussed in the next section.

Here are some examples of table expressions. Most of them are presented without additional discussion; however, we remark that Examples 3–7 all illustrate the relational join operation (see Chapter 2 if you need to refresh your memory regarding joins). *Note:* To make the examples a trifle more realistic, we prefix each one with an appropriate SELECT clause (thus in fact converting it into a *query specification* rather than a pure table expression), but it must be clearly understood that the SELECT clause is not part of the table expression per se.

Example 1: Get part numbers for all parts supplied.

```
SELECT SP.PNO
FROM   SP
```

Or if duplicate elimination is required:

```
SELECT DISTINCT SP.PNO
FROM   SP
```

DISTINCT causes redundant duplicate rows to be eliminated from the result. The alternative to DISTINCT is ALL. ALL is assumed if nothing is specified.

Example 2: Get supplier numbers for suppliers in Paris with status > 20.

```
SELECT  S.SNO
FROM    S
WHERE   S.CITY = 'Paris'
AND     S.STATUS > 20
```

Example 3: Get all supplier-number/part-number combinations such that the supplier and part in question are located in the same city.

```
SELECT  S.SNO, P.PNO
FROM    S, P
WHERE   S.CITY = P.CITY
```

Example 4: Get all supplier-number/part-number combinations such that the supplier city follows the part city in alphabetical order.

```
SELECT  S.SNO, P.PNO
FROM    S, P
WHERE   S.CITY > P.CITY
```

Example 5: Get all supplier-number/part-number combinations such that the supplier and part in question are located in the same city, but omitting suppliers with status 20.

```
SELECT  S.SNO, P.PNO
FROM    S, P
WHERE   S.CITY = P.CITY
AND     S.STATUS <> 20
```

Example 6: Get all pairs of city names such that a supplier located in the first city supplies a part stored in the second city.

```
SELECT  DISTINCT S.CITY, P.CITY
FROM    S, SP, P
WHERE   S.SNO = SP.SNO
AND     SP.PNO = P.PNO
```

Note that this example involves a join of three tables.

Example 7: Get all pairs of supplier numbers such that the two suppliers concerned are located in the same city.

```
SELECT  FIRST.SNO, SECOND.SNO
FROM    S FIRST, S SECOND
WHERE   FIRST.CITY = SECOND.CITY
```

This example involves a join of table S with itself (over matching cities), as we now explain. Suppose for a moment that we had two separate copies of table S, the "first" copy and the "second" copy. Then the logic of the query is as follows: We need to be able to examine all possible pairs of supplier rows, one from the first copy of S and one from the second, and to retrieve the two supplier numbers from such a pair of rows when the city values are equal. We therefore need to be able to reference two supplier rows at the same time. In order to distinguish between the two references, we introduce two *range variables* FIRST and SECOND, each of which "ranges over" table S (for the duration of the evaluation of the containing expression). At any particular time, FIRST represents some row from the "first" copy of table S, and SECOND represents some row from the "second" copy. The result of the query is found by examining all possible pairs of FIRST/SECOND values and checking the WHERE condition in every case:

```
---   ---
SNO   SNO
---   ---
S1    S1
S1    S4
S2    S2
S2    S3
S3    S2
S3    S3
S4    S1
S4    S4
S5    S5
```

We can tidy up this result by extending the WHERE clause as follows:

```
SELECT  FIRST.SNO,  SECOND.SNO
FROM    S FIRST, S SECOND
WHERE   FIRST.CITY = SECOND.CITY
AND     FIRST.SNO < SECOND.SNO
```

The effect of the condition FIRST.SNO < SECOND.SNO is twofold:

(a) It eliminates pairs of supplier numbers of the form (x, x);

(b) it guarantees that the pairs (x,y) and (y, x) will not both appear. Result:

```
---   ---
SNO   SNO
---   ---
S1    S4
S2    S3
```

This is the first example we have seen in which the explicit use of range variables has been necessary.* However, it is never wrong to introduce such variables, even when they are not explicitly required, and sometimes they can help to make the statement clearer. (They can also save writing, if table names are on the lengthy side.) In general, a range variable is a variable

---

*The first in the present section, that is. Another can be found in Section 10.4 (Example 6).

that ranges over some specified table—i.e., a variable whose only permitted values are the rows of that table. In other words, if range variable *R* ranges over table *T,* then, at any given time, *R* represents some row *r* of *T.* For example, the query "Get supplier numbers for suppliers in Paris with status > 20" (Example 2 above) could alternatively have been expressed as follows:

```
SELECT  SX.SNO
FROM    S SX
WHERE   SX.CITY = 'Paris'
AND     SX.STATUS > 20
```

The range variable here is SX, and it ranges over table S.

As a matter of fact, SQL *always* requires queries to be formulated in terms of range variables. If no such variables are specified explicitly, then SQL assumes the existence of *implicit* variables with the same name(s) as the corresponding table(s). For example, the query

```
SELECT  T.C
FROM    T
.....
```

is treated by SQL as if it had been expressed as follows:

```
SELECT  T.C
FROM    T T
.....
```

—in other words, "T" itself is a default range variable name, representing a range variable called T that ranges over the table called T.

Note: The SQL standard uses the term "correlation variable" in place of the more orthodox term "range variable." A name such as SX in the example above is referred to as a "correlation name." In this book, however, we will generally stick with "range variable."

Example 8: For each part supplied, get the part number and the total shipment quantity for that part.

```
SELECT  PNO, SUM ( SP.QTY )
FROM    SP
GROUP   BY SP.PNO
```

```
           ---   ----
Result:    PNO
           ---   ----
           P1     600
           P2    1000
           P3     400
           P4     500
           P5     500
           P6     100
```

   The GROUP BY operator conceptually rearranges the table represented by the FROM clause (and WHERE clause, if specified—see Example 9 below) into the minimum number of groups (or partitions) such that within any one group all rows have the same value for the GROUP BY column. In the example, table SP is grouped so that one group contains all the rows for part P1, another contains all the rows for part P2, and so on. The result is a *grouped table*. (Grouped views, already discussed in Section 9.3, are a special case of a grouped table.)

   If a SELECT clause is applied to a grouped table (as in the example), then each expression in the "selection" (see Section 8.2) in that SELECT clause must be *single-valued per group;* e.g., it can be a reference to the GROUP BY column itself (or an arithmetic expression involving that column), or a literal, or a function such as SUM that operates on all values in a given column within a group and reduces those values to a single scalar value.

   A table can be grouped by any combination of its columns.

Example 9: For each part supplied, get the part number, maximum quantity, and minimum quantity supplied of that part, excluding shipments by supplier S1.

```
SELECT  SP.PNO, MAX ( SP.QTY ), MIN ( SP.QTY )
FROM    SP
WHERE   SP.SNO <> 'S1'
GROUP   BY SP.PNO
```

Result:

PNO	---	---
P1	300	300
P2	400	200
P4	300	300
P5	400	400

Rows that do not satisfy the WHERE clause are eliminated before any grouping is done.

Example 10: Get part numbers for all parts supplied by more than one supplier.

```
SELECT  SP.PNO
FROM    SP
GROUP   BY SP.PNO
HAVING  COUNT(*) > 1
```

The HAVING clause is "a WHERE-clause for groups"; i.e., HAVING is used to eliminate groups, just as WHERE is used to eliminate rows. Thus, if HAVING is specified, GROUP BY should have been specified also.* Expressions in a HAVING clause must be single-valued per group (in practice they are almost invariably aggregate function references, as in the example).

A Comprehensive Example

We conclude this section with a comprehensive example that shows how many (by no means all) of the features discussed above can be used together in a single expression. We also give a conceptual algorithm (i.e., a sketch of a formal definition) for the evaluation of table expressions in general.

Example: For all red and blue parts such that the total quantity supplied is greater than 350 (excluding from the total all shipments for which the quantity is less than or equal to 200), get the part number, the weight in grams, the color, and the maximum quantity supplied of that part. (This is the example shown at the end of Section 10.2. We assume for the sake of the example that weights are given in table P in pounds.)

```
SELECT P.PNO, 'Weight in grams =', P.WEIGHT * 454, P.COLOR,
            'Max shipped quantity =', MAX ( SP.QTY )
FROM    P, SP
WHERE   P.PNO = SP.PNO
AND     ( P.COLOR = 'Red' OR P.COLOR = 'Blue')
AND     SP.QTY > 200
GROUP   BY P.PNO, P.WEIGHT, P.COLOR
HAVING SUM ( SP.QTY ) > 350
```

Explanation: The clauses of a SELECT-expression are applied in the order suggested by that in which they are written—with the sole exception of the SELECT clause itself, which is applied last. In the example, therefore, we can imagine the result being constructed as follows.

1. *FROM:* The FROM clause is evaluated to yield a new table that is the Cartesian product of tables P and SP. *Note:* The Cartesian product of a set of tables T1, T2, . . . (in that order) is a table consisting of all possible rows *t* such that *t* is the concatenation of a row *t1* from T1, a row *t2* from T2, etc.

2. *WHERE:* The result of Step 1 is reduced by the elimination of all rows that do not satisfy the WHERE clause. In the example, rows not satisfying the condition

---

*It is in fact possible, though unusual, to specify HAVING and not GROUP BY; the effect is then simply to consider the entire table as if it were a single group.

```
    P.PNO = SP.PNO AND
( P.COLOR = 'Red' OR P.COLOR = 'Blue') AND
    SP.QTY > 200
```

are eliminated.

3. *GROUP BY:* The result of Step 2 is grouped by values of the column(s) named in the GROUP BY clause. In the example, those columns are P.PNO, P.WEIGHT, and P.COLOR.

4. *HAVING:* Groups not satisfying the condition

```
SUM ( SP.QTY ) > 350
```

are eliminated from the result of Step 3.

5. *SELECT:* Each group in the result of Step 4 generates a single result row, as follows. First, the part number, weight, color, and maximum quantity are extracted from the group. Second, the weight is converted to grams. Third, the two literal strings "Weight in grams =" and "Max shipped quantity =" are inserted at the appropriate points in the row.

Comment: To return to the GROUP BY clause for a moment: In theory P.PNO alone would be sufficient as the grouping column in this example, since P.WEIGHT and P.COLOR are themselves single-valued per part number. However, SQL is not aware of this latter fact, and will raise an error condition if P.WEIGHT and P.COLOR are omitted from the GROUP BY clause, because they *are* mentioned in the SELECT clause. The basic problem here is that SQL still does not properly support primary keys (even though primary keys can now be defined within CREATE TABLE). See Appendix F. *End of comment.*

10.6 SEARCH CONDITIONS

Search conditions are used in WHERE and HAVING clauses to qualify or disqualify specific rows (or groups of rows, in the case of HAVING) for subsequent processing. For a given row (or group), a given search condition evaluates to *true*, *false*, or *unknown*. The rows (or groups) that qualify are precisely those for which the condition evaluates to *true*.

The syntax of a search condition is as follows:

```
search-condition
    ::=    boolean-term
       |   search-condition OR boolean-term

boolean-term
    ::=    boolean-factor
       |   boolean-term AND boolean-factor
```

```
boolean-factor
    ::=    [ NOT ] boolean-primary

boolean-primary
    ::=    predicate | ( search-condition )
```

Thus, a search condition is basically a collection of *predicates*, combined together using the Boolean operators AND, OR, and NOT, and parentheses to enforce a desired order of evaluation. A predicate, in turn, is one of the following:

- a comparison predicate
- a BETWEEN predicate
- a LIKE predicate
- a test for null
- an IN predicate
- an all-or-any predicate
- an existence text

(not all official standard terms). We refer to the first five categories above as unquantified predicates, the other two as quantified predicates (again not the official terms). Section 10.7 deals with unquantified predicates and Sections 10.8 and 10.9 with quantified predicates.

10.7   UNQUANTIFIED PREDICATES

Comparison Predicates

Comparison predicates come in two different formats. The first is:

```
scalar-expression   comparison   scalar-expression
```

where "comparison" is any of the scalar comparison operators $=$, $<>$ (not equals), $<$, $>$, $<=$, or $>=$. If the comparison predicate appears in the context of a WHERE clause, then the scalar expressions must not include any aggregate function references.

The second format is:

```
scalar-expression   comparison   subquery
```

where a subquery is basically just a parenthesized query specification (see Section 10.2), except that:

(a) The query specification in question *must* represent a table of just one column (unless it appears as the argument to EXISTS—see Section 10.9); and also

(b) In this particular context—i.e., the second format of a comparison predicate—that table must also have at most one row.

Here is an example:

```
SELECT  S.SNO
FROM    S
WHERE   S.CITY =
      ( SELECT  S.CITY
        FROM    S
        WHERE   S.SNO = 'S1' )
```

("supplier numbers for suppliers who are located in the same city as supplier S1"). A subquery in a comparison predicate should (as already indicated) return just a single scalar value. If instead it returns no value at all, the predicate evaluates to *unknown;* if it returns multiple values, an error occurs.

Comments:

There are a number of additional restrictions on the use of subqueries within a comparison predicate:

1. The comparison predicate must be written as shown, with the subquery appearing after the comparison operator, not before it. For example, the following is ***ILLEGAL***:

```
SELECT  S.SNO
FROM    S
WHERE   ( SELECT  S.CITY
          FROM    S
          WHERE   S.SNO = 'S1' ) = S.CITY
```

2. It is not possible to compare two subqueries.

3. Although subqueries in general can include GROUP BY and HAVING clauses, those clauses are not permitted in this context.

4. The FROM clause in the subquery must not identify a grouped view.

Note also that "subquery" is not all that felicitous a term, since the result table must have *a single column* (unless it represents the argument to EXISTS—see Section 10.9), whereas a general query returns a table of multiple columns. "Column expression" might have been a better term. See Appendix F.

End of comments.

BETWEEN Predicates

The syntax of a BETWEEN predicate is

```
scalar-expression [ NOT ] BETWEEN scalar-expression
                            AND      scalar-expression
```

The BETWEEN predicate

```
y BETWEEN x AND z
```

is defined to be semantically equivalent to

```
x <= y AND y <= z
```

The BETWEEN predicate

```
y NOT BETWEEN x AND z
```

is defined to be semantically equivalent to

```
NOT ( y BETWEEN x AND z )
```

Example:

```
SELECT P.PNO
FROM   P
WHERE  P.WEIGHT BETWEEN 16 AND 19
```

LIKE Predicates

The LIKE predicate is intended for simple pattern-matching—i.e., for testing a given string to see whether it conforms to some prescribed pattern (specified as an atom, *not* as a general scalar expression). Syntax:

```
column-reference [ NOT ] LIKE atom [ ESCAPE atom ]
```

The column reference must identify a column of type string. Here is an example:

```
SELECT P.PNO, P.PNAME
FROM   P
WHERE  P.PNAME LIKE 'C%'
```

("part numbers and names for parts whose names begin with the letter C").

Result:

PNO	PNAME
P5	Cam
P6	Cog

The atom following LIKE must represent a character string. Provided no ESCAPE clause is specified, characters within that string are interpreted as follows:

- The underscore character (_) stands for *any single character.*
- The percent character (%) stands for *any sequence of n characters* (where *n* may be zero).
- All other characters stand for themselves.

In the example, therefore, the SELECT-expression will return rows from table P for which the PNAME value begins with an upper case C and has any sequence of zero or more characters following that C. Here are some more examples:

ADDRESS LIKE '%Berkeley%'   —will evaluate to *true* if ADDRESS contains the string "Berkeley" anywhere inside it

SNO LIKE 'S__'   —will evaluate to *true* if SNO is exactly 3 characters long and the first is "S"

PNAME LIKE '%c___'   —will evaluate to *true* if PNAME is 4 characters long or more and the last but three is "c"

STRING LIKE '_%' ESCAPE '\'   —will evaluate to *true* if STRING begins with an underscore character (see below)

In this last example, the backslash character "\ " has been specified as the escape character, which means that the special interpretation given to the characters "_" and "%" can be disabled if desired by preceding such characters with a backslash character. The atom in an ESCAPE clause must represent a single character.

Finally, the LIKE predicate

    x NOT LIKE y [ESCAPE z]

is defined to be semantically equivalent to

    NOT (x LIKE y [ESCAPE z])

Tests for Null

Recall from Chapter 3 that, at least for the purposes of WHERE and HAVING, *nothing* is considered to be equal to null—not even null itself. Likewise, nothing is considered to be less than null, or greater than null, or . . . , etc. In other words, when a null is compared with some value in evaluating a comparison predicate, then the result is never *true* (even if that other value is also null); rather, the result is the *unknown* truth value in every case. The interaction among the three truth values is defined by the following truth tables (to repeat from Chapter 3):

```
NOT |                AND | T | ? | F            OR  | T | ? | F
----+---              ----+---+---+---           ----+---+---+---
  T | F                 T | T | ? | F             T | T | T | T
  ? | ?                 ? | ? | ? | F             ? | T | ? | ?
  F | T                 F | F | F | F             F | T | ? | F
```

A special predicate of the form

```
column-reference IS NULL
```

is provided for testing for the presence of nulls. For example:

```
SELECT  S.SNO
FROM    S
WHERE   S.STATUS IS NULL
```

Note that the syntax "S.STATUS = NULL" is illegal, because (as already explained) nothing, not even null itself, is considered to be equal to null for the purposes of WHERE or HAVING.

The predicate

```
x IS NOT NULL
```

is defined to be semantically equivalent to

```
NOT ( x IS NULL )
```

IN Predicates

Like comparison predicates, IN predicates come in two different formats. The first is really just a shorthand for a combination of comparison predicates:

```
scalar-expression [ NOT ] IN ( atom-commalist )
```

The commalist must contain at least two atoms. Here is an example of the use of an IN predicate (first format):

```
SELECT  P.PNO
FROM    P
WHERE   P.WEIGHT IN ( 12, 16, 17 )
```

The IN predicate

```
x IN ( a, b, ..., z )
```

is defined to be semantically equivalent to

```
x = a OR x = b OR ... OR x = z
```

The second IN predicate format is

```
scalar-expression [ NOT ] IN subquery
```

This format (without the NOT) is defined to be semantically identical to

```
scalar-expression =ANY subquery
```

(see Section 10.8). However, IN is perhaps intuitively easier to understand than =ANY. Here is an example of the use of IN with a subquery:

```
SELECT  S.SNAME
FROM    S
WHERE   S.SNO IN
      ( SELECT SP.SNO
        FROM   SP
        WHERE  SP.PNO = 'P2' )
```

("names of suppliers who supply part P2"). For further discussion of this format, see the next section.

Finally, the IN predicate

```
x NOT IN rhs
```

(where "rhs" is either a parenthesized commalist of atoms or a subquery) is defined to be semantically equivalent to

```
NOT ( x IN rhs )
```

10.8 SUBQUERIES

The syntax of a subquery is:

```
( SELECT [ ALL | DISTINCT ]  selection  table-expression )
```

where the table expression must represent a single-column table (except in the context of EXISTS—see Section 10.9). The semantics of a subquery are identical to those of a query specification (see Section 10.2), except for the single-column restriction; in particular, the rule that DISTINCT must not appear more than once at a given level of nesting applies to subqueries also (see Section 8.2). Note that the enclosing parentheses are considered part of the syntax of the subquery. Subqueries are used:

- in comparison predicates (see Section 10.7)
- in IN predicates (see Section 10.7)
- in any-or-all predicates (see Section 10.9)
- in existence tests (see Section 10.9)

A simple example of the use of IN with a subquery was given at the end of Section 10.7. Here is a more complex example, showing one subquery nested inside another.

Example 1: Get supplier names for suppliers who supply at least one red part.

```
SELECT  S.SNAME
FROM    S
WHERE   S.SNO IN
        ( SELECT  SP.SNO
          FROM    SP
          WHERE   SP.PNO IN
                  ( SELECT  P.PNO
                    FROM    P
                    WHERE   P.COLOR = 'Red' ) )
```

For interest, here is the same example with all explicit table name qualifiers omitted:

```
SELECT  SNAME
FROM    S
WHERE   SNO IN
        ( SELECT  SNO
          FROM    SP
          WHERE   PNO IN
                  ( SELECT  PNO
                    FROM    P
                    WHERE   COLOR = 'Red' ) )
```

In this formulation, each unqualified column name is *implicitly* qualified by a table name (or range variable name) from the "nearest" applicable FROM clause. (For full details of how implicit qualifiers are determined, the reader is referred to the official standard documents. Explicit qualification is to be recommended in practice if there is any possible doubt.)

Example 2: Get supplier names for suppliers who supply part P2.

```
SELECT  S.SNAME
FROM    S
WHERE   'P2' IN
        ( SELECT  SP.PNO
          FROM    SP
          WHERE   SP.SNO = S.SNO )
```

This example differs from the previous ones in that the inner subquery cannot be evaluated once and for all before the outer query is evaluated, because that inner subquery depends on a *variable*, namely S.SNO, whose value changes as the system examines different rows of table S. Conceptually, therefore, evaluation proceeds as follows:

(a) The system examines some row of table S; let us assume this is the row for S1. The variable S.SNO thus currently has the value S1, so the system evaluates the inner subquery

```
        ( SELECT  SP.PNO
          FROM    SP
          WHERE   SP.SNO = 'S1' )
```

to obtain the set (P1,P2,P3,P4,P5,P6). Now it can complete its processing for S1; it will select the SNAME value for S1, namely Smith, if and
only if P2 is in this set (which of course it is).

(b) Next the system moves on to repeat this kind of processing for another
supplier row, and so on, until all rows of table S have been dealt with.

A subquery such as the one in this example is said to be a *correlated*
subquery. A correlated subquery is one whose value depends upon some
variable that receives its value in some outer query; such a subquery therefore has to be evaluated repeatedly (once for each value of the variable in
question), instead of once and for all. *Note:* Another example of a correlated subquery has already been given in Section 10.4 (Example 6).

Example 3: Get supplier numbers for suppliers who supply at least one part
supplied by supplier S2.

```
SELECT DISTINCT SPX.SNO
FROM    SP SPX
WHERE   SPX.PNO IN
      ( SELECT SPY.PNO
        FROM    SP SPY
        WHERE   SPY.SNO = 'S2' )
```

This example involves two distinct references to table SP, so at least one of
the two must be by means of an explicit range variable name (see Section
10.5, Example 7, for a discussion of range variables). For explicitness we
have used explicit range variables (SPX and SPY) for both references.

10.9   QUANTIFIED PREDICATES

All-or-Any Predicates

An all-or-any predicate has the general form

```
scalar-expression   quantified-comparison   subquery
```

where a quantified comparison is any one of the normal scalar comparisons
=, < >, <, >, < =, > =, followed by one of the key words ALL or
ANY (or SOME; SOME is just a different spelling for ANY). An all-or-
any predicate evaluates to *true* if and only if the corresponding comparison
predicate without the ALL (respectively ANY)—

```
scalar-expression   comparison   scalar-value
```

—evaluates to *true* for all (respectively any) of the scalar values in the column represented by the subquery. (*Note:* If that column is empty, the ALL
predicates return *true,* the ANY predicates return *false.*) Here is an example:

```
SELECT  DISTINCT SP.SNO
FROM    SP
WHERE   SP.QTY >ALL
      ( SELECT SP.QTY
        FROM    SP
        WHERE   SP.SNO = 'S1' )
```

("supplier numbers for suppliers who supply at least one part in a quantity greater than every quantity in which supplier S1 supplies a part").

> *Comment:* All-or-any predicates are error-prone. A very natural English language formulation of the foregoing query would use the word "any" in place of "every," which could easily lead to the (incorrect) use of the quantified comparison >ANY instead of >ALL. In addition, all-or-any predicates are logically unnecessary, since they can always be recast in the form of existence tests anyway. (At least, this statement is true *provided* the column returned by the subquery on the right hand side of the comparison does not contain any nulls. It is not true otherwise. See Example 4 at the end of this section.) *End of comment.*

Existence Tests

An existence test is a predicate of the form

```
EXISTS subquery
```

The predicate evaluates to *false* if the subquery evaluates to the empty set, the value *true* otherwise.* *Note:* In this particular context (only), the subquery is allowed to use "SELECT *" (or any other form of SELECT clause) instead of "SELECT scalar-expression," even if the result table has more than one column. Indeed, "SELECT *" is the normal case.

Example 1: Get supplier names for suppliers who supply at least one part.

```
SELECT  S.SNAME
FROM    S
WHERE   EXISTS
      ( SELECT *
        FROM    SP
        WHERE   SP.SNO = S.SNO )
```

---

*Note that SQL suffers from a logical inconsistency here. If it is *not known* whether some particular data exists (e.g., whether any shipment exists with quantity 1000, say), then the corresponding existence test should return *unknown*. However, "EXISTS subquery" will return *false* in such a case. See Example 4 below.

Example 2: Get supplier names for suppliers who do not supply at least one part.

```
SELECT  S.SNAME
FROM    S
WHERE   NOT EXISTS
      ( SELECT *
        FROM    SP
        WHERE   SP.SNO = S.SNO )
```

Example 3: Get supplier names for suppliers who supply all parts.

```
SELECT  S.SNAME
FROM    S
WHERE   NOT EXISTS
      ( SELECT *
        FROM    P
        WHERE   NOT EXISTS
              ( SELECT *
                FROM    SP
                WHERE   S.SNO = SP.SNO
                AND     SP.PNO = P.PNO ) )
```

Example 4: Get supplier numbers for suppliers who supply at least one part in a quantity greater than every quantity in which supplier S1 supplies a part. (Same as the ">ALL example shown earlier in this section)

```
SELECT  DISTINCT SPX.SNO
FROM    SPX
WHERE   NOT EXISTS
      ( SELECT *
        FROM    SP SPY
        WHERE   SPY.SNO = 'S1'
        AND     SPY.QTY >= SPX.QTY )
```

("select supplier numbers from shipments SPX such that there does not exist a shipment SPY for supplier S1 with a greater or equal quantity").

As suggested earlier, however, the NOT EXISTS version and the >ALL version are unfortunately not quite equivalent, as we now explain. Suppose table SP contains just two rows, namely (S1,P1,null) and (S2,P2,100). First, consider the >ALL formulation. The subquery returns a column containing just one value, namely null; the ALL predicate therefore returns *unknown,* and the overall result of the SELECT statement is the empty set (no supplier numbers are retrieved at all). In the case of the NOT EXISTS formulation, by contrast, we need to consider each row of table SP in turn:

- For the row (S1,P1,null), the argument to the EXISTS reference evaluates to the empty set; the EXISTS reference therefore returns *false,* the NOT EXISTS therefore returns *true,* and supplier number S1 therefore appears in the final result.

- For the row (S2,P2,100), exactly the same is true, so supplier number S2 also appears in the final result.

The basic problem is that, if it is unknown whether there exists any data that satisfied some condition, a test for existence should return *unknown*. EXISTS, however, returns *false*.

11

Embedded SQL

11.1 INTRODUCTION

As explained in Section 3.2, the ANSI X3H2 standard document includes a series of "annexes" or appendixes defining an "embedded" version of SQL—i.e., a version of SQL designed for direct incorporation into host programs (specifically, host programs written in COBOL, FORTRAN, Pascal, or PL/I). Although not part of the official standard per se, embedded SQL in many ways represents the most immediately visible aspect of the entire proposal. In this chapter we consider embedded SQL in detail. For definiteness we base our discussions on PL/I, but of course most of the ideas translate into other host languages with only minor changes. Section 11.2 presents a complete embedded SQL-PL/I program; Section 11.3 discusses the detailed language points illustrated by that example.

11.2 A COMPLETE EXAMPLE

A host language program with embedded SQL statements—an "embedded SQL host program"—consists of an otherwise standard host program plus a set of embedded SQL declare sections, a set of embedded cursor definitions, a set of embedded exception declarations, and a set of embedded SQL statements. In Fig. 11.1 we show an embedded SQL version of the

```
SQLEX: PROC OPTIONS (MAIN) ;

       EXEC SQL BEGIN DECLARE SECTION ;

       /* program input */

       DCL GIVENPNO       CHAR(6) ;
       DCL GIVENCIT       CHAR(15) ;
       DCL GIVENINC       DECIMAL(3) ;
       DCL GIVENLVL       DECIMAL(3) ;

       /* targets for "FETCH SUPPLIER" */

       DCL SNO            CHAR(5) ;
       DCL SNAME          CHAR(20) ;
       DCL STATUS         DECIMAL(3) ;
       DCL CITY           CHAR(15) ;

       /* SQL return code variable */

       DCL SQLCODE        FIXED BINARY(15) ;

       EXEC SQL END DECLARE SECTION ;

       /* housekeeping variables */

       DCL DISP           CHAR(7) ;
       DCL MORE_SUPPLIERS BIT(1) ;

       /* exception declarations */

       EXEC SQL WHENEVER NOT FOUND CONTINUE ;
       EXEC SQL WHENEVER SQLERROR  CONTINUE ;

       /* database exception handler */

       ON CONDITION ( DBEXCEPTION )
       BEGIN ;
          PUT SKIP LIST ( SQLCODE ) ;
          EXEC SQL ROLLBACK WORK ;
          PUT SKIP LIST ( SQLCODE ) ;
          GO TO QUIT ;
       END ;

       /* cursor definition */

       EXEC SQL DECLARE Z CURSOR FOR
          SELECT S.SNO, S.SNAME, S.STATUS, S.CITY
          FROM   S
          WHERE  S.SNO IN
               ( SELECT SP.SNO
                 FROM   SP
                 WHERE  SP.PNO = :GIVENPNO ) ;
```

Fig. 11.1 Embedded SQL example (part 1 of 2)

```
/* main program logic */

GET LIST ( GIVENPNO, GIVENCIT, GIVENINC, GIVENLVL ) ;
EXEC SQL OPEN Z ;
IF NOT ( SQLCODE = 0 )
THEN SIGNAL CONDITION ( DBEXCEPTION ) ;
MORE_SUPPLIERS = '1'B ;
DO WHILE ( MORE_SUPPLIERS ) ;
    EXEC SQL FETCH Z INTO :SNO, :SNAME, :STATUS, :CITY ;
    SELECT ;              /* a PL/I SELECT, not a SQL SELECT */
    WHEN ( SQLCODE = 100 )
        MORE_SUPPLIERS = '0'B ;
    WHEN NOT ( SQLCODE = 100 | SQLCODE = 0 )
        SIGNAL CONDITION ( DBEXCEPTION ) ;
    WHEN ( SQLCODE = 0 )
        DO ;
            DISP = 'bbbbbbb' ;
            IF CITY = GIVENCIT
            THEN
                DO ;
                    EXEC SQL UPDATE S
                             SET     STATUS = S.STATUS + :GIVENINC
                             WHERE   S.SNO = :SNO ;
                    IF NOT ( SQLCODE = 0 )
                    THEN SIGNAL CONDITION ( DBEXCEPTION ) ;
                    DISP = 'UPDATED' ;
                END ;
            ELSE
                IF STATUS < GIVENLVL
                THEN
                    DO ;
                        EXEC SQL DELETE
                                 FROM   SP
                                 WHERE  SP.SNO = :SNO ;
                        IF NOT ( SQLCODE = 0 | SQLCODE = 100 )
                        THEN SIGNAL CONDITION ( DBEXCEPTION ) ;
                        EXEC SQL DELETE
                                 FROM   S
                                 WHERE  S.SNO = :SNO ;
                        IF NOT ( SQLCODE = 0 )
                        THEN SIGNAL CONDITION ( DBEXCEPTION ) ;
                        DISP = 'DELETED' ;
                    END ;
                PUT SKIP LIST
                        ( SNO, SNAME, STATUS, CITY, DISP ) ;
        END ;    /* WHEN ( SQLCODE = 0 ) ... */
    END ;    /* PL/I SELECT */
END ;    /* DO WHILE */
EXEC SQL CLOSE Z ;
EXEC SQL COMMIT WORK ;
QUIT:   RETURN ;
    END ;   /* SQLEX */
```

Fig. 11.1 Embedded SQL example (part 2 of 2)

example from Chapter 7 (Fig. 7.1). The detailed explanations of the next section are in terms of that example (for the most part).

11.3   POINTS ARISING

1. Embedded SQL statements are prefixed by EXEC SQL (so that they can easily be distinguished from statements of the host language), and are terminated as follows:

COBOL	—END-EXEC
FORTRAN	—absence of continuation character (i.e., no explicit terminator)
Pascal	—semicolon
PL/I	—semicolon

2. An executable SQL statement can appear wherever an executable host statement can appear. Note the qualifier "executable" here: DECLARE CURSOR is not an executable statement, nor is WHENEVER (see paragraph 8. below), and nor are BEGIN and END DECLARE SECTION.

3. SQL statements (from now on we will usually drop the "embedded") can include references to host variables. Such references must be prefixed with a colon to distinguish them from SQL column names. They must not be qualified or subscripted, and must identify scalars, not arrays or structures. They can appear in SQL data manipulation statements in the same positions that parameters can appear in manipulative statements in the module language (see Section 6.2).

4. All host variables that will be referenced in SQL statements must be defined within an embedded SQL declare section, which is delimited by the BEGIN and END DECLARE SECTION statements (see Fig. 11.1). Such host variable definitions are deliberately limited to certain simple forms (e.g., arrays and structures are not permitted); the reader is referred to the standard document for details. A given program can include any number of embedded SQL declare sections. A host variable must not appear in an embedded SQL statement before it is defined.

5. Every embedded SQL program must include a host variable called SQLCODE (SQLCOD in FORTRAN). After any SQL statement has been executed, a numeric status indicator is returned to the program in SQLCODE. See Section 6.2 for details of SQLCODE values.

6. Host variables must have a data type compatible with the SQL data type of columns they are to be compared with or assigned to or from. Data type compatibility is defined in Section 6.2.

7. Host variables and SQL columns can have the same name.

8. Every SQL statement should in principle be followed by a test of the returned SQLCODE value. The WHENEVER statement is provided to simplify this process. The WHENEVER statement has the syntax:

```
EXEC SQL WHENEVER  condition  action  terminator
```

where "terminator" is as explained in paragraph 1. above, "condition" is either SQLERROR or NOT FOUND, and "action" is either CONTINUE or a GO TO statement.* WHENEVER is not an executable statement; rather, it is a directive to the SQL language processor. "WHENEVER condition GO TO label" causes that processor to insert an "IF condition GO TO label" statement after each executable SQL statement it encounters. "WHENEVER condition CONTINUE" causes it not to insert any such statements, the implication being that the programmer will insert such statements by hand. The two "conditions" are defined as follows:

```
NOT FOUND    means    SQLCODE = 100
SQLERROR     means    SQLCODE < 0
```

Each WHENEVER statement the SQL processor encounters on its sequential scan through the program text (for a particular condition) overrides the previous one it found (for that condition).

All exception testing in the sample program (Fig. 11.1) is done explicitly, for tutorial reasons.

9. A cursor must not appear in an embedded SQL statement before it is defined.

10. Indicator variables can (and must) be used in a manner precisely analogous to the way indicator parameters are used in the module language (see Section 6.3). For example:

```
EXEC SQL SELECT P.WEIGHT
         INTO    :WEIGHT INDICATOR :WEIGHT_INDIC
         FROM    P
         WHERE   P.PNO = :PNO ;
```

---

*"GO TO" can be spelled as shown here, as two words, or as one word without the space ("GOTO").

12

Future Extensions

12.1 INTRODUCTION

The ANSI and ISO SQL standards committees are currently at work on a proposed extended version of the existing SQL standard called SQL2. In this chapter, we take a brief look at the SQL2 proposals. The reader is cautioned that the proposals *are* only proposals at this stage; they will undoubtedly change in a number of ways before they achieve official standard status (if they ever do). Nevertheless, it seems worthwhile to spend a little time on them in this book, if only because they do give some indication as to how the committees are currently thinking, and hence as to how the standard is likely to evolve over the next several years.

At the time of writing, it looks as if the proposals are likely to go for public review some time in 1989. Note, however, that they do represent a *major* extension to the existing standard, and hence a *major* (multi-year) implementation effort; any prospective implementation is likely to require rather careful staging. Indeed, it is possible that the standards committees will propose some such staging themselves. Furthermore, the proposals are still somewhat fluid at the time of writing; hence, there does not seem to be a great deal of point in trying to be meticulously precise and detailed in trying to describe them at this stage. The discussions of this chapter are therefore deliberately more superficial than those in earlier parts of the book.

Before getting into details, we make a couple of general observations:

1. The proposed extensions (unlike the existing standard) do permit data definition operations such as CREATE TABLE to be executed from within an application program. As a consequence, the "schema definition language" of the existing standard is now totally redundant and could be discarded.

2. The proposed extensions (unlike the existing standard) do include a full set of "embedded SQL" facilities (not only for the languages discussed earlier in this book—COBOL, FORTRAN, Pascal, and PL/I—but also for Ada and C). As a consequence, the "module language" of the existing standard is likewise now totally redundant and could be discarded also.

The rest of this chapter discusses certain aspects of the proposed extensions in more detail. Section 12.2 covers definitional aspects and Section 12.3 covers manipulative aspects. Section 12.4 is concerned with one specific (and rather important) aspect, namely *orthogonality*.

One last introductory point: We deliberately do not devote much space to explaining the underlying relational concepts (e.g., domains, theta-join, outer join, set intersection, etc.) that are being addressed by some of the proposed extensions. A tutorial on such material can be found in many places; see, e.g., the author's book *An Introduction to Database Systems: Volume I* (4th edition, Addison-Wesley, 1985).

12.2   DEFINITIONAL EXTENSIONS

- Partial support is provided for the relational concept of *domains*. Domains can be created and dropped (CREATE DOMAIN, DROP DOMAIN). Column definitions (in CREATE and ALTER TABLE) can specify a user-defined domain instead of one of the builtin data types such as INTEGER. Domains in SQL2 thus provide the ability to factor out scalar-level data type definitions. They also provide:
  - some domain integrity support (i.e., constraints to be satisfied by all columns defined on the domain)
  - limited "strong type checking" on comparisons (in particular, on joins)
  - limited ability to define valid operators for specified domains and to define the domain of the result of scalar expressions

  They still do not provide "enumerated types" or full user-defined data type support.

- The following new builtin data types are supported:

VARCHAR	(varying length strings)
NCHAR	(national strings)
DATETIME	(absolute dates and times)
INTERVAL	(date and time intervals)

- In addition to the "schema definition" operations in the current standard (CREATE SCHEMA, CREATE TABLE, CREATE VIEW, GRANT [= create authorization]), the following "schema manipulation" operations are also supported:

  ```
  DROP SCHEMA
  DROP TABLE
  DROP VIEW
  REVOKE        [= drop authorization]
  ALTER TABLE  [add/drop column, add/drop constraints, modify defaults]
  CREATE DOMAIN, DROP DOMAIN
  CREATE ASSERTION, DROP ASSERTION
  ```

  All schema definition and schema manipulation operations can be used from within an application program.

- Referential integrity support is extended to include CASCADE, SET NULL, and SET DEFAULT delete and update rules. (Although this is not the place to go into details, it must be said that the SQL2 referential integrity proposals are unfortunately far more complex than they need to be, at least in their present form.)

- As suggested above by the appearance of CREATE and DROP ASSERTION in the list of "schema manipulation" operations, general integrity constraints (i.e., integrity constraints of arbitrary complexity, involving any number of tables) are supported. *Note:* A side-effect of this extension is that there is now a lot of redundancy in the language in this area:

  - "NOT NULL" constraints are a special case of single-column CHECK constraints

  - single-column CHECK constraints are a special case of table-level CHECK constraints

  - table-level CHECK constraints are a special case of general integrity constraints (i.e., assertions)

  UNIQUE and PRIMARY KEY constraints can also be regarded as a special case of assertions; however, special-casing is probably desirable for these constraints, because they are so fundamental. FOREIGN KEY constraints would be a special case also, except that they include the ability to specify what the system is to do if an attempt is made to violate them—which CREATE ASSERTION, at least in its present form, does not.

12.3   MANIPULATIVE EXTENSIONS

- Several new scalar operators are supported—arithmetic, comparison, and component extraction operators for dates and times; a string concatenation operator (‖); an operator to extract a substring from a given string (SUBSTRING); an operator to search for a substring in a given string (INDEX); an operator to return the length of a string (LENGTH); and so on.

- An extended string pattern-matching comparison operator, SIMILAR TO, is supported.

- Manipulative statements generally are now defined to return an extensive set of feedback information if an exception occurs—not just an implementation-defined negative SQLCODE value as at present, but a SQL2-defined character string value in a special variable called SQLSTATE and a SQL2-defined row of values in a special table called SQL_DIAGNOSTICS. SQLCODE is now a "deprecated feature," meaning that it is a feature of the existing standard that is scheduled to be dropped at some future time. *Aside:* The only other "deprecated feature" at the time of writing is the ability to specify an integer instead of a column reference in an ORDER BY clause.

- A set of "schema information tables" (in effect, system-defined views of the system catalog) are supported. The schema information tables currently defined are as follows (the names should be broadly self-explanatory):

```
ACCESSIBLE_TABLES
TABLE_PRIVILEGES
ACCESSIBLE_COLUMNS
COLUMN_PRIVILEGES
CONSTRAINT_DEFS      [sic]
CONSTRAINT_COLUMNS
DOMAIN_DEFINITIONS
```

- The ability to assign a name to a derived column is supported. Here are two examples:

```
SELECT X + Y AS Z, ...
  ...


SELECT T.Z + 1, ...
FROM    ( SELECT X + Y FROM ... ) AS T ( Z )
  ...
```

In the first example, the final result table—i.e., the table retrieved by the SELECT—has a single (derived) column called Z. In the second example, the table identified in the FROM clause of the outer SELECT is a (derived) table called T, with a single (derived) column called T.Z.

(The second example also illustrates the point that the FROM clause can now include general table-expressions as well as simple table names. See further examples below and in Section 12.4.)

■ Scroll cursors are supported. A scroll cursor is an extended version of the existing cursor, a version for which not only "FETCH NEXT" but also "FETCH PREVIOUS" and other cursor movement operations are supported (note, however, that the table associated with such a cursor will be read-only). A cursor is defined to be a scroll cursor by the appearance of the key word SCROLL in the cursor definition. For example:

```
DECLARE X SCROLL CURSOR
     FOR SELECT ... etc.
```

The FETCH statement is extended to include a "fetch orientation" specification, as follows:

```
FETCH [ fetch-orientation ] cursor INTO target-commalist
```

where "fetch orientation" is one of the following:

```
NEXT
PRIOR
FIRST
LAST
ABSOLUTE scalar-expression
RELATIVE scalar-expression
```

(NEXT is the default, and is the only legal option if the cursor is not a scroll cursor.) NEXT, PRIOR, FIRST, and LAST are self-explanatory. For the other two cases, let n be the result of evaluating the scalar expression (which must be of type exact numeric); n must not be zero. ABSOLUTE n moves the cursor to the nth row (counting backward from the end if n is negative). RELATIVE n moves the cursor to the nth row from the current position (again, counting backward if n is negative).

■ A new kind of query expression, namely "joined table," is supported. Joined tables provide direct and explicit support for various kinds of join (in particular, natural join and outer join). Here is the syntax (somewhat simplified):

```
table [ NATURAL ] [ INNER | LEFT | RIGHT | FULL ] JOIN table
                                      [ ON search-condition ]
```

LEFT, RIGHT, and FULL mean left, right, and full *outer* join, respectively; INNER (which is the default) means inner join. If NATURAL is specified, the appropriate natural join is computed *on the basis of common column names* (the ON clause must be omitted in this case);

otherwise, the appropriate "theta-join" is computed (the ON clause must not be omitted in this case). Here is an example:

```
SELECT *
FROM   ( S NATURAL LEFT JOIN SP )
```

The "SELECT * FROM" seems somewhat obtrusive, but is apparently required. More to the point, however, note that this example cannot be expressed *at all* in the existing standard. The best that can be done today is something along the following lines (note, however, that this expression produces blanks and zeros instead of nulls in the result):

```
SELECT S.SNO, S.SNAME, S.STATUS, S.CITY, SP.PNO, SP.QTY
FROM   S, SP
WHERE  S.SNO = SP.SNO

UNION

SELECT S.SNO, S.SNAME, S.STATUS, S.CITY, '       ', 0000000000
FROM   S
WHERE  NOT EXISTS
     ( SELECT *
       FROM    SP
       WHERE   SP.SNO = S.SNO )
```

■ Query expressions can also involve explicit INTERSECT (set intersection) and EXCEPT (set difference) operators as well as the UNION operator. Like UNION, INTERSECT and EXCEPT can also include an ALL qualifier to specify that redundant duplicates are not to be eliminated. All three operators (UNION, INTERSECTION, and EXCEPT) also have a CORRESPONDING version to indicate that the operation is to be performed on the basis of common column names. A version of OUTER UNION is also supported. Simplified syntax:

```
table  op  [ ALL ]  [ CORRESPONDING ]  table
```

where "op" is UNION or INTERSECT or EXCEPT or OUTER UNION; if it is OUTER UNION, ALL and CORRESPONDING must be omitted. *Note:* Unfortunately, the two "tables" must be specified via SELECT-expressions, not just as simple table names. For example:

```
SELECT *
FROM   ( ( SELECT * FROM X ) UNION ( SELECT * FROM Y ) )
 ...
```

An expression of the form

```
X UNION Y
```

would appear preferable!

■ The ability to deactivate (and subsequently reactivate) individual integrity constraints is supported. For example, the statement

`SET CHECK47, CHECK82 CONSTRAINTS OFF`

will cause checking of integrity constraints CHECK47 and CHECK82 to be suspended (until such time as they are set ON again). This facility thus allows some integrity checking not to be done at the time of the relevant update operation, but rather to be deferred to some later time—e.g., to end of transaction. Such a feature could be useful in connexion with referential constraint cycles, for example.

- The COMMIT and ROLLBACK WORK operations, together with a new operation (SET TRANSACTION), are no longer considered to be data manipulation operations per se but instead constitute a new language, the "transaction management language." The SET TRANSACTION statement allows the user to specify the transaction "status" (READ ONLY or READ WRITE) and transaction "consistency level" (0, 2, or 4, corresponding respectively to what are usually known as "express read," "cursor stability," and "repeatable read"). Note, incidentally, that support for consistency levels less than 4 means that serializability can no longer be guaranteed and can therefore no longer be considered a requirement.

- Temporary base tables and temporary views are supported. A temporary table (base table or view) is a table that is created during a user session and destroyed at the end of that session, and is totally private to the user in question; it does not need to be registered in the catalog or subjected to the usual recovery and concurrency controls (and associated overhead) that apply to other, more permanent tables. *Note:* The concept of "session" is not defined, however.

- "Dynamic SQL" is supported. Dynamic SQL provides the ability for an application to generate (and then execute) SQL statements dynamically, i.e., during application execution. Such a facility is extremely important in the construction of generalized applications. *Note* (for readers who may be familiar with the dynamic SQL facilities of the IBM products DB2 and SQL/DS): The SQL2 dynamic SQL feature is based on the facilities of SQL/DS—i.e., "extended" dynamic SQL—rather than those of DB2.

- Finally, SQL2 manipulative operations are much more *orthogonal* than the existing standard. As indicated in Section 12.1, this is such a significant point that we devote a separate section to it (Section 12.4).

12.4   ORTHOGONALITY

Standard SQL is not a very orthogonal language. Many of the detailed criticisms made earlier in this book are essentially specific instances of this general—and very broad—complaint. Orthogonality means *independence:* A language is orthogonal if independent concepts are kept independent and are not mixed together in confusing ways. One example of *lack* of orthogonality (one among many, and one that unfortunately still applies to SQL2) is provided by the rule in existing SQL to the effect that the argument to a function such as SUM cannot be another function reference (see Appendix F for further discussion of this particular case).

Orthogonality is desirable because the less orthogonal a language is, the more complicated it is and (paradoxically but simultaneously) the less powerful it is. "Orthogonal design maximizes expressive power while avoiding deleterious superfluities" (from A. van Wijngaarden et al., eds., *Revised Report on the Algorithmic Language Algol 68*, Springer-Verlag, 1976). As already indicated, SQL as currently defined is extremely deficient in this regard. SQL2 is somewhat better. We summarize below some of the major improvements (not all) in this general area.

- Query expressions are no longer limited to appearing only in the context of a cursor definition. Instead, they are now also permitted in all of the following contexts:

  - within CREATE VIEW (as the view-defining expression)
  - in a subquery (i.e., a subquery is now just a query expression in parentheses—except that in most contexts, the result of evaluating the subquery must still be a single-column table)
  - within INSERT (multiple-row format—i.e., INSERT . . . SELECT) to define the rows to be inserted
  - in a "joined table" expression (see Section 12.3) to define one of the tables to be joined
  - in a UNION (or OUTER UNION or INTERSECT or EXCEPT) expression to define one of the tables to be UNIONed (or . . .)
  - within a FROM clause (as a "derived table")

  The last of these requires some additional explanation. The general syntax of the FROM clause is still

  ```
  FROM table-reference-commalist
  ```

  but "table reference" is now extended as follows (simplifying somewhat once again):

  ```
  table-reference
      ::=    table [ [ AS ] ... See Section 12.3 ]
           | ( query-expression ) [ AS ... See Section 12.3 ]
           | joined-table
  ```

  The first form is basically as in standard SQL today (except for the optional noiseword AS); the second and third forms introduce the idea that, instead of limiting the operands of FROM to be named tables, they can instead be *table-valued expressions*. For example:

```
SELECT MAX ( T.CITY )
FROM    ( SELECT S.CITY FROM S
          UNION
          SELECT P.CITY FROM P ) AS T ( CITY )
```

Note, however, that UNION (and INTERSECT and EXCEPT and OUTER UNION) are still illegal in a SELECT *statement* (i.e., a singleton SELECT).

Comment: The foregoing extension, though desirable so far as it goes, still fails to recognize the basic point that a table name *ought* to be regarded as just a special case of a general table (or query) expression. See Appendix F. *End of comment.*

The syntactic category "query specification" now has meaning only as a component of a query expression (basically, a query specification is just a query expression that does not include any [OUTER] UNIONs or INTERSECTs or EXCEPTs—it is no longer particularly interesting in its own right).

- The argument to a function that includes DISTINCT is no longer limited to being a column reference but can instead be any scalar expression.

- The restrictions on the number of times DISTINCT can appear within a given expression have been dropped.

- The restrictions regarding grouped views (e.g., a FROM clause that includes a reference to a grouped view cannot include any other table references) have been dropped. In fact, the term "grouped view" has been dropped entirely.

- To return to query expressions once again: As stated in Chapter 10, query expressions can be regarded as being at the top of the syntax tree. The following simplified explanation indicates how very much more orthogonal matters are in this area in SQL2.

  - a query expression is basically a collection of terms connected together by means of the operators UNION, and/or INTERSECT, and/or EXCEPT (each with or without ALL and with or without CORRESPONDING), and/or OUTER UNION

  - each term in a query expression is either a query specification or a "table value expression"

  - a query specification is basically just a SELECT–FROM–WHERE– GROUP BY–HAVING expression; a "table value expression" is basically just a list of one or more "row value expressions"

- a row value expression is basically a list of one or more scalar expressions
- a scalar expression (in addition to all of the obvious cases—arithmetic expressions, etc.) can be a subquery
- finally, as explained earlier, a subquery is basically just a query expression in parentheses

One consequence of all of the above, incidentally, is that an UPDATE statement can update one value in the database from another in SQL2 (this is not possible in the existing standard).

A Set of Sample Problems

A.1 INTRODUCTION

In this appendix we present a testbed of sample problems for readers who wish to try their hand at writing some standard SQL code. The problems are based (for the most part) on the exercises from the book *A Guide to DB2* (3rd edition, Addison-Wesley, 1989). Most of them involve the "suppliers-parts-projects" database (see Fig. A.1). That database contains information concerning suppliers (S), parts (P), and projects (J). Suppliers, parts, and projects are uniquely identified by supplier number (SNO), part number (PNO), and project number (JNO), respectively. The significance of an SPJ (shipment) row is that the specified supplier supplies the specified part to the specified project in the specified quantity (and the combination SNO-PNO-JNO uniquely identifies such a row).

A.2 DATA DEFINITION

A.2.1 Write a suitable schema (i.e., set of CREATE TABLE statements) for the suppliers-parts-projects database.

A.2.2 Create a view consisting of project information for projects that are located in London (only).

A.2.3 Define table SP of the suppliers-and-parts database as a view of table SPJ of the suppliers-parts-projects database.

S	SNO	SNAME	STATUS	CITY
	S1	Smith	20	London
	S2	Jones	10	Paris
	S3	Blake	30	Paris
	S4	Clark	20	London
	S5	Adams	30	Athens

P	PNO	PNAME	COLOR	WEIGHT	CITY
	P1	Nut	Red	12	London
	P2	Bolt	Green	17	Paris
	P3	Screw	Blue	17	Rome
	P4	Screw	Red	14	London
	P5	Cam	Blue	12	Paris
	P6	Cog	Red	19	London

J	JNO	JNAME	CITY
	J1	Sorter	Paris
	J2	Punch	Rome
	J3	Reader	Athens
	J4	Console	Athens
	J5	Collator	London
	J6	Terminal	Oslo
	J7	Tape	London

SPJ	SNO	PNO	JNO	QTY
	S1	P1	J1	200
	S1	P1	J4	700
	S2	P3	J1	400
	S2	P3	J2	200
	S2	P3	J3	200
	S2	P3	J4	500
	S2	P3	J5	600
	S2	P3	J6	400
	S2	P3	J7	800
	S2	P5	J2	100
	S3	P3	J1	200
	S3	P4	J2	500
	S4	P6	J3	300
	S4	P6	J7	300
	S5	P2	J2	200
	S5	P2	J4	100
	S5	P5	J5	500
	S5	P5	J7	100
	S5	P6	J2	200
	S5	P1	J4	100
	S5	P3	J4	200
	S5	P4	J4	800
	S5	P5	J4	400
	S5	P6	J4	500

Fig.A.1 The suppliers-parts-projects database

A.2.4 Create a view from the suppliers-parts-projects database consisting of all projects (project number and city columns only) that are supplied by supplier S1 or use part P1.

A.2.5 Create a view consisting of supplier numbers and part numbers for suppliers and parts that are not located in the same city.

A.2.6 Given the view definition:

```
CREATE VIEW SUMMARY ( SNO, PNO, MAXQ, MINQ, AVGQ )
    AS SELECT SPJ.SNO, SPJ.PNO,
              MAX ( SPJ.QTY ), MIN ( SPJ.QTY ), AVG ( SPJ.QTY )
       FROM   SPJ
       GROUP  BY SPJ.SNO, SPJ.PNO
       HAVING SUM ( SPJ.QTY ) > 50
```

state which of the following query expressions and update operations are legal and, for those that are, give the translated equivalents:

```
(a)    SELECT *
       FROM    SUMMARY
```

```
(b)    SELECT *
       FROM    SUMMARY
       WHERE   SUMMARY.SNO <> 'S1'
```

```
(c)    SELECT *
       FROM    SUMMARY
       WHERE   SUMMARY.MAXQ > 250

(d)    SELECT SUMMARY.MAXQ - SUMMARY.MINQ, SUMMARY.SNO, SUMMARY.PNO
       FROM    SUMMARY
       WHERE   SUMMARY.SNO = 'S1'
       AND     SUMMARY.PNO = 'P1'

(e)    SELECT SUMMARY.SNO
       FROM    SUMMARY
       GROUP   BY SUMMARY.SNO

(f)    SELECT SUMMARY.SNO, SUMMARY.MAXQ
       FROM    SUMMARY
       GROUP   BY SUMMARY.SNO, SUMMARY.MAXQ

(g)    SELECT S.SNO, SUMMARY.AVGQ
       FROM    S, SUMMARY
       WHERE   S.SNO = SUMMARY.SNO

(h)    UPDATE SUMMARY
       SET     SNO = 'S2'
       WHERE   SUMMARY.SNO = 'S1'

(i)    UPDATE SUMMARY
       SET     SUMMARY.MAXQ = 1000
       WHERE   SUMMARY.SNO = 'S1'

(j)    DELETE
       FROM    SUMMARY
       WHERE   SUMMARY.SNO = 'S1'
```

A.3   DATA MANIPULATION: RETRIEVAL OPERATIONS

Write query expressions for the following:

Simple Queries

A.3.1 Get full details of all projects.

A.3.2 Get full details of all projects in London.

A.3.3 Get supplier numbers for suppliers who supply project J1.

A.3.4 Get all shipments where the quantity is in the range 300 to 750 inclusive.

A.3.5 Get a list of all part-color/part-city combinations, with duplicate color/city pairs eliminated.

A.3.6 Get all shipments where the quantity is nonnull.

A.3.7 Get project numbers and cities where the city has an "o" as the second letter of its name.

Joins

A.3.8 Get all supplier-number/part-number/project-number triples such that the indicated supplier, part, and project are all located in the same city.

A.3.9 Get all supplier-number/part-number/project-number triples such that the indicated supplier, part, and project are not all located in the same city.

A.3.10 Get all supplier-number/part-number/project-number triples such that no two of the indicated supplier, part, and project are located in the same city.

A.3.11 Get part numbers for parts supplied by a supplier in London.

A.3.12 Get part numbers for parts supplied by a supplier in London to a project in London.

A.3.13 Get all pairs of city names such that a supplier in the first city supplies a project in the second city.

A.3.14 Get part numbers for parts supplied to any project by a supplier in the same city as that project.

A.3.15 Get project numbers for projects supplied by at least one supplier not in the same city.

A.3.16 Get all pairs of part numbers such that some supplier supplies both the indicated parts.

Subqueries

A.3.17 Get project names for projects supplied by supplier S1.

A.3.18 Get colors of parts supplied by supplier S1.

A.3.19 Get part numbers for parts supplied to any project in London.

A.3.20 Get project numbers for projects using at least one part available from supplier S1.

A.3.21 Get supplier numbers for suppliers supplying at least one part supplied by at least one supplier who supplies at least one red part.

A.3.22 Get supplier numbers for suppliers with a status lower than that of supplier S1.

A.3.23 Get supplier numbers for suppliers supplying some project with part P1 in a quantity greater than the average shipment quantity of part P1 for that project.

EXISTS

A.3.24 Repeat number A.3.19 to use EXISTS in your solution.

A.3.25 Repeat number A.3.20 to use EXISTS in your solution.

A.3.26 Get project numbers for projects not supplied with any red part by any London supplier.

A.3.27 Get project numbers for projects supplied entirely by supplier S1.

A.3.28 Get part numbers for parts supplied to all projects in London.

A.3.29 Get supplier numbers for suppliers who supply the same part to all projects.

A.3.30 Get project numbers for projects supplied with at least all parts available from supplier S1.

For the next four (numbers A.3.31–A.3.34), convert the SQL expression shown back into an English equivalent.

A.3.31
```
SELECT  DISTINCT SPJX.JNO
FROM    SPJ SPJX
WHERE   NOT EXISTS
        ( SELECT *
          FROM    SPJ SPJY
          WHERE   SPJY.JNO = SPJX.JNO
          AND     NOT EXISTS
                  ( SELECT *
                    FROM    SPJ SPJZ
                    WHERE   SPJZ.PNO = SPJY.PNO
                    AND     SPJZ.SNO = 'S1' ) )
```

A.3.32
```
SELECT  DISTINCT SPJX.JNO
FROM    SPJ SPJX
WHERE   NOT EXISTS
        ( SELECT *
          FROM    SPJ SPJY
          WHERE   EXISTS
                  ( SELECT *
                    FROM    SPJ SPJA
                    WHERE   SPJA.SNO = 'S1'
                    AND     SPJA.PNO = SPJY.PNO )
          AND     NOT EXISTS
                  ( SELECT *
                    FROM    SPJ SPJB
                    WHERE   SPJB.SNO = 'S1'
                    AND     SPJB.PNO = SPJY.PNO
                    AND     SPJB.JNO = SPJX.JNO ) )
```

A.3.33
```
SELECT  DISTINCT SPJX.JNO
FROM    SPJ SPJX
WHERE   NOT EXISTS
        ( SELECT *
          FROM    SPJ SPJY
          WHERE   EXISTS
                  ( SELECT *
                    FROM    SPJ SPJA
                    WHERE   SPJA.PNO = SPJY.PNO
                    AND     SPJA.JNO = SPJX.JNO )
          AND     NOT EXISTS
                  ( SELECT *
                    FROM    SPJ SPJB
                    WHERE   SPJB.SNO = 'S1'
                    AND     SPJB.PNO = SPJY.PNO
                    AND     SPJB.JNO = SPJX.JNO ) )
```

A.3.34
```
SELECT  DISTINCT SPJX.JNO
FROM    SPJ SPJX
WHERE   NOT EXISTS
        ( SELECT *
          FROM    SPJ SPJY
```

```
WHERE   EXISTS
        ( SELECT *
          FROM    SPJ SPJA
          WHERE   SPJA.SNO = SPJY.SNO
          AND     SPJA.PNO IN
                  ( SELECT P.PNO
                    FROM    P
                    WHERE   P.COLOR = 'Red' )
          AND     NOT EXISTS
                  ( SELECT *
                    FROM    SPJ SPJB
                    WHERE   SPJB.SNO = SPJY.SNO
                    AND     SPJB.JNO = SPJX.JNO ) ) )
```

Builtin Functions

A.3.35 Get the total number of projects supplied by supplier S1.

A.3.36 Get the total quantity of part P1 supplied by supplier S1.

A.3.37 For each part being supplied to a project, get the part number, the project number, and the corresponding total quantity.

A.3.38 Get project numbers for projects whose city is first in the alphabetic list of such cities.

A.3.39 Get project numbers for projects supplied with part P1 in an average quantity greater than the greatest quantity in which any part is supplied to project J1.

A.3.40 Get supplier numbers for suppliers supplying some project with part P1 in a quantity greater than the average quantity in which part P1 is supplied to that project.

Union

A.3.41 Construct a list of all cities in which at least one supplier, part, or project is located.

A.3.42 Show the result of the following:

```
SELECT P.COLOR
FROM   P
UNION
SELECT P.COLOR
FROM   P
```

A.3.43 Repeat the previous exercise with UNION ALL in place of UNION.

A.4 DATA MANIPULATION: UPDATE OPERATIONS

Write INSERT, DELETE, or UPDATE statements (as appropriate) for each of the following problems.

A.4.1 Change the color of all red parts to orange.

A.4.2 Delete all projects for which there are no shipments.

A.4.3 Increase the shipment quantity by 10 percent for all shipments by suppliers that supply a red part.

A.4.4 Delete all projects in Rome.

A.4.5 Insert a new supplier (S10) into table S. The name and city are "Lopez" and "New York," respectively; the status is not yet known.

A.4.6 Construct a table containing a list of part numbers for parts that are supplied either by a London supplier or to a London project.

A.4.7 Construct a table containing a list of project numbers for projects that are either located in London or are supplied by a London supplier.

A.4.8 Add 10 to the status of all suppliers whose status is currently less than that of supplier S4.

A.5 EMBEDDED SQL

A.5.1 Write an embedded SQL program to list all suppliers, in supplier number order. Each supplier should be immediately followed in the listing by all projects for projects supplied by that supplier, in project number order.

A.5.2 Revise your solution to number A.5.1 to do the following in addition: (a) Increase the status by 50 percent for any supplier who supplies more than two projects; (b) delete any supplier who does not supply any projects at all.

A.5.3 (Harder.) Given the tables

```
CREATE TABLE PARTS
    ( PNO ... NOT NULL,
      DESCRIPTION ...,
      PRIMARY KEY ( PNO ) )

CREATE TABLE PART_STRUCTURE
    ( MAJOR_PNO ... NOT NULL,
      MINOR_PNO ... NOT NULL,
      QTY         ...,
      PRIMARY KEY ( MAJOR_PNO, MINOR_PNO ),
      FOREIGN KEY ( MAJOR_PNO ) REFERENCES PARTS,
      FOREIGN KEY ( MINOR_PNO ) REFERENCES PARTS )
```

where PART_STRUCTURE shows which parts (MAJOR_PNO) contain which other parts (MINOR_PNO) as first-level components, write an embedded SQL program to list all component parts of a given part, to all levels (the "parts explosion" problem).

A.6 ANSWERS

In this section we present a set of possible answers to the problems of Sections A.2–A.5. The solutions shown are not necessarily the only ones possible.

```
A.2.1    CREATE TABLE S
              ( SNO      CHAR(5)       NOT NULL,
                SNAME    CHAR(20)      DEFAULT '    ',
                STATUS   DECIMAL(3)    DEFAULT 0,
                CITY     CHAR(15)      DEFAULT '    ',
                PRIMARY KEY ( SNO ) )

         CREATE TABLE P
              ( PNO      CHAR(6)       NOT NULL,
                PNAME    CHAR(20)      DEFAULT '    ',
                COLOR    CHAR(6)       DEFAULT '    ',
                WEIGHT   DECIMAL(3)    DEFAULT -1,
                CITY     CHAR(15)      DEFAULT '    ',
                PRIMARY KEY ( PNO ) )

         CREATE TABLE J
              ( JNO      CHAR(4)       NOT NULL,
                JNAME    CHAR(10)      DEFAULT '    ',
                CITY     CHAR(15)      DEFAULT '    ',
                PRIMARY KEY ( JNO ) )

         CREATE TABLE SPJ
              ( SNO      CHAR(5)       NOT NULL,
                PNO      CHAR(6)       NOT NULL,
                JNO      CHAR(4)       NOT NULL,
                QTY      DECIMAL(5)    DEFAULT -1,
                PRIMARY KEY ( SNO, PNO, JNO ),
                FOREIGN KEY ( SNO ) REFERENCES S,
                FOREIGN KEY ( PNO ) REFERENCES P,
                FOREIGN KEY ( JNO ) REFERENCES J )
```

```
A.2.2    CREATE VIEW LONDON_PROJECTS ( JNO, JNAME, CITY )
              AS SELECT J.JNO, J.JNAME, J.CITY
                 FROM   J
                 WHERE  J.CITY = 'London'
```

```
A.2.3    CREATE VIEW SP ( SNO, PNO, QTY )
              AS SELECT SPJ.SNO, SPJ.PNO, SUM ( SPJ.QTY )
                 FROM   SPJ
                 GROUP  BY SPJ.SNO, SPJ.PNO
```

```
A.2.4    CREATE VIEW JC ( JNO, CITY )
              AS SELECT DISTINCT J.JNO, J.CITY
                 FROM   J, SPJ
                 WHERE  J.JNO = SPJ.JNO
                 AND  ( SPJ.SNO = 'S1' OR
                        SPJ.PNO = 'P1' )
```

```
A.2.5    CREATE VIEW NON_COLOCATED ( SNO, PNO )
              AS SELECT S.SNO, P.PNO
                 FROM   S, P
                 WHERE  S.CITY <> P.CITY
```

A.2.6 Only (a), (b), and (d) are legal. Translated version of (d):

```
SELECT MAX ( SPJ.QTY ) - MIN ( SPJ.QTY ), SPJ.SNO, SPJ.PNO
FROM   SPJ
WHERE  SPJ.SNO = 'S1'
AND    SPJ.PNO = 'P1'
GROUP  BY SPJ.SNO, SPJ.PNO
HAVING SUM ( SPJ.QTY ) > 50
```

```
A.3.1.   SELECT J.JNO, J.JNAME, J.CITY
         FROM   J
```

A.3.2
```
SELECT  J.JNO, J.JNAME, J.CITY
FROM    J
WHERE   J.CITY = 'London'
```

A.3.3
```
SELECT  DISTINCT SPJ.SNO
FROM    SPJ
WHERE   SPJ.JNO = 'J1'
ORDER   BY SPJ.SNO
```

A.3.4
```
SELECT  SPJ.SNO, SPJ.PNO, SPJ.JNO, SPJ.QTY
FROM    SPJ
WHERE   SPJ.QTY BETWEEN 300 AND 750
```

A.3.5
```
SELECT  DISTINCT P.COLOR, P.CITY
FROM    P
```

A.3.6
```
SELECT  SPJ.SNO, SPJ.PNO, SPJ.JNO, SPJ.QTY
FROM    SPJ
WHERE   SPJ.QTY IS NOT NULL
```

A.3.7
```
SELECT  J.JNO, J.CITY
FROM    J
WHERE   J.CITY LIKE '_o%'
```

A.3.8
```
SELECT  S.SNO, P.PNO, J.JNO
FROM    S, P, J
WHERE   S.CITY = P.CITY
AND     P.CITY = J.CITY
```

A.3.9
```
SELECT  S.SNO, P.PNO, J.JNO
FROM    S, P, J
WHERE   NOT
      ( S.CITY = P.CITY AND P.CITY = J.CITY )
```

A.3.10
```
SELECT  S.SNO, P.PNO, J.JNO
FROM    S, P, J
WHERE   S.CITY <> P.CITY
AND     P.CITY <> J.CITY
AND     J.CITY <> S.CITY
```

A.3.11
```
SELECT  DISTINCT SPJ.PNO
FROM    SPJ, S
WHERE   SPJ.SNO = S.SNO
AND     S.CITY = 'London'
```

A.3.12
```
SELECT  DISTINCT SPJ.PNO
FROM    SPJ, S, J
WHERE   SPJ.SNO = S.SNO
AND     SPJ.JNO = J.JNO
AND     S.CITY = 'London'
AND     J.CITY = 'London'
```

A.3.13
```
SELECT  DISTINCT S.CITY, J.CITY
FROM    S, SPJ, J
WHERE   S.SNO = SPJ.SNO
AND     SPJ.JNO = J.JNO
```

A.3.14
```
SELECT  DISTINCT SPJ.PNO
FROM    SPJ, S, J
WHERE   SPJ.SNO = S.SNO
AND     SPJ.JNO = J.JNO
AND     S.CITY = J.CITY
```

```
A.3.15   SELECT  DISTINCT J.JNO
         FROM    SPJ, S, J
         WHERE   SPJ.SNO = S.SNO
         AND     SPJ.JNO = J.JNO
         AND     S.CITY <> J.CITY

A.3.16   SELECT  SPJX.PNO, SPJY.PNO
         FROM    SPJ SPJX, SPJ SPJY
         WHERE   SPJX.SNO = SPJY.SNO
         AND     SPJX.PNO > SPJY.PNO

A.3.17   SELECT  J.JNAME
         FROM    J
         WHERE   J.JNO IN
                 ( SELECT  SPJ.JNO
                   FROM    SPJ
                   WHERE   SPJ.SNO = 'S1' )

A.3.18   SELECT  DISTINCT P.COLOR
         FROM    P
         WHERE   P.PNO IN
                 ( SELECT  SPJ.PNO
                   FROM    SPJ
                   WHERE   SPJ.SNO = 'S1' )

A.3.19   SELECT  DISTINCT SPJ.PNO
         FROM    SPJ
         WHERE   SPJ.JNO IN
                 ( SELECT  J.JNO
                   FROM    J
                   WHERE   J.CITY = 'London' )

A.3.20   SELECT  DISTINCT SPJ.JNO
         FROM    SPJ
         WHERE   SPJ.PNO IN
                 ( SELECT  SPJ.PNO
                   FROM    SPJ
                   WHERE   SPJ.SNO = 'S1' )

A.3.21   SELECT  DISTINCT SPJ.SNO
         FROM    SPJ
         WHERE   SPJ.PNO IN
                 ( SELECT  SPJ.PNO
                   FROM    SPJ
                   WHERE   SPJ.SNO IN
                         ( SELECT  SPJ.SNO
                           FROM    SPJ
                           WHERE   SPJ.PNO IN
                                 ( SELECT  P.PNO
                                   FROM    P
                                   WHERE   P.COLOR = 'Red' ) ) )

A.3.22   SELECT  S.SNO
         FROM    S
         WHERE   S.STATUS <
                 ( SELECT  S.STATUS
                   FROM    S
                   WHERE   S.SNO = 'S1' )

A.3.23   SELECT  DISTINCT SPJX.SNO
         FROM    SPJ SPJX
         WHERE   SPJX.PNO = 'P1'
         AND     SPJX.QTY >
                 ( SELECT AVG ( SPJY.QTY )
```

```
                FROM     SPJ SPJY
                WHERE    SPJY.PNO = 'P1'
                AND      SPJY.JNO = SPJX.JNO )
```

A.3.24
```
        SELECT DISTINCT SPJ.PNO
        FROM     SPJ
        WHERE    EXISTS
             ( SELECT *
               FROM     J
               WHERE    J.JNO = SPJ.JNO
               AND      J.CITY = 'London' )
```

A.3.25
```
        SELECT DISTINCT SPJX.JNO
        FROM     SPJ SPJX
        WHERE    EXISTS
             ( SELECT *
               FROM     SPJ SPJY
               WHERE    SPJY.PNO = SPJX.PNO
               AND      SPJY.SNO = 'S1' )
```

A.3.26
```
        SELECT J.JNO
        FROM     J
        WHERE    NOT EXISTS
             ( SELECT *
               FROM     SPJ
               WHERE    SPJ.JNO = J.JNO
               AND      SPJ.PNO IN
                    ( SELECT P.PNO
                      FROM     P
                      WHERE    P.COLOR = 'Red' )
               AND      SPJ.SNO IN
                    ( SELECT S.SNO
                      FROM     S
                      WHERE    S.CITY = 'London' ) )
```

A.3.27
```
        SELECT DISTINCT SPJX.JNO
        FROM     SPJ SPJX
        WHERE    NOT EXISTS
             ( SELECT *
               FROM     SPJ SPJY
               WHERE    SPJY.JNO = SPJX.JNO
               AND      SPJY.SNO <> 'S1' )
```

A.3.28
```
        SELECT DISTINCT SPJX.PNO
        FROM     SPJ SPJX
        WHERE    NOT EXISTS
             ( SELECT *
               FROM     J
               WHERE    J.CITY = 'London'
               AND      NOT EXISTS
                    ( SELECT *
                      FROM     SPJ SPJY
                      WHERE    SPJY.PNO = SPJX.PNO
                      AND      SPJY.JNO = J.JNO ) )
```

A.3.29
```
        SELECT DISTINCT SPJX.SNO
        FROM     SPJ SPJX
        WHERE    EXISTS
             ( SELECT P.PNO
               FROM     SPJ SPJY
               WHERE    NOT EXISTS
                    ( SELECT J.JNO
                      FROM     J
                      WHERE    NOT EXISTS
```

```
                          ( SELECT *
                            FROM     SPJ SPJZ
                            WHERE    SPJZ.SNO = SPJX.SNO
                            AND      SPJZ.PNO = SPJY.PNO
                            AND      SPJZ.JNO = J.JNO ) ) )
```

A.3.30   SELECT DISTINCT SPJX.JNO
          FROM   SPJ SPJX
          WHERE   NOT EXISTS
                   (SELECT SPJY.PNO
                     FROM   SPJ SPJY
                     WHERE   SPJY.SNO = 'S1'
                     AND   NOT EXISTS
                              (SELECT *
                                FROM   SPJ SPJZ
                                WHERE   SPJZ.PNO = SPJY.PNO
                                AND   SPJZ.JNO = SPJX.JNO))

A.3.31 Get project numbers for projects that use only parts that are available from supplier S1.

A.3.32 Get project numbers for projects that are supplied by supplier S1 with some of every part that supplier S1 supplies.

A.3.33 Get project numbers for projects such that at least some of every part they use is supplied to them by supplier S1.

A.3.34 Get project numbers for projects that are supplied by every supplier who supplies some red part.

A.3.35   SELECT COUNT (DISTINCT SPJ.JNO)
          FROM   SPJ
          WHERE   SPJ.SNO = 'S1'

A.3.36   SELECT SUM (SPJ.QTY)
          FROM   SPJ
          WHERE   SPJ.PNO = 'P1'
          AND   SPJ.SNO = 'S1'

A.3.37   SELECT SPJ.PNO, SPJ.JNO, SUM (SPJ.QTY)
          FROM   SPJ
          GROUP   BY SPJ.PNO, SPJ.JNO

A.3.38   SELECT J.JNO
          FROM   J
          WHERE   J.CITY =
                   (SELECT MIN (J.CITY)
                     FROM   J)

A.3.39   SELECT SPJ.JNO
          FROM   SPJ
          WHERE   SPJ.PNO = 'P1'
          GROUP   BY SPJ.JNO
          HAVING AVG (SPJ.QTY) >
                   (SELECT MAX (SPJ.QTY)
                     FROM   SPJ
                     WHERE   SPJ.JNO = 'J1')

A.3.40   SELECT DISTINCT SPJX.SNO
          FROM   SPJ SPJX
          WHERE   SPJX.PNO = 'P1'
          AND   SPJX.QTY >
                   (SELECT AVG (SPJY.QTY)
                     FROM   SPJ SPJY
                     WHERE   SPJY.PNO = 'P1'
                     AND   SPJY.JNO = SPJX.JNO)

A.3.41
```
SELECT S.CITY FROM S
UNION
( SELECT P.CITY FROM P
UNION
SELECT J.CITY FROM J )
ORDER  BY 1
```

A.3.42 The result consists of the set (Red,Green,Blue)—i.e., duplicates are eliminated.

A.3.43 The result consists of 6 Reds, 2 Greens, and 4 Blues.

A.4.1
```
UPDATE P
SET    COLOR = 'Orange'
WHERE  P.COLOR = 'Red'
```

A.4.2
```
DELETE
FROM   J
WHERE  J.JNO NOT IN
       ( SELECT SPJ.JNO
         FROM   SPJ )
```

A.4.3
```
CREATE TABLE REDS
       ( SNO   CHAR(5),
         PRIMARY KEY ( SNO ) )

INSERT INTO REDS ( SNO )
       SELECT DISTINCT SPJ.SNO
       FROM   SPJ, P
       WHERE  SPJ.PNO = P.PNO
       AND    P.COLOR = 'Red'

UPDATE SPJ
SET    QTY = SPJ.QTY * 1.1
WHERE  SPJ.SNO IN
       ( SELECT REDS.SNO
         FROM   REDS )
```

A.4.4
```
DELETE
FROM   SPJ
WHERE  'Rome' =
       ( SELECT J.CITY
         FROM   J
         WHERE  J.JNO = SPJ.JNO )

DELETE
FROM   J
WHERE  J.CITY = 'Rome'
```

Note that the "DELETE FROM J" will fail (in general) if the corresponding shipments are not deleted from SPJ first.

A.4.5
```
INSERT
INTO   S ( SNO, SNAME, CITY )
VALUES ( 'S10', 'Lopez', 'New York' )
```

A.4.6
```
CREATE TABLE LP
       ( PNO CHAR(6),
         PRIMARY KEY ( PNO ) )

INSERT INTO LP ( PNO )
       SELECT DISTINCT SPJ.PNO
       FROM   SPJ
       WHERE  SPJ.SNO IN
              ( SELECT S.SNO
```

```
                        FROM    S
                        WHERE   S.CITY = 'London' )
              OR        SPJ.JNO IN
                      ( SELECT J.JNO
                        FROM    J
                        WHERE   J.CITY = 'London' )
```

A.4.7   CREATE TABLE LJ
```
                    ( JNO   CHAR(4),
                      PRIMARY KEY ( JNO ) )

            INSERT INTO LJ ( JNO )
                    SELECT J.JNO
                    FROM    J
                    WHERE   J.CITY = 'London'
                    OR      J.JNO IN
                          ( SELECT DISTINCT SPJ.JNO
                            FROM    SPJ
                            WHERE   SPJ.SNO IN
                                  ( SELECT S.SNO
                                    FROM    S
                                    WHERE   S.CITY = 'London' ) )
```
A.4.8   SELECT S.STATUS
```
            FROM    S
            WHERE   S.SNO = 'S4'
```

Suppose the result is 20. Then:

```
    UPDATE S
    SET     STATUS = S.STATUS + 10
    WHERE   S.STATUS < 20
```

A.5.1 We show an outline solution only. First the cursor definitions:

```
    EXEC SQL DECLARE CS CURSOR FOR
            SELECT S.SNO, S.SNAME, S.STATUS, S.CITY
            FROM    S
            ORDER   BY S.SNO ;

    EXEC SQL DECLARE CJ CURSOR FOR
            SELECT J.JNO, J.JNAME, J.CITY
            FROM    J
            WHERE   J.JNO IN
                  ( SELECT SPJ.JNO
                    FROM    SPJ
                    WHERE   SPJ.SNO = :CS_SNO )
            ORDER BY J.JNO ;
```

where the host variable CS_SNO contains a supplier number value, fetched via
cursor CS. The logic is essentially as follows:

```
    EXEC SQL OPEN CS ;
    DO for all S records accessible via CS ;
       EXEC SQL FETCH CS INTO :CS_SNO, :CS_SN, :CS_ST, :CS_SC ;
       print CS_SNO, CS_SN, CS_ST, CS_SC ;
       EXEC SQL OPEN CJ ;
       DO for all J records accessible via CJ ;
          EXEC SQL FETCH CJ INTO :CJ_JNO, :CJ_JN, :CJ_JC ;
          print CJ_JNO, CJ_JN, CJ_JC ;
       END ;
       EXEC SQL CLOSE CJ ;
    END ;
    EXEC SQL CLOSE CS ;
```

A.5.2 The relevant embedded SQL statements are:

```
EXEC SQL UPDATE S
         SET    STATUS = S.STATUS * 1.5
         WHERE  S.SNO = :CS_SNO ;

EXEC SQL DELETE
         FROM   S
         WHERE  S.SNO = :CS_SNO ;
```

A.5.3 We present a recursive solution:

```
        GET LIST ( GIVENPNO ) ;
        CALL RECURSION ( GIVENPNO ) ;
        RETURN ;

RECURSION: PROC ( UPPER_PNO ) RECURSIVE ;
     DCL UPPER_PNO ... ;
     DCL LOWER_PNO ... INITIAL ( 'bbbbbb' ) ;
     EXEC SQL DECLARE C CURSOR FOR
              SELECT MINOR_PNO
              FROM   PART_STRUCTURE
              WHERE  MAJOR_PNO = :UPPER_PNO
              AND    MINOR_PNO > :LOWER_PNO
              ORDER  BY MINOR_PNO ;

     DO forever ;
        print UPPER_PNO ;
        EXEC SQL OPEN C ;
        EXEC SQL FETCH C INTO :LOWER_PNO ;
        IF not found THEN RETURN ;
        IF found THEN
        DO ;
           EXEC SQL CLOSE C ;
           CALL RECURSION ( LOWER_PNO ) ;
        END ;
     END ;
END ; /* of RECURSION */
```

For further discussion of this problem, see the author's book *Relational Database: Selected Writings* (Addison-Wesley, 1986).

A SQL Grammar

B.1 INTRODUCTION

Any formal language definition, standard or otherwise, necessarily involves two parts, a syntactic part and a semantic part—where (loosely speaking) *syntax* is how you say it and *semantics* is what it means. In the SQL standard (and in this book), the syntactic part of the language is defined by means of a BNF grammar, together with certain additional "syntax rules" expressed in English prose; the semantic part is defined purely by a set of "general rules" expressed (again) in English prose. We note in passing that other, more formal, definitional techniques do exist; however, such matters are beyond the scope of this book.

A language is thus certainly not just syntax. Nevertheless, it is always convenient to have a summary of the syntax of a language—i.e., a complete BNF grammar—for ease of reference. Despite this fact, the official standard document does not include any such summary. We therefore present one in this appendix.

The grammar that follows deliberately does not always use the same terminology as the official standard, for reasons explained in Section 3.5. It does use the "-list" and "-commalist" constructs (again, see Section 3.5 for details). It also uses a few simplifying abbreviations, namely "exp" for expression, "spec" for specification, "ref" for reference, and "def" for definition. The following are all defined to be *identifiers* in this grammar:

```
authorization-identifier
column
cursor
module
parameter
procedure
range-variable
```

The following are terminal categories (i.e., are undefined) with respect to this grammar:

```
data-type
identifier
integer
literal
```

We present the grammar top-down (more or less).

Note: In the interests of clarity and brevity, our grammar does not accurately reflect all of the syntactic limitations of SQL but is instead rather permissive, in the sense that it allows the generation of certain constructs that are not legal in SQL. For example, it permits the argument to an aggregate function such as AVG to consist of a reference to another such function, which standard SQL does not allow. It also makes no attempt to distinguish between numeric expressions and character string expressions (e.g., the operators "+" and "−" do not apply to character strings). Our reason for making these simplifications is that SQL is a very context-sensitive language, and attempts to reflect context sensitivity in BNF tend to lead to a rather unwieldy set of production rules.

B.2   SCHEMA DEFINITION LANGUAGE

```
schema
   ::=    CREATE SCHEMA
          AUTHORIZATION user
          [ schema-element-list ]

schema-element
   ::=    base-table-def
        | view-def
        | grant-operation

base-table-def
   ::=    CREATE TABLE base-table ( base-table-element-commalist )

base-table-element
   ::=    column-def
        | table-constraint-def

column-def
   ::=    column  data-type
          [ DEFAULT literal | USER | NULL ]
          [ column-constraint-def-list ]
```

```
column-constraint-def
    ::=   NOT NULL [ UNIQUE | PRIMARY KEY ]
        | CHECK ( search-condition )
        | REFERENCES base-table [ ( column-commalist ) ]

table-constraint-def
    ::= { UNIQUE | PRIMARY KEY } ( column-commalist )
        | CHECK ( search-condition )
        | FOREIGN KEY ( column-commalist )
                REFERENCES base-table [ ( column-commalist ) ]

view-def
    ::=   CREATE VIEW view [ ( column-commalist ) ]
            AS query-spec
          [ WITH CHECK OPTION ]

grant-operation
    ::=   GRANT privileges ON table TO grantee-commalist
            [ WITH GRANT OPTION ]

privileges
    ::=   ALL [ PRIVILEGES ] | operation-commalist

operation
    ::=   SELECT | INSERT | DELETE
        | UPDATE [ ( column-commalist ) ]
        | REFERENCES [ ( column-commalist ) ]

grantee
    ::=   PUBLIC | user
```

B.3   MODULE LANGUAGE

```
module-def
    ::=   MODULE [ module ]
          LANGUAGE { COBOL | FORTRAN | PASCAL | PLI }
          AUTHORIZATION user
        [ cursor-def-list ]
          procedure-def-list

cursor-def
    ::=   DECLARE cursor CURSOR FOR query-exp [ order-by-clause ]

order-by-clause
    ::=   ORDER BY ordering-spec-commalist

ordering-spec
    ::=   { integer | column-ref } [ ASC | DESC ]

procedure-def
    ::=   PROCEDURE  procedure  parameter-def-list ;
          manipulative-statement ;

parameter-def
    ::=   parameter  data-type  | SQLCODE
```

B.4 MANIPULATIVE STATEMENTS

```
manipulative-statement
    ::=    close-statement
         | commit-statement
         | delete-statement-positioned
         | delete-statement-searched
         | fetch-statement
         | insert-statement
         | open-statement
         | rollback-statement
         | select-statement
         | update-statement-positioned
         | update-statement-searched

close-statement
    ::=    CLOSE cursor

commit-statement
    ::=    COMMIT WORK

delete-statement-positioned
    ::=    DELETE FROM table WHERE CURRENT OF cursor

delete-statement-searched
    ::=    DELETE FROM table [ where-clause ]

fetch-statement
    ::=    FETCH cursor INTO target-commalist

insert-statement
    ::=    INSERT INTO table [ ( column-commalist ) ]
              { VALUES ( insert-atom-commalist ) | query-spec }

insert-atom
    ::=    atom | NULL

open-statement
    ::=    OPEN cursor

rollback-statement
    ::=    ROLLBACK WORK

select-statement
    ::=    SELECT [ ALL | DISTINCT ] selection
           INTO target-commalist
           table-exp

update-statement-positioned
    ::=    UPDATE table SET assignment-commalist
           WHERE CURRENT OF cursor

assignment
    ::=    column = { scalar-exp | NULL }

update-statement-searched
    ::=    UPDATE table SET assignment-commalist
           [ where-clause ]
```

B.5 QUERY EXPRESSIONS

```
query-exp
    ::=   query-term
        | query-exp UNION [ ALL ] query-term

query-term
    ::=   query-spec | ( query-exp )

query-spec
    ::=   SELECT [ ALL | DISTINCT ]  selection  table-exp

selection
    ::=   scalar-exp-commalist | *

table-exp
    ::=   from-clause
        [ where-clause ]
        [ group-by-clause ]
        [ having-clause ]

from-clause
    ::=   FROM table-ref-commalist

table-ref
    ::=   table [ range-variable ]

where-clause
    ::=   WHERE search-condition

group-by-clause
    ::=   GROUP BY column-ref-commalist

having-clause
    ::=   HAVING search-condition
```

B.6 SEARCH CONDITIONS

```
search-condition
    ::=   boolean-term
        | search-condition OR boolean-term

boolean-term
    ::=   boolean-factor
        | boolean-term AND boolean-factor

boolean-factor
    ::=   [ NOT ] boolean-primary

boolean-primary
    ::=   predicate | ( search-condition )

predicate
    ::=   comparison-predicate
        | between-predicate
        | like-predicate
        | test-for-null
        | in-predicate
        | all-or-any-predicate
        | existence-test
```

```
comparison-predicate
   ::=   scalar-exp  comparison  { scalar-exp  | subquery }

comparison
   ::=   = | <> | < | > | <= | >=

between-predicate
   ::=   scalar-exp [ NOT ] BETWEEN scalar-exp AND scalar-exp

like-predicate
   ::=   column-ref [ NOT ] LIKE atom [ ESCAPE atom ]

test-for-null
   ::=   column-ref IS [ NOT ] NULL

in-predicate
   ::=   scalar-exp [ NOT ] IN
         { subquery | atom [, atom-commalist ] }

all-or-any-predicate
   ::=   scalar-exp  comparison [ ALL | ANY | SOME ]  subquery

existence-test
   ::=   EXISTS subquery

subquery
   ::=   ( SELECT [ ALL | DISTINCT ]  selection  table-exp )
```

B.7   SCALAR EXPRESSIONS

```
scalar-exp
   ::=   term
       | scalar-exp { + | - } term

term
   ::=   factor
       | term { * | / } factor

factor
   ::=   [ + | - ] primary

primary
   ::=   atom
       | column-ref
       | function-ref
       | ( scalar-exp )

atom
   ::=   parameter-ref
       | literal
       | USER

parameter-ref
   ::=   parameter [ [ INDICATOR ] parameter ]

function-ref
   ::=   COUNT(*)
       | distinct-function-ref
       | all-function-ref
```

```
distinct-function-ref
    ::=    { AVG | MAX | MIN | SUM | COUNT } ( DISTINCT column-ref )

all-function-ref
    ::=    { AVG | MAX | MIN | SUM | COUNT } ( [ ALL ] scalar-exp )
```

B.8 MISCELLANEOUS

```
table
    ::=    base-table | view

base-table
    ::=    [ user . ] identifier

view
    ::=    [ user . ] identifier

user
    ::=    authorization-identifier

column-ref
    ::=    [ column-qualifier . ] column

column-qualifier
    ::=    table | range-variable

target
    ::=    parameter-ref
```

Language Levels and Conformance

The original SQL standard document defined two language levels; an "Integrity Enhancement Feature" was added later.

- The Integrity Enhancement Feature consists of all those parts of the language having to do with any of the following:
  - default values
  - CHECK constraints
  - primary and foreign key support
- Level 2 is the complete SQL language, minus the Integrity Enhancement Feature.
- Level 1 is a subset of level 2. (At least, that is the intent; but it does not necessarily follow that a Level 1 program will execute correctly under a Level 2 implementation.) As mentioned in Chapter 1, Level 1 is intended to be (approximately) "the intersection of existing implementations"; a program that restricts itself to Level 1—if that were possible— should thus enjoy maximum portability.

The main differences between Level 1 and Level 2 are as follows. In level 1:

1. The interleaved execution of concurrent transactions is not guaranteed to be serializable.

2. Identifiers are required to be up to 12 characters in length (instead of 18).

3. An authorization identifier qualifier is not permitted on table names.

4. Every column must be explicitly declared to be NOT NULL. (The intent here seems to be to exclude support for nulls. However, nulls can still be *generated*—e.g., if an aggregate function such as SUM is applied to an empty set.)

5. USER is not supported.

6. Correlated subqueries are not supported; i.e., a subquery cannot include a reference to a range variable that is defined (implicitly or explicitly) outside that subquery.

7. ALL (as an alternative to DISTINCT) is supported only implicitly.

8. DISTINCT cannot be applied to the argument of any function except COUNT.

9. The "not equals" comparison operator $<>$ is not supported.

10. The ESCAPE clause and the NOT LIKE predicate "x NOT LIKE y" are not supported.

11. EXISTS is not supported.

12. Whether two nulls are considered equal for the purposes of GROUP BY is implementation-defined.

13. Whether or not a given view or cursor permits updates is implementation-defined.

14. Schemas per se are not supported. Instead, the implementation is free to specify its own mechanism for associating an authorization identifier with a specific CREATE TABLE, CREATE VIEW, or GRANT operation.

15. UNIQUE constraints on base tables are not supported. Instead, the implementation is free to specify its own mechanism for enforcing uniqueness constraints.

16. REAL, DOUBLE PRECISION, and NUMERIC data types are not supported.

17. The check option is not supported.

18. The grant option is not supported.

19. On a "not found" exception, SQLCODE is set to an implementation-defined nonnegative value (not necessarily $+100$). If an error occurs during the execution of a given SQL statement, the effect on the database is im-

plementation-defined (Level 2, by contrast, specifies that there should be *no* effect).

20. UNION is not supported.

21. "ASC" ordering in ORDER BY is supported only implicitly. Numeric ordering specifications (instead of explicit column references) are not supported.

22. INSERT . . . SELECT is not supported.

23. UPDATE . . . WHERE CURRENT and DELETE . . . WHERE CURRENT are not supported.

24. The only parameter data type supported is CHARACTER.

The SQL language defined by the standard is said to be "conforming SQL language." A SQL implementation is said to be a "conforming SQL implementation" if it processes conforming SQL language according to the specifications of the standard. Thus, a conforming SQL implementation must support, either at Level 1 or at Level 2, at least all of the following:

- The schema definition language
- At least one of:
  - the module language
  - "direct" (interactive) invocation of all standard SQL data manipulation statements
  - embedded SQL COBOL, and/or embedded SQL FORTRAN, and/or embedded SQL Pascal, and/or embedded SQL PL/I
- The Integrity Enhancement Feature (optional)

However, a conforming implementation is explicitly permitted:

- To provide support for additional facilities not specified in the standard
- To provide options to process conforming SQL language in a nonconforming manner
- To provide options to process nonconforming SQL language

Note also that many aspects of standard SQL are explicitly stated to be either undefined or implementation-defined (and certain aspects are *im*plicitly undefined also—presumably unintentionally). Even if two implementations are both conforming, therefore, there is still no guarantee of application portability.

The standard specifically does not define the method or time of binding between database objects and references to such objects from within application programs.

The X/OPEN
SQL Dialect

D.1 INTRODUCTION

X/OPEN is a consortium of vendors responsible for standards in the UNIX world. In 1987, X/OPEN adopted a version of SQL (based on the ANSI/ISO standard but not identical to it) as a standard for interacting with relational databases in the UNIX environment. In this appendix we present a summary (certainly incomplete) of significant differences between X/OPEN's "portable SQL" and the ANSI/ISO standard.

D.2 STANDARD FEATURES NOT SUPPORTED IN X/OPEN

- Explicit schemas and modules are not supported.
- Comments are not permitted within embedded SQL statements.
- The character string data type must be spelled CHAR, not CHARACTER. The length specification must not be omitted.
- The integer data type must be spelled INTEGER, not INT.
- The decimal data type must be spelled DECIMAL, not DEC. The precision and scale specifications must not be omitted.

- The float data type always has precision 15. The precision specification must be omitted.

- The data types REAL, DOUBLE PRECISION, and NUMERIC are not supported.

- User-defined default values are not supported.

- UNIQUE constraints in CREATE TABLE are not supported (instead, X/OPEN enforces uniqueness via "UNIQUE indexes").

- PRIMARY KEY specifications are not supported.

- FOREIGN KEY (and/or REFERENCES) specifications are not supported.

- CHECK constraints are not supported.

- The check option on CREATE VIEW is not supported.

- The optional PRIVILEGES key word (in GRANT ALL PRIVILEGES) is not supported.

- The REFERENCES privilege is not supported.

- The grant option is not supported.

- In the WHENEVER statement, "GOTO" must be so spelled (i.e., without a space between the "GO" and the "TO").

- The synonym SOME for ANY is not supported.

- The optional INDICATOR key word is not supported.

- Indicator variables cannot be used in a WHERE or HAVING clause.

- The ESCAPE option on LIKE is not supported.

- The argument to an aggregate function such as SUM cannot include a "correlated reference," i.e., a reference to a range variable that is defined (explicitly or implicitly) outside the scope of that function reference.

- The argument to an aggregate function such as SUM cannot explicitly include the key word ALL.

- The ALL option on UNION is not supported.

- Every argument column in a UNION operation must be a *named column* (e.g., it cannot be specified as a literal).

D.3 X/OPEN FEATURES NOT SUPPORTED IN THE STANDARD

- Embedded SQL support for C is provided.

- Consecutive underscores are permitted in user-defined names.

- User-defined names and SQL key words are case-insensitive (i.e., they can be entered in upper or lower case or any mixture).

- The following data definition statements are supported in addition to those defined in the ANSI/ISO standard: CREATE [UNIQUE] INDEX, DROP INDEX, DROP TABLE, DROP VIEW, ALTER TABLE (to add a column), and REVOKE.

- Data definition statements can be included in application programs.

- Columns that are constrained to be "unique" do not have to be NOT NULL.

- The WHENEVER statement includes support for the SQLWARNING condition.

- For feedback information, an entire *SQL Communications Area* (SQLCA) is required, not just SQLCODE. (The SQLCA includes SQLCODE as one component.) The corresponding statement IN-CLUDE SQLCA is supported.

- An approximate numeric value can be assigned to an exact numeric column or variable.

- An expression such as x UNION y UNION z is legal in X/OPEN (i.e., it is not necessary, nor is it permitted, to group the UNIONs into pairs by means of parentheses).

D.4   INCOMPATIBILITIES

- Authorization identifiers are limited to a maximum of 8 characters in X/OPEN.

- If a given cursor will be used for UPDATE or DELETE CURRENT operations, X/OPEN requires a FOR UPDATE clause in the definition of that cursor.

- X/OPEN does not guarantee transaction serializability (it supports only the "cursor stability" consistency level).

- X/OPEN and ANSI/ISO have different sets of reserved words. For details, see the appropriate official documents.

Appendix E

The DB2 SQL Dialect

E.1 INTRODUCTION

Outside the ANSI and ISO committees per se, the biggest influence on the direction in which the SQL standard is likely to develop is unquestionably wielded by IBM, in the shape of its (highly successful) mainline product DB2. In this appendix we present a summary (certainly incomplete) of significant differences between the current DB2 dialect of SQL (as of DB2 Version 2 Release 1) and the current ANSI/ISO standard. For a thorough description of the DB2 version, the reader is referred to the book *A Guide to DB2*, by C. J. Date and Colin J. White (Addison-Wesley, 3rd edition, 1989).

E.2 STANDARD FEATURES NOT SUPPORTED IN DB2

- Explicit schemas and modules are not supported.
- Comments are not permitted within embedded SQL statements.
- The NUMERIC data type is not supported.
- User-defined default values are not supported.
- UNIQUE constraints in CREATE TABLE are not supported (instead, DB2 enforces uniqueness via "UNIQUE indexes"). PRIMARY KEY

constraints are supported, however—though only at the level of a "table constraint," not as part of an individual column definition.

- The REFERENCES specification (as part of an individual column definition) is not supported. FOREIGN KEY specifications (at the level of a "table constraint") are supported, however. Foreign keys in DB2 are required to reference primary keys, not just candidate keys.

- CHECK constraints are not supported.

- The REFERENCES privilege is not supported (the ALTER privilege is used for the purpose instead).

- The optional INDICATOR key word is not supported.

- Indicator variables cannot be used in a WHERE or HAVING clause.

- The ESCAPE option on LIKE is not supported.

- In DB2, if the argument to an aggregate function such as SUM includes DISTINCT, then the function reference must appear in isolation—i.e., it cannot be an operand in a larger arithmetic expression such as SUM(DISTINCT F) + 3. This restriction does not exist in the standard.

E.3   DB2 FEATURES NOT SUPPORTED IN THE STANDARD

- The characters #, @, and $ can appear in an identifier wherever a letter can appear. Consecutive underscores can also appear. DB2 also supports "delimited identifiers" (see the IBM manuals for details).

- The following data definition statements are supported in addition to those defined in the ANSI/ISO standard: CREATE [UNIQUE] INDEX, DROP INDEX, DROP TABLE, DROP VIEW, and ALTER TABLE.

- The standard also does not include any of the more "physical" data definition statements that are supported in DB2—CREATE/DROP DATABASE, CREATE/DROP TABLESPACE, CREATE/DROP STOGROUP, etc. The standard also does not include any of the more "physical" operands on CREATE TABLE, such as EDITPROC, FIELDPROC, VALIDPROC, "IN tablespace," etc.

- Data definition statements can be included in application programs.

- The following DB2 data types are not supported in the standard:

```
VARCHAR (and LONG VARCHAR)
GRAPHIC
VARGRAPHIC (and LONG VARGRAPHIC)
DATE
TIME
TIMESTAMP
```

The concept of "durations" also does not exist in the standard.

- DB2 provides extensive support for dates, times, and timestamps.

- The DB2 concept of system-defined default values does not exist in the standard; the specification NOT NULL WITH DEFAULT on CREATE (or ALTER) TABLE is a DB2 extension.

- Columns that are constrained to be "unique" do not have to be NOT NULL.

- DB2's support for foreign keys includes (a) "constraint names" for foreign key constraints, (b) additional delete rules (CASCADE and SET NULL), and (c) support for constraint cycles.

- The WHENEVER statement includes support for the SQLWARNING condition.

- For feedback information, an entire *SQL Communications Area* (SQLCA) is provided (the SQLCA includes SQLCODE—required by the standard—as one component). The corresponding statement INCLUDE SQLCA is supported.

- An approximate numeric value can be assigned to an exact numeric column or variable.

- DB2 supports hexadecimal constants.

- DB2 supports a concatenate operator ($||$).

- DB2 supports numerous scalar builtin functions, such as SUBSTR, LENGTH, etc.

- DB2 supports the scalar comparison operators $\sim =$, $\sim <$, and $\sim >$ as alternative representations of $<>$, $> =$, and $< =$, respectively.

- The standard SELECT statement is strictly a singleton SELECT—i.e., it retrieves a single row. Multiple-row retrieval must be done by means of a cursor. DB2 supports a standalone multiple-row SELECT (for interactive use).

- DB2 allows qualified references of the form "R.*" (where R is a range variable) in a SELECT clause. DB2 also allows references of the form "*" (or "R.*") in a SELECT clause to appear in conjunction with other items.

- In DB2, the commalist of constants in an IN condition (first format) must contain at least one constant; in the standard, it must contain at least two. DB2 also allows the argument to IN to be a single scalar expression, in which case the IN is interpreted as "$=$".

- UNION in the standard includes very severe restrictions regarding "union-compatibility" (basically, corresponding columns must have *identical* descriptions). In DB2, corresponding columns are required to be compatible only in the sense that they can legally be compared with one another.

- An expression such as *x* UNION *y* UNION *z* is legal in DB2 (it is not necessary to group the UNIONs into pairs by means of parentheses).

- DB2 supports the use of explicitly defined range variables in UPDATE and DELETE as well as in SELECT.

- The standard does not include any definition of the system catalog.

- The standard does not support the COMMENT or LABEL statements.

- The standard does not support synonyms (CREATE SYNONYM, DROP SYNONYM).

- The only privileges defined in the standard are SELECT, INSERT, UPDATE, DELETE, REFERENCES, and ALL. DB2 supports numerous additional privileges (see the IBM manuals for details). In addition, the DB2 GRANT statement allows a commalist of table names (not just one, as in the standard) to be specified in the ON clause, and allows that commalist to be optionally preceded by the noiseword TABLE (not permitted in the standard). DB2 also allows privileges to be REVOKEd (the standard does not include a REVOKE statement).

- The standard does not support the SET CURRENT SQLID statement.

- Certain restrictions on the use of view columns in the standard are relaxed in DB2. For example, if column C of view V is derived from an expression such as A + B, then in the standard an aggregate function reference of the form SUM (DISTINCT C) is (tacitly) illegal. In DB2, however, this restriction is relaxed if—and only if—the function reference appears within a statement that "meets certain special criteria" (this is the phrase used in the DB2 manual). Details of those "special criteria" are beyond the scope of this appendix, however. The reader is referred to the DB2 manual for more information.

- DB2's rules regarding view updatability are slightly more permissive than those of the standard, as follows:

  (a) In DB2, if a column of the view is derived from a constant or an expression that does not involve an aggregate function, then INSERT operations are not allowed, and UPDATE operations are not allowed on that column, but DELETE operations are allowed, and so are UPDATE operations on other columns. In the standard, such a view cannot be updated at all.

  (b) In DB2, if the WHERE clause in the view definition includes a subquery *and the FROM clause in that subquery refers to the base table on which the view is defined*, then the view is not updatable.

> In the standard, a view cannot be updated if its definition involves any subquery whatsoever.

- The FOR UPDATE clause on a cursor definition is not included in the standard.

- The embedded SQL statement DECLARE TABLE is not included in the standard.

- The standard requires host variables that will be used within embedded SQL statements to be defined within an "embedded SQL declare section," bracketed by BEGIN and END DECLARE SECTION statements. DB2 does not have this requirement.

- DB2 allows host variables to be elements of a structure, and also supports the use of structure variables where a commalist of scalars is required (e.g., in the VALUES clause on INSERT).

- The colon marker (":") on host variables can be omitted in DB2 in contexts where no ambiguity can arise (e.g., on the INTO clause in FETCH). It is always required in the standard.

- The standard does not support an explicit LOCK TABLE statement.

- All dynamic SQL features—the statements PREPARE, DESCRIBE, and EXECUTE, the SQL Descriptor Area (SQLDA), the special INCLUDE statement for incorporating the SQLDA into host programs, the miscellaneous associated facilities (DECLARE STATEMENT, special form of OPEN, etc.)—are excluded from the standard.

- DB2 supports partitioned tables. The standard does not.

- The standard does not support the EXPLAIN statement.

- The standard defines host language interfaces for COBOL, FORTRAN, Pascal, and PL/I (only). It also restricts the range of data types accessible from each of those languages; for example, INTEGER data is not accessible from PL/I in the standard (of course, this is probably an error in the standard). DB2 does not have such restrictions.

E.4   INCOMPATIBILITIES

- The standard and DB2 have different sets of reserved words.

- Authorization identifiers are limited to a maximum of 8 characters in DB2.

- String constants are varying length in DB2 but fixed length in the standard.

- In DB2, updates against a view V are checked against the check option (if any) specified for V and also against the check option (if any) specified for each view W (if any) on which V is defined. In other words, the check option is inheritable in DB2. This is not the case with the standard (nor was it with DB2, prior to Version 1 Release 3).

- The DB2 concept that there is an implicit WHENEVER statement for each condition—NOT FOUND, SQLERROR, also SQLWARNING— at the start of the program text, specifying CONTINUE in each case, is not supported in the standard.

- In some circumstances, if an error occurs on retrieval, DB2 will generate a null and will set the indicator variable to -2. It is not clear whether this is permitted by the standard or not.

- The DB2 rules determining the binding of range variables to their corresponding table are not identical to those of the standard. The details are beyond the scope of this appendix; we merely observe that the behavior of DB2 may be unpredictable (and in some cases is certainly incorrect) if a FROM clause (a) mentions the same table twice and introduces an explicit range variable in one of the two mentions only (e.g., FROM S, S SX), or (b) mentions two tables and introduces explicit range variables for both, each having the same name as the other table (e.g., FROM S P, P S). The standard handles these cases (and all others like them) correctly.

- (Another illustration of the preceding point.) Suppose for the sake of the example that fields S.CITY and P.CITY (supplier city and part city) of the suppliers-and-parts database are renamed as S.SCITY and P.PCITY. Consider the following SELECT statement:

```
SELECT  SNO
FROM    S
WHERE   NOT EXISTS
      ( SELECT *
        FROM    P
        WHERE   PCITY = SCITY )
```

This SELECT is valid in the standard but not in DB2 (the standard recognizes that the reference to SCITY is implicitly qualified by table name S, but DB2 does not; "correlated references" in DB2 are never unqualified).

- The key word WORK in COMMIT and ROLLBACK is optional in DB2 but required in the standard. The COMMIT and ROLLBACK statements are illegal in DB2 under IMS batch, IMS/DC, and CICS.

- The standard requires all concurrent executions of interleaved transactions to be serializable (i.e., equivalent to some serial execution of those same transactions, running them one at a time). DB2 cannot provide such a guarantee if any of the transactions in question executes under CS isolation level.

E.5   OTHER IBM DIALECTS

IBM has its own standard version of SQL, SAA ("Systems Application Architecture") SQL. It also has at least three database products in addition to DB2 that support some dialect of SQL, namely SQL/DS (for the VSE and VM environments), SQL/400 (for the OS/400 environment), and the OS/2 Extended Edition Database Manager (for the OS/2EE environment). At the time of writing, however:

- SAA SQL and the official SQL standard both include features that the other does not. For example, SAA SQL includes CREATE and DROP INDEX statements; the SQL standard includes UNIQUE specifications on CREATE TABLE.

- None of IBM's SQL products supports everything in SAA SQL exactly as prescribed by the SAA SQL standard—each of them has its own sanctioned deviations. For example, the semantics of GRANT TO PUBLIC are different in DB2 and in SAA SQL.

- With the possible exception of SQL/400, every one of those products supports SQL features that are not in SAA and SQL features that are not supported by any of the other products. For example, the DB2 LABEL statement is not included in SAA; the DB2 rules regarding legal view retrievals are not supported by either SQL/DS or the OS/2 Database Manager.

- As a consequence, no two of IBM's SQL products supports exactly the same dialect of SQL.

Further details are beyond the scope of this appendix.

An Annotated SQL Critique

This appendix consists of an annotated version of a paper that was previously published (under the title "A Critique of the SQL Database Language") in the author's book *Relational Database: Selected Writings* (Addison-Wesley, 1986), and prior to that in *ACM SIGMOD Record*, Vol. 14, No. 3 (November 1984). It is reprinted here (with permission) in essentially unchanged form, except that a number of comments have been added, as will be seen. *Note:* Numbers in square brackets (e.g., [10]) are references to papers and other publications listed in the "References" section at the end of the paper.

The abstract of the original paper was as follows:

The ANSI Database Committee (X3H2) is currently at work on a proposed standard relational database language (RDL), and has adopted as a basis for that activity a definition of the "Structured Query Language" SQL from IBM [10]. Moreover, numerous hardware and software vendors (in addition to IBM) have already released or at least announced products that are based to a greater or lesser extent on the SQL language as defined by IBM. There can thus be little doubt that the importance of that language will increase significantly over the next few years. Yet the language is very far from perfect. The purpose of this paper is to present a critical analysis of the language's major shortcomings, in the hope that it may be possible to remedy some of the deficiencies before their influence becomes too all-pervasive. The paper's standpoint is primarily that of formal computer languages in general, rather than that of database languages specifically.

Comment: The deficiencies were not remedied, for the most part. Most of the criticisms in the original paper do still apply to the version of SQL that was adopted as the official standard—which is of course the reason for reprinting the paper here. *End of comment.*

Note: Unlike the rest of this book, this appendix uses "record" and "field" as synonyms for "row" and "column."

F.1 INTRODUCTION

The relational language SQL (the name is usually pronounced "sequel"), pioneered in the IBM prototype System R [1] and subsequently adopted by IBM and others as the basis for numerous commercial implementations, represents a major advance over older database languages such as the DL/I language of IMS and the DML and DDL of the Data Base Task Group (DBTG) of CODASYL. Specifically, SQL is far easier to use than those older languages; as a result, users in a SQL system (both end-users and application programmers) can be far more productive than they used to be in those older systems (improvements of up to 20 times have been reported). Among the strongpoints of SQL that lead to such improvements are the following:

- Simple data structure
- Powerful operators
- Short initial learning period
- Improved data independence
- Integrated data definition and data manipulation
- Double mode of use
- Integrated catalog
- Compilation and optimization

Comment: These strongpoints were elaborated in an appendix to the original paper. However, that appendix is omitted here. *End of comment.*

The language does have its weak points too, however. In fact, it cannot be denied that SQL in its present form leaves rather a lot to be desired—

even that, in some important respects, it fails to realize the full potential of the relational model. The purpose of this paper is to describe and examine some of those weak points, in the hope that such aspects of the language may be improved before their influence becomes too all-pervasive.

> *Comment:* A pious hope. As already indicated, most of the criticisms that follow apply equally to the SQL standard. *End of comment.*

Before getting into details, I should like to make one point absolutely clear: *The criticisms that follow should not be construed as criticisms of the original designers and implementers of the SQL language.* The paper is intended solely as a critique of the SQL language as such, and nothing more. Note also that the paper applies specifically to the dialect of SQL implemented by IBM in its products SQL/DS, DB2, and QMF. It is entirely possible that some specific point does not apply to some other implemented dialect. However, most points of the paper do apply to most of the dialects currently implemented, so far as I am aware.

The remainder of the paper is divided into the following sections:

- Lack of orthogonality: expressions
- Lack of orthogonality: builtin functions
- Lack of orthogonality: miscellaneous items
- Formal definition
- Mismatch with host languages
- Missing function
- Mistakes
- Aspects of the relational model not supported
- Summary and conclusions

Reference [3] gives some background material—specifically, a set of principles that apply to the design of programming languages in general and database languages in particular. Many of the criticisms that follow are expressed in terms of those principles. *Note:* Some of the points apply to interactive SQL only and some to embedded SQL only, but most apply to both. I have not bothered to spell out the distinctions; the context makes it clear in every case. Also, the structure of the paper is a little arbitrary, in the sense that it is not really always clear which heading a particular point belongs under. There is also some repetition (I hope not too much), for essentially the same reason.

F.2   LACK OF ORTHOGONALITY: EXPRESSIONS

It is convenient to begin by introducing some nonSQL terms.

- A *table-expression* is a SQL expression that yields a table—for example, the expression

```
SELECT *
FROM    EMP
WHERE   EMP.DEPTNO = 'D3'
```

  Comment: "Table expression" here is intended to be more general than "table expression" as defined in the standard (see Chapter 10). Similarly for "scalar expression" (see below). *End of comment.*

- A *column-expression* is a SQL expression that yields a single column—for example, the expression

```
SELECT EMP.EMPNO
FROM    EMP
WHERE   EMP.DEPTNO = 'D3'
```

  A column-expression is a special case of a table-expression.

- A *row-expression* is a SQL expression that yields a single row—for example, the expression

```
SELECT *
FROM    EMP
WHERE   EMP.EMPNO = 'E2'
```

  A row-expression is a special case of a table-expression.

- A *scalar-expression* is a SQL expression that yields a single scalar value—for example, the expression

```
SELECT AVG ( EMP.SALARY )
FROM    EMP
```

  or the expression

```
SELECT EMP.SALARY
FROM    EMP
WHERE   EMP.EMPNO = 'E2'
```

  A scalar-expression is a special case of a row-expression and a special case of a column-expression.

Note that these four kinds of expression correspond to the four classes of data object (table, column, row, scalar) supported by SQL. Note too that (as pointed out in [3]) the four classes of object can be partially ordered as follows:

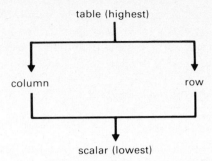

(columns are neither higher nor lower than rows with respect to this ordering).

As explained in [3] (again), a language should provide, for each class of object it supports, at least all of the following:

- A constructor function, i.e., a means for constructing an object of the class from literal (constant) values and/or variables of lower classes;

- A means for comparing two objects of the class;

- A means for assigning the value of one object in the class to another;

- A selector function, i.e., a means for extracting component objects of lower classes from an object of the given class;

- A general, recursively defined syntax for expressions that exploits to the full any closure properties the object class may possess.

The table below shows that SQL does not really measure up to these requirements.

opn obj	constructor	compare	assign	selector	gen expr
table	no	no	only via INSERT – SELECT	yes	no (see below)
column	only as arg to IN (host vbles & consts only)	no	no	yes	no
row	only in INSERT & UPDATE (host vbles & consts only)	no	only to/ from set of host scalars	(yes)	no
scalar	N/A	yes	only to/ from host scalar	(yes)	no

Let us consider table-expressions in more detail. The SELECT state-ment, which, since it yields a table, may be regarded as a table-expression (possibly of a degenerate form, e.g., as a column-expression), currently has the following structure:

```
SELECT scalar-expression-commalist
FROM   table-name-commalist
WHERE  predicate
```

(ignoring numerous minor details). Notice that it is just *table-names* that appear in the FROM clause. Completeness suggests that it should be *table-expressions* (as Gray puts it [8], "anything in computer science that is not recursive is no good"). This is not just an academic consideration, by the way; on the contrary, there are several practical reasons as to why such recursiveness is desirable.

Comment: The proposed SQL2 extensions—but not the standard per se—do address this criticism, partially. *End of comment.*

▪   First, consider the relational algebra. Relational algebra possesses the important property of *closure*—that is, relations form a closed system under the operations of the algebra, in the sense that the result of apply-ing any of those operations to any relation(s) is itself another relation. As a consequence, the operands of any given operation are not con-strained to be real ("base") relations only, but rather can be any alge-braic expression. Thus, the relational algebra allows the user to write *nested relational expressions*—and this feature is useful for precisely the same reasons that nested expressions are useful in ordinary arithmetic.

▪   Now consider SQL. SQL is a language that supports, directly or indi-rectly, all of the operations of the relational algebra (i.e., SQL is "rela-tionally complete"). However, the table-expressions of SQL (which are the SQL equivalent of the expressions of the relational algebra) *cannot* be arbitrarily nested. Let us consider the question of exactly which cases SQL does support. Simplifying matters slightly, the expression SELECT–FROM–WHERE is the SQL version of the nested algebraic expression

```
projection ( restriction ( product ( table1, table2, ... ) ) )
```

(the product corresponds to the FROM clause, the restriction to the WHERE clause, and the projection to the SELECT clause; table1, table2, . . . are the tables identified in the FROM clause—and note that, as we pointed out earlier, these are simple table-names, not more complex expressions). Likewise, the expression

```
SELECT ... FROM ... WHERE ...
UNION
SELECT ... FROM ... WHERE ...
  .....
```

is the SQL version of the nested algebraic expression

```
union ( tabexp1, tabexp2, ... )
```

where tabexp1, tabexp2, . . . are in turn table-expressions of the form shown earlier (i.e., projections of restrictions of products of named tables). But it is not possible to formulate direct equivalents of any other nested algebraic expressions. Thus, for example, it is not possible to write a direct equivalent in SQL of the nested expression

```
restriction ( projection ( table ) )
```

Instead, the user has to recast the expression into a semantically equivalent (but syntactically different) form in which the restriction is applied before the projection. What this means in practical terms is that the user may have to expend time and effort transforming the "natural" formulation of a given query into some different, and arguably less "natural," representation (see Example below). What is more, the user is therefore also required to understand exactly when such transformations are valid. This may not always be intuitively obvious. For example, is a projection of a union always equivalent to the union of two projections?

Example: Given the two tables

```
NYC ( EMPNO, DEPTNO, SALARY )
SFO ( EMPNO, DEPTNO, SALARY )
```

(representing New York and San Francisco employees, respectively), list EMPNO for all employees.

"Natural" formulation (projection of a union):

```
SELECT EMPNO FROM ( NYC UNION SFO )
```

SQL formulation (union of two projections):

```
SELECT EMPNO FROM NYC
UNION
SELECT EMPNO FROM SFO
```

Note in passing that allowing both formulations of the query would enable different users to perceive and express the same problem in different ways. (Of course, both formulations should ideally translate to the same internal representation, for otherwise the choice between them would no longer be arbitrary.)

- The foregoing example tacitly makes use of the fact that a simple table-reference (i.e., a table-name) *ought* to be just a special case of a general table-expression. Thus I wrote

`NYC UNION SFO`

instead of

`SELECT * FROM NYC UNION SELECT * FROM SFO`

(which current SQL would require). It would be highly desirable for SQL to allow the expression "SELECT * FROM T" to be replaced by simply "T" wherever it appears, in the style of more conventional languages. In other words, SELECT should be regarded as a *statement* whose function is to retrieve a table (represented by a table-expression). Table-expressions per se—in particular, *nested* table-expressions—should not require the "SELECT * FROM." Among other things, this change would improve the usability of the EXISTS builtin function (see later). It would also be clear that INTO and ORDER BY are clauses of the SELECT *statement* and not part of a table- (or column-) expression; the question of whether they can appear in a nested expression would then simply not arise, thus avoiding the need for a rule that looks arbitrary but is in fact not.

Comment: The foregoing criticism still applies to SQL2, except partially in the (limited) special context of a "joined table." *End of comment.*

- A nested table-expression is permitted—in fact required—in current SQL as the argument to EXISTS (but strangely enough not as the argument to the other builtin functions; this point is discussed in the next section). Nested *column-expressions* ("subqueries") are (a) *required* with the ANY and ALL operators (includes the IN operator, which is just a different spelling for =ANY); and (b) *permitted* with scalar comparison operators (<, >, =, etc.), if and only if the column-expression yields a column having at most one row. Moreover, the nested expression is allowed to include GROUP BY and HAVING in case (a) but not in case (b). More arbitrariness.

- Elsewhere I have proposed some extensions to SQL to support the outer join operation [4]. The details of that proposal do not concern us here; what does concern us is the following. If the user needs to compute an outer join of three or more relations, then (a) that outer join is constructed by performing a sequence of *binary* outer joins (e.g., join relations A and B, then join the result and relation C); and (b) it is essential that the user indicate the sequence in which those binary joins are performed, because different sequences will produce different results, in general. Indicating the required sequence is done, precisely, by writing a suitable nested expression. Thus, nested expressions are *essential* if SQL is to provide direct (i.e., single-statement) support for general outer joins of more than two relations.

Comment: SQL2 does support general outer joins of more than two relations, and uses a syntactic trick (details beyond the scope of this appendix) to specify the required nesting. *End of comment.*

- Another example (involving outer join again): Part of the proposal for supporting outer join in reference [4] involves the use of a new clause, the PRESERVE clause, whose function is to preserve rows from the indicated table that would not otherwise participate in the result of the SELECT. Consider the tables

```
COURSE    ( COURSENO, SUBJECT )
OFFERING ( COURSENO, OFFNO, LOCATION )
```

and consider the query "List all algebra courses, with their offerings if any." The two SELECT statements following (neither of which is valid in current SQL, of course) represent two attempts to formulate this query:

```
SELECT    ALGEBRA.COURSENO,
          OFFERING.OFFNO, OFFERING.LOCATION
FROM     ( SELECT COURSE.COURSENO
          FROM    COURSE
          WHERE   COURSE.SUBJECT = 'Algebra' ) ALGEBRA,
          OFFERING
WHERE     ALGEBRA.COURSENO = OFFERING.COURSENO
PRESERVE ALGEBRA

SELECT    COURSE.COURSENO, OFFERING.OFFNO, OFFERING.LOCATION
FROM      COURSE, OFFERING
WHERE     COURSE.COURSENO = OFFERING.COURSENO
AND       COURSE.SUBJECT = 'Algebra'
PRESERVE COURSE
```

Each of these statements does list all algebra courses, together with their offerings, for all such courses that do have any offerings. The first also lists algebra courses that do not have any offerings, concatenated with nulls in the OFFERING positions; i.e., it preserves information for those courses (note the introduced name ALGEBRA, which is used to refer to the result of evaluating the inner expression). The second, by contrast, preserves information not only for *algebra* courses with no offerings, *but also for all courses for which the subject is not algebra* (regardless of whether those courses have any offerings or not). In other words, the first preserves information for algebra courses only (as required), the second produces a lot of unnecessary output. And note that the first cannot even be formulated (as a single statement) if nested expressions are not supported.

Comment: SQL2 does support the introduction of user-defined names for intermediate results (both tables and columns), as discussed in Chapter 12 of this book. *End of comment.*

■ In fact, SQL does already support nested expressions in a kind of "under the covers" sense. Consider the following example:

Base table:

```
S ( SNO, SNAME, STATUS, CITY )
```

View definition:

```
CREATE VIEW LS
    AS SELECT S.SNO, S.SNAME, S.STATUS
       FROM    S
       WHERE   S.CITY = 'London'
```

Query (Q1):

```
SELECT *
FROM    LS
WHERE   LS.STATUS > 50
```

Resulting SELECT statement (Q2):

```
SELECT  S.SNO, S.SNAME, S.STATUS
FROM    S
WHERE   S.STATUS > 50
AND     S.CITY = 'London'
```

The SELECT statement Q2 is obtained from the original query Q1 by a process usually described as "merging"—statement Q1 is "merged" with the SELECT in the view definition to produce statement Q2. To the naive user this looks a little bit like magic. But in fact what is going on is simply that the reference to LS in the FROM clause in Q1 is being replaced by the expression that *defines* LS as follows:

```
SELECT *
FROM ( SELECT S.SNO, S.SNAME, S.STATUS
       FROM    S
       WHERE   S.CITY = 'London' )
WHERE   S.STATUS > 50
```

This explanation, though both accurate and easy to understand, cannot conveniently be used in describing or teaching SQL, precisely because SQL does not support nesting at the external or user's level.

■ UNION is not permitted in a subquery, and hence (among other things) cannot be used in the definition of a view (although strangely enough it *can* be used to define the scope for a cursor in embedded SQL). So a view cannot be "any derivable relation," and the relational closure property breaks down. Likewise, INSERT . . . SELECT cannot be used to assign the union of two relations to another relation. Yet another consequence of the special treatment given to UNION is that it is not possible to apply a builtin function such as AVG to a union. See the following section.

Comment: The foregoing restrictions regarding UNION do not apply to SQL2. *End of comment.*

I conclude this discussion of SQL expressions by noting a few additional (and apparently arbitrary) restrictions.

Comment: All of the following restrictions are relaxed in SQL2. *End of comment.*

- The predicate C BETWEEN A AND B is equivalent to the predicate A < = C AND C < = B—*except* that B (but not A or C!) can be a column-expression (subquery) in the second formulation but not in the first.

- The predicate "field comparison subquery" must be written in the order shown and not the other way around; i.e., the expression "subquery comparison field" is illegal.

- If we regard SELECT, UPDATE, and INSERT all as special kinds of assignment statement—in each case, the value of some expression is being assigned to some variable (a newly created variable, in the case of INSERT)—then source values for those assignments can be specified as scalar-expressions (involving database fields, host variables, constants, and scalar operators) for SELECT and UPDATE, but must be specified as simple host variables or constants for INSERT. Thus, for example, the following is valid:

```
SELECT :X + 1
FROM   T
   . . .
```

and so is:

```
UPDATE T
SET    F = :X + 1
   . . .
```

but the following is not:

```
INSERT INTO T ( F )
       VALUES ( :X + 1 )
```

- Given the tables:

```
S ( SNO, SNAME, STATUS, CITY )
P ( PNO, PNAME, COLOR, WEIGHT, CITY )
```

the SELECT statement

```
SELECT  P.COLOR
FROM    P
WHERE   P.CITY =
        ( SELECT  P.CITY
          FROM    P
          WHERE   P.PNO = 'P1' )
```

is legal, but the UPDATE statement

```
UPDATE  P
SET     COLOR = 'Blue'
WHERE   P.CITY =
        ( SELECT  P.CITY
          FROM    P
          WHERE   P.PNO = 'P1' )
```

is not. Worse, neither is the UPDATE statement

```
UPDATE  P
SET     CITY =
        ( SELECT  S.CITY
          FROM    S
          WHERE   S.SNO = 'S1' )
WHERE   ...
```

Even worse, given:

```
EMP      ( EMPNO, SALARY )
BONUSES  ( EMPNO, BONUS )
```

the following (potentially very useful) UPDATE is also illegal:

```
UPDATE  EMP
SET     SALARY = EMP.SALARY +
                ( SELECT  BONUSES.BONUS
                  FROM    BONUSES
                  WHERE   BONUSES.EMPNO = EMP.EMPNO )
```

(Actually there is a slight problem in this last example. Suppose a given employee number, say e, appears in the EMP table but not in the BONUSES table. Then the parenthesized expression will evaluate to the empty set for employee e. SQL will probably therefore consider the bonus for e to be null, and so will set e's salary to null as well—whereas what is wanted is clearly for e's salary to remain unchanged. To fix this problem, we need to replace the parenthesized expression by (say)

```
ROWMAX ( ( SELECT ... EMP.EMPNO ) , 0 )
```

where ROWMAX is a function that operates by (a) ignoring any of its arguments that evaluate to null and then (b) returning the maximum of those that are left, if any, or null otherwise. Note that ROWMAX is different in kind from the builtin functions currently provided in SQL—it is in fact a scalar-valued function, whose arguments are scalar-expressions.)

F.3   LACK OF ORTHOGONALITY: BUILTIN FUNCTIONS

Frankly, there is so much confusion in this area that it is difficult to criticize it coherently. The basic point, however, is that the argument to a function such as SUM is a column of scalar values and the result is a single scalar value; hence, orthogonality dictates that (a) any column-expression should be permitted as the argument, and (b) the function-reference should be permitted in any context in which a scalar can appear. However, (a) the argument is in fact specified in a most unorthodox manner, which means in turn that (b) function references can actually appear only in a rather small set of special-case situations. In particular, function-references cannot appear nested inside other function-references. In addition to this fact, functions are subject to a large number of peculiar and apparently arbitrary restrictions.

Before getting into details, I should point out that SQL in fact supports two distinct categories of function, not however in any uniform syntactic style. The two categories can be referred to, informally, as *column* and *table* functions, respectively. I discuss each in turn.

Column Functions

Column functions are the ones that one usually thinks of whenever functions are mentioned in connexion with SQL. A column function is a function that reduces an entire column of scalar values to a single value. The functions in this category are COUNT [excluding COUNT(*)], SUM, AVG, MAX, and MIN. A functional notation is used to represent these functions; however, as suggested above, the scoping rules for representing the argument are somewhat unconventional. Consider the following database (suppliers and parts):

```
S   ( SNO, SNAME, STATUS, CITY )
P   ( PNO, PNAME, COLOR, WEIGHT, CITY )
SP  ( SNO, PNO, QTY )
```

and consider also the following query:

```
SELECT SUM ( SP.QTY )
FROM    SP
```

The argument to SUM here is in fact the entire column of QTY values in table SP, and a more conventional syntax would accordingly be:

```
SUM ( SELECT SP.QTY
         FROM   SP )
```

(though once again the keyword SELECT seems rather obtrusive; SP.QTY FROM SP, or—even better—simply SP.QTY, would be more orthodox). As another example, the query:

```
SELECT SUM ( SP.QTY )
FROM   SP
WHERE  SP.PNO = 'P2'
```

would more conventionally be expressed as

```
SUM ( SELECT SP.QTY
         FROM   SP
         WHERE  SP.PNO = 'P2' )
```

or (better) as:

```
SUM ( SP.QTY WHERE SP.PNO = 'P2' )
```

As it is, the argument has to be determined by reference to the context. An immediate consequence of this fact is that a query such as "Find parts supplied in a total quantity greater than 1000" cannot be expressed in a natural style. First, the syntax:

```
SELECT SP.PNO
FROM   SP
WHERE  SUM ( SP.QTY ) > 1000
```

clearly does not work, either with SQL's rules for argument scope or with any other rules. The most logical formulation (but still retaining a SQL-like style) is:

```
SELECT DISTINCT SPX.PNO
FROM   SP SPX
WHERE  SUM ( SELECT SPY.QTY
                FROM   SP SPY
                WHERE  SPY.PNO = SPX.PNO )
          > 1000
```

(The DISTINCT is required because of SQL's rules concerning duplicate elimination.) However, the normal SQL formulation would be:

```
SELECT SP.PNO
FROM   SP
GROUP  BY SP.PNO
HAVING SUM ( SP.QTY ) > 1000
```

Note that the user is not really interested in grouping per se in this query; by writing GROUP BY, he or she is in effect telling the system how to *execute* the query, instead of simply stating what the query *is*. In other words, the statement begins to look more like a prescription for solving the problem, rather than a simple description of what the problem is.

More important, it is necessary to introduce the HAVING clause, the justification for which is not immediately apparent to the user ("Why can't I use a WHERE clause?"). *The HAVING clause—and the GROUP BY clause also, come to that (see later)—are needed in SQL ONLY as a consequence of the column-function argument scoping rules.* As a matter of fact, it is possible to produce a SQL formulation of this example that does not use GROUP BY or HAVING at all, and is fairly close to "the most logical formulation" suggested earlier:

```
SELECT DISTINCT SPX.PNO
FROM    SP SPX
WHERE   1000 <
      ( SELECT SUM ( SPY.QTY )
        FROM    SP SPY
        WHERE   SPY.PNO = SPX.PNO )
```

As mentioned earlier, current SQL requires the predicate in the outer WHERE clause to be written as shown (i.e., in the order "constant–comparison–subquery," instead of the other way around).

An important consequence of all of the foregoing is that *SQL cannot support arbitrary retrievals on arbitrary views.* Consider the following example.

View definition:

```
CREATE VIEW PQ ( PNO, TOTQTY )
    AS SELECT SP.PNO, SUM ( SP.QTY )
       FROM    SP
       GROUP  BY SP.PNO
```

Attempted query:

```
SELECT *
FROM    PQ
WHERE   SP.TOTQTY > 1000
```

This statement is invalid, because the "merging" process described earlier leads to something like the following:

```
SELECT SP.PNO, SUM ( SP.QTY )
FROM    SP
WHERE   SUM ( SP.QTY ) > 1000
GROUP  BY SP.PNO
```

and this is not a legal SELECT statement. Likewise, the attempted query:

```
SELECT AVG ( PQ.TOTQTY )
FROM    PQ
```

also does not work, for similar reasons.

The following is another striking example of the unobviousness of the scoping rules. Consider the following two queries:

```
SELECT SUM ( SP.QTY )          SELECT SUM ( SP.QTY )
FROM    SP                     FROM    SP
                               GROUP   BY SP.PNO
```

In the first case, the query returns a single value; the argument to the SUM invocation is the entire QTY column. In the second case, the query returns multiple values; the SUM function is invoked multiple times, once for each of the groups created by the GROUP BY clause. (Notice, incidentally, how the meaning of the syntactic construct "SUM (SP.QTY)" is dependent on the context.) In fact, SQL is moving out of the strict tabular framework of the relational model in this second example and introducing a new kind of data object, viz. *a set of tables* (which is of course not the same thing as a table at all). GROUP BY converts a table into a set of tables. In the example, SUM is then applied to (a column within) each member of that set. A more logical syntax might look something like the following:

```
APPLY ( SUM, SELECT QTY
             FROM ( GROUP SP BY SP.PNO ) )
```

where "GROUP SP BY SP.PNO" produces the set of tables, "SELECT QTY FROM (. . .)" extracts a corresponding set of columns, and APPLY applies the function specified as its first argument to each column in the set of columns specified as its second argument, producing a set of scalars— i.e., another column. (I am not suggesting a concrete syntax here, only indicating a possible direction for a systematic development of such a syntax.)

As a matter of fact, GROUP BY would be logically unnecessary in the foregoing example anyway if column function invocations were more systematic:

```
SELECT DISTINCT SPX.PNO, SUM ( SELECT SPY.QTY
                               FROM    SP SPY
                               WHERE   SPY.PNO = SPX.PNO )
        FROM    SP SPX
```

This formulation also shows, incidentally, that it might be preferable to declare range variables such as SPX and SPY by means of separate statements before they are used. As it is, the use of such variables may well precede their definition, possibly by a considerable amount. Although there is nothing logically wrong with this, it does make the statements difficult to read (and write) on occasion.

Yet another consequence of the scoping rules (already touched on a couple of times) is that it is not possible to nest column function references. Extending the earlier example of generating the total quantity per part (i.e., a column of values, each of which is a total quantity), suppose we now wanted to find the *average* total quantity per part—i.e., the average of that column of values. The logical formulation is something like:

```
AVG ( APPLY ( SUM, SELECT QTY
                    FROM ( GROUP SP BY SP.PNO ) ) )
```

But (as already stated) existing SQL cannot handle this problem at all in a single expression.

Let us now leave the scoping rules and consider some additional points. Each of SUM, AVG, MAX, and MIN can optionally have its argument qualified by the operator DISTINCT. (COUNT *must* have its argument so qualified, though it would seem that there is no intrinsic justification for this requirement. For MAX and MIN such qualification is legal but has no semantic effect.) If and only if DISTINCT is *not* specified, then the column argument can be a "computed" column, i.e., the result of an arithmetic expression—for example:

```
SELECT AVG ( X + Y )
FROM   T
   ...
```

(X and Y here must be column-names or constants, incidentally, not arbitrary scalar-expressions.) And if and only if DISTINCT is *not* specified (again), the function reference can itself be an operand in an arithmetic expression—for example:

```
SELECT AVG ( X ) * 3
FROM   T
   ...
```

Comment: This latter restriction does not apply to the standard. *End of comment.*

In current SQL, nulls are always eliminated from the argument to a column function, regardless of whether DISTINCT is specified. However, this should be regarded as a property of the existing functions specifically, rather than as a necessary property of all column functions. In fact, it would be better *not* to ignore nulls but to introduce a new function whose effect is to reduce a given column to another in which nulls have been eliminated—and, of course, to allow that new function to be used completely orthogonally.

Table Functions

Table functions are functions that operate on an entire table (not necessarily just on a single column). There are four functions in this category, two that return a scalar value and two that return another table. The two that return a scalar value are COUNT(*) and EXISTS.

- COUNT(*) is basically very similar to the column functions discussed above. Thus, most of the comments made above apply here also. For example, the query:

```
SELECT COUNT(*)
FROM   SP
```

would more logically be expressed as

```
COUNT ( SELECT *
        FROM   SP )
```

or (better) as:

```
COUNT ( SP )
```

COUNT(*) does *not* ignore nulls (i.e., all-null rows) in its argument, unlike the column functions.

- EXISTS, interestingly enough, does use a more logical syntax. For example:

```
SELECT *
FROM   S
WHERE  EXISTS
       ( SELECT *
         FROM   SP
         WHERE  SP.SNO = S.SNO )
```

—though the EXISTS argument would look better if the "SELECT * FROM" could be elided:

```
SELECT *
FROM   S
WHERE  EXISTS ( SP WHERE SP.SNO = S.SNO )
```

or (better still):

```
S WHERE EXISTS ( SP WHERE SP.SNO = S.SNO )
```

EXISTS takes a table as its argument (though that table *must* be expressed as a SELECT-expression, not just as a table-name) and returns the value *true* if that table is nonempty, *false* otherwise. (A table that contains only nulls—i.e., all-null rows—is not considered to be empty, incidentally.) Because there is currently no BOOLEAN or BIT data type in SQL, EXISTS can be used only in a WHERE clause, not (e.g.) in a SELECT clause (lack of orthogonality once again).

Now I turn to the functions that return another table, viz. DISTINCT and UNION.

- DISTINCT takes a table and returns another which is a copy of that first table except that redundant duplicate rows have been removed (rows that are entirely null are considered to be duplicates of one another in this process—that is, the result will contain at most one all-null row). Once again the syntax is unconventional. For instance:

```
SELECT DISTINCT SP.SNO
FROM    SP
```

instead of:

```
DISTINCT ( SELECT SP.SNO
           FROM    SP )
```

or (better):

```
DISTINCT ( SP.SNO )
```

There is an apparently arbitrary restriction that DISTINCT may appear at most once in any given SELECT statement.

Comment: This latter restriction is partially eased in the standard: DISTINCT can appear at most once *at a given level of nesting*, but can appear multiple times at multiple levels. *End of comment.*

- UNION takes two tables (each of which must be represented by means of a SELECT-expression, not just as a simple table-name) and produces another table that is their union. It is written as an infix operator. Because of the unorthodox syntax, it is not possible (as mentioned before) to apply a column function such as AVG to a union of two columns.

  Note: I consider UNION, alone of the operators of the relational algebra, as a function in SQL merely because of the special syntactic treatment it is given. SQL is really a hybrid of the relational algebra and the relational calculus; it is not precisely the same as either, though it does lean somewhat toward the calculus.

F.4 LACK OF ORTHOGONALITY: MISCELLANEOUS ITEMS

Indicator Variables

Let F be a database field that can accept null values, and let HF be a corresponding host variable, with associated indicator variable HN. Then:

```
SELECT F
INTO    :HF:HN
   ...
```

is legal, and so are

```
INSERT ...
VALUES ( :HF:HN ... )
```

and

```
UPDATE ...
SET     F = :HF:HN
 ...
```

But the following is not:

```
SELECT ... ( or UPDATE or DELETE )
 ...
WHERE   F = :HF:HN
```

Comment: It is legal in the standard, though it may not do what the user expects. *End of comment.*

References to Current Data

Let C be a cursor that currently identifies a record of table T. Then it is possible to designate the "CURRENT OF C"—i.e., the record currently identified by C—as the target of an UPDATE or DELETE statement, e.g., as follows:

```
UPDATE T
SET    ...
WHERE  CURRENT OF C
```

Incidentally, a more logical formulation would be

```
UPDATE CURRENT OF C
SET    ...
```

Specifying the table-name T is redundant (this point is recognized in the syntax of FETCH, see later), and in any case "CURRENT OF C" is not the same kind of construct as the more usual WHERE-predicate (e.g., "SALARY > 20000"). Nor is it permitted to combine "CURRENT OF C" with other predicates and write (e.g.) "WHERE CURRENT OF C AND SALARY > 20000." But to return to the main argument: Although the (first) UPDATE statement above is legal, the analogous SELECT statement

```
SELECT ...
FROM   T
WHERE  CURRENT OF C
```

is not. Moreover, fields within the "CURRENT OF C" cannot even be referenced (let alone be retrieved)—e.g., the following is also illegal:

```
SELECT  *
FROM    EMP
WHERE   DEPTNO =
       ( SELECT  DEPT.DEPTNO
         FROM    DEPT
         WHERE   CURRENT OF D )
```

Turning now to the FETCH statement, we have here an example of *bundling.* "FETCH C INTO . . . " is effectively a shorthand for a sequence of two distinct operations—

```
STEP C TO NEXT

SELECT * INTO ... WHERE CURRENT OF C
```

—the first of which (STEP) advances C to the next record in T in accordance with the ordering associated with C, and the second of which (SELECT) then retrieves that record. (Note that that SELECT does not logically require any FROM clause, incidentally.) Replacing the FETCH statement by two more primitive statements in this way would have a number of advantages:

(a) It is clearer;

(b) It is a more logical structure (incidentally, "FETCH C" does not really make intuitive sense—it is not the *cursor* that is being fetched);

(c) It would allow SELECTs of individual fields of the current record (i.e., "SELECT field-name" as well as "SELECT *");

(d) It would allow selective (and repeated) access to that current record (e.g., "SELECT F" followed by "SELECT G," both selecting fields of the same record);

(e) It would be extendable to other kinds of STEP operation—e.g., STEP C TO PREVIOUS (say).

In fact I would go further. First, note that "CURRENT OF C" is an example of a row-expression. Let us therefore introduce a (new) FETCH statement, whose argument is a row-expression (as opposed to SELECT, whose argument is a table-expression), and whose function is to retrieve the row represented by that expression. Next, outlaw SELECT where FETCH is really intended. Next, introduce "(row-expression).field-name"—e.g., (CURRENT OF C).F—as a new form of scalar-expression. Finally, support all of these constructs orthogonally. Thus, for example, all of the following would be legal:

```
FETCH CURRENT OF C INTO ...

FETCH (CURRENT OF C).F INTO ...
```

```
SELECT  *
FROM    EMP
WHERE   EMP.DEPTNO = (CURRENT OF D).DEPTNO

UPDATE  CURRENT OF C
SET     ...

DELETE  CURRENT OF C
```

The examples illustrate the point that "CURRENT OF C" is really a very clumsy notation, incidentally, but an improved syntax is beyond the scope of this paper. See reference [5] for a preferable alternative.

ORDER BY in Cursor Declaration

Specifying ORDER BY in the declaration of cursor C means that the statements UPDATE/DELETE . . . CURRENT OF C are illegal (in fact, the declaration of C cannot include a FOR UPDATE clause if ORDER BY is specified). The rationale for this restriction is that ORDER BY may cause the program to operate on a copy instead of on the actual data, and hence that updates and deletes would be meaningless; but the restriction is unfortunate, to say the least. Consider a program that needs to process employees in department number order and needs to update some of them as it goes. The user is forced to code along the following lines:

```
EXEC SQL DECLARE C CURSOR FOR
                  SELECT EMP.EMPNO, EMP.DEPTNO, ...
                  FROM    EMP
                  ORDER  BY DEPTNO ;

EXEC SQL OPEN C ;
DO for all records accesible via C ;
    EXEC SQL FETCH C INTO :EMPNO, :DEPTNO, ... ;
    if this record needs updating, then
    EXEC SQL UPDATE EMP
             SET    ...
             WHERE  EMP.EMPNO = :EMPNO
/* instead of WHERE  CURRENT OF C */ ;
    END ;
    EXEC SQL CLOSE C ;
```

The UPDATE statement here is an "out-of-the-blue" UPDATE, not the CURRENT form. Problems:

(a) The update will be visible through cursor C if and only if C is running through the real data, not a copy.

(b) If cursor C is running through the real data, and if the UPDATE changes the value of DEPTNO, the effect on the position of cursor C within the table is apparently undefined.

I cannot help pointing out also that the FOR UPDATE clause is a little mysterious (its real significance is not immediately apparent); it is also logically unnecessary. The whole of this area smacks of a most unfortunate loss of physical data independence.

Comment: The X3H2 committee eliminated the FOR UPDATE clause but did not provide anything to replace it. *End of comment.*

The NULL Constant

The keyword NULL may be regarded as a "builtin constant," whose value, of course, is null. However, it cannot appear in all positions in which a scalar constant can appear. For example, the statement

```
SELECT F, NULL
FROM   T
```

is illegal. This is unfortunate, since the ability to select NULL is precisely what is required in order to construct an outer join (in the absence of direct system support for such an operation). See reference [4].

Empty Sets

Let T be a table-expression. If T happens to evaluate to an empty set, then what happens depends on the context in which T appears. For example, consider the expressions

```
SELECT EMP.SALARY              SELECT AVG ( EMP.SALARY )
FROM   EMP                     FROM   EMP
WHERE  EMP.DEPTNO = 'D3'       WHERE  EMP.DEPTNO = 'D3'
```

and

and suppose that department D3 currently has no employees. Note that the second of these expressions represents the application of the AVG function to the result of the first; as pointed out earlier, it would more logically be written as

```
AVG ( SELECT EMP.SALARY
      FROM   EMP
      WHERE  EMP.DEPTNO = 'D3')
```

- The statement

```
EXEC SQL SELECT EMP.SALARY
         INTO   :S:SN
         FROM   EMP
         WHERE  EMP.DEPTNO = 'D3' ;
```

gives "not found" (SQLCODE = +100, host variables S and SN unchanged).

- The statement

```
EXEC SQL SELECT AVG ( EMP.SALARY )
         INTO   :S:SN
         FROM   EMP
         WHERE  EMP.DEPTNO = 'D3' ;
```

sets host variable SN to an unspecified negative value to indicate that the value of the expression is null. The effect on host variable S is unspecified.

- The statement

```
EXEC SQL SELECT ...
         INTO   :S:SN
         FROM   ...
         WHERE  field IN
                ( SELECT EMP.SALARY
                  FROM   EMP
                  WHERE  EMP.DEPTNO = 'D3' ) ;
```

gives "not found" (at the *outer* level).

- The statement

```
EXEC SQL SELECT ...
         INTO   :S:SN
         FROM   ...
         WHERE  field =
                ( SELECT EMP.SALARY
                  FROM   EMP
                  WHERE  EMP.DEPTNO = 'D3' ) ;
```

also gives "not found" at the outer level, though there is a good argument for treating this case as an error, as follows: The parenthesized expression "(SELECT EMP.SALARY ...)" should really be regarded as a shorthand for the expression "*UNIQUE* (SELECT EMP.SALARY ...)," where UNIQUE is a quantifier (analogous to EXISTS) meaning "there exists *exactly one*"—or, in other words, a function whose effect is to return the single element from a singleton set, and to raise an error if that set does not in fact contain exactly one member. Note that an error *would* be raised in the example if the parenthesized expression yielded a set having *more than one* member (which in general, of course, it would).

- The statement

```
EXEC SQL SELECT ...
         INTO   :S:SN
         FROM   ...
         WHERE  field =
                ( SELECT AVG ( EMP.SALARY )
                  FROM   EMP
                  WHERE  EMP.DEPTNO = 'D3' ) ;
```

also gives "not found" at the outer level.

Inconsistent Syntax

Compare the following:

```
SELECT * FROM T ...

UPDATE        T ...

DELETE    FROM T ...

INSERT    INTO T ...

( FETCH C ... )
```

A more consistent approach would be to define "table-expressions" (as suggested earlier in this paper), and then to recognize that SELECT, UPDATE, etc., are each *operators*, one of whose arguments is such a table-expression. (A problem that immediately arises is that a simple table-name is currently *not* a valid table-expression!—i.e., instead of being able to write simply "T," the user has to write "SELECT * FROM T." This point has been mentioned before, and is of course easily remedied.)

Note too that the syntax "UPDATE T SET F = . . ." does not extend very nicely to a form of UPDATE in which an entire record is replaced en bloc ("SET * = . . ."?). And this touches on yet another point, viz: SQL currently provides whole-record SELECT (and FETCH) and INSERT operators, but no whole-record UPDATE operator. (DELETE of course *must* be a "whole-record" operation, by definition.)

Long Fields (LONG VARCHAR, or VARCHAR(n) with n > 254)

Comment: The following restrictions do not apply to standard SQL. Standard SQL does not support varying strings of any kind. *End of comment.*

Long fields are subject to numerous restrictions. Here are some of them (this may or may not be an exhaustive list). A long field:

- Cannot be referenced in a predicate
- Cannot be indexed
- Cannot be referenced in SELECT DISTINCT
- Cannot be referenced in GROUP BY
- Cannot be referenced in ORDER BY
- Cannot be referenced in COUNT, MAX, or MIN (note that SUM and AVG would make no sense anyway)
- Cannot be involved in a UNION

- Cannot be involved in a "subquery" (i.e., column-expression)
- Cannot be INSERTed from a constant or SELECT-expression
- Cannot be UPDATEd from a constant (UPDATE from NULL is legal, however)

UNION Restrictions

Union is not permitted on long fields or in a subquery (in particular, in a view definition). Also, the data types of corresponding items in a UNION must be *exactly* the same:

- If the data type is DECIMAL(p,q), then p must be the same for both items and q must be the same for both items
- If the data type is CHAR(n), then n must be the same for both items
- If the data type is VARCHAR(n), then n must be the same for both items
- If NOT NULL applies to either item, then it must apply to both items

Given these restrictions, it is particularly unfortunate that a character string constant such as "ABC" is treated as a *varying* string (maximum length 3, in this example).

Comment: Character string constants are treated as fixed length in the standard. The above restrictions are eliminated in SQL2. *End of comment.*

Note also that UNION always eliminates duplicates. There is no "DISTINCT/ALL" option as there is with a simple SELECT; and if there were, the default would have to be DISTINCT (for compatibility reasons), whereas the default for a simple SELECT is ALL.

Comment: The standard does support ALL. (So too does DB2, as of Version 1 Release 3.) *End of comment.*

GROUP BY Restrictions

GROUP BY:

- Only works to one level (it can construct a "set of tables" but not a "set of sets of tables," etc.)
- Can only have simple fields as arguments (unlike ORDER BY)

The fact is, as indicated earlier in the discussion of functions, an orthogonal treatment of GROUP BY would require a thorough treatment of an entirely new kind of data object, namely the "set of tables"—presumably a major undertaking.

NULL Anomalies

- Null values are implemented by hidden fields in the database. However, it is necessary to expose those fields in the interface to a host language such as PL/I, because PL/I has no notion of null (in the SQL sense, that is). As an example, if F and G are two fields in table T, the UPDATE statement to set F equal to G is:

```
EXEC SQL UPDATE T
         SET    F = G ...
```

—but the UPDATE statement to set F equal to a host variable H (with corresponding null indicator variable HN) is:

```
EXEC SQL UPDATE T
         SET    F = :H:HN ...
```

(assuming in both cases that the source of the assignment might be null).

- Indicator variables are not permitted in all contexts where host variables can appear (as already discussed).

- To test in a WHERE clause whether a field is null, SQL provides the special comparison "field IS NULL." It is not intuitively obvious why the user has to write "field IS NULL" and not "field = NULL"— especially as the syntax "field = NULL" *is* used in the SET clause of the UPDATE statement to update a field to the null value. (In fact, the WHERE clause "WHERE field = NULL" is syntactically illegal.)

- Null values are considered as duplicates of each other for the purposes of UNIQUE and DISTINCT and ORDER BY but not for the purposes of WHERE and HAVING and GROUP BY. Null values are also considered as greater than all nonnull values for the purposes of ORDER BY but not for the purposes of WHERE.

  Comment: The standard considers two nulls to be duplicates of each other for the purposes of GROUP BY. DB2 now does the same. The statement above regarding GROUP BY applied to DB2 Version 1 Release 1. *End of comment.*

- Nulls are always eliminated from the argument to a builtin function such as SUM or AVG, regardless of whether DISTINCT is specified in the function reference—except for the case of COUNT(*), which counts all rows, including duplicates and including all-null rows. Thus, for example, given:

```
SELECT AVG ( S.STATUS ) FROM S   —   Result: x

SELECT SUM ( S.STATUS ) FROM S   —   Result: y

SELECT COUNT(*)         FROM S   —   Result: z
```

there is no guarantee that $x = y/z$.

- Likewise, the function reference SUM (F) is *not* semantically equivalent to the expression

```
f1 + f2 + ... + fn
```

where f1, f2, . . . , fn are the values appearing in field F at the time the function is evaluated. Perhaps even more counterintuitively, the expression

```
SUM ( F1 + F2 )
```

is not equivalent to the expression

```
SUM ( F1 ) + SUM ( F2 )
```

Host Variables

Host variables are permitted wherever constants are permitted, also in the INTO clause of SELECT and FETCH, but nowhere else. In particular, table-names and field-names cannot be represented by host variables.

Introduced Names

The user can introduce names (''aliases''—actually range variables) for tables—e.g., FROM T TX—but not for scalars. This latter could easily be done via the SELECT clause—e.g., SELECT F FX. Such a facility would be particularly useful when the scalar is in fact represented by an operational expression—e.g., SELECT A + B C, D + E F, ... The names C, F, . . . could be used in WHERE or ORDER BY or GROUP BY or as an inherited name in CREATE VIEW (etc., etc.).

Comment: As mentioned earlier, the foregoing capability is included in SQL2. *End of comment.*

Legal INSERTs/UPDATEs/DELETEs

Certain INSERT, UPDATE, and DELETE statements are not allowed. For example, consider the requirement "Delete all suppliers with a status less than the average." The statement:

```
DELETE
FROM    S
WHERE   STATUS <
        ( SELECT AVG ( S.STATUS )
          FROM    S )
```

is illegal: The FROM clause in the subquery is not allowed to refer to the table against which the DELETE is to be done. Likewise, the UPDATE statement:

```
UPDATE  S
SET     STATUS = 0
WHERE   S.STATUS <
        ( SELECT AVG ( S.STATUS )
          FROM    S )
```

is also illegal, for analogous reasons. Third, the statement

```
INSERT INTO T
       SELECT * FROM T
```

(which might be regarded as a perfectly natural way to "double up" on the contents of table T) is also illegal, again for analogous reasons.

F.5   FORMAL DEFINITION

As indicated earlier in this paper, it would be misleading to suggest that SQL does not possess a formal definition. However, as was also indicated earlier, that definition [10] was produced "after the fact." In some respects, therefore, it represents a definition of the way implementations actually work rather than the way a "pure" language ought to be (although it must be said that many of the criticisms of the present paper have indeed been addressed in [10]). At the same time it provides definitive answers to some questions that are not in agreement with the way IBM SQL actually works! Furthermore, there still appear to be some areas where the definition is not yet precise enough. Examples of all of these aspects are given below.

> *Comment:* At the time this paper was originally written, the draft proposed SQL standard was much "purer" than the version that was eventually adopted as the actual standard. The standard per se does not "address many of the criticisms of the present paper." *End of comment.*

Cursor Positioning

Let C be a cursor that is currently associated with a set of records of type R. Suppose moreover that the ordering associated with C is defined by values of field R.F. If C is positioned on a record r and r is deleted, C goes into the "before" state—i.e., it is now positioned "before" record r1, where r1 is the immediate successor of r with respect to the ordering associated with C—or, if there is no such successor record, then it goes into the "after" state—i.e., it is "after" the last record in the set. (*Note:* The "after" state is possible even if the set is empty.)

Questions:

(a) If C is "before r1" and a new record r is inserted with a value of R.F such that r logically belongs between r1 and r1's predecessor (if any), what happens to C? [Answer: Implementation-defined.]

(b) Does it make a difference if the new record r logically precedes or follows the old record r that C was positioned on before that record was deleted? [Answer: Implementation-defined.]

(c) Does it make a difference if C was actually running through a copy of the real set of records? [Answer: Implementation-defined.]

   Note for cases (a)–(c) that it *is* guaranteed that the next "FETCH C" will retrieve record r1 (provided no other DELETEs etc. occur in the interim).

(d) What if the new r is not an INSERTed record but an UPDATEd record? [Answer: Not defined.]

(e) If C is positioned on a record r and the value of field F in that record is updated (not via cursor C, of course), what happens to C? [Answer: Not defined.]

LOCK Statement

Does LOCK SHARED acquire an S lock or an SIX lock [9]? If the answer is S, are updates permitted? When are locks acquired via LOCK TABLE released?

Name Resolution

First, consider the two statements:

```
SELECT  SNO
FROM    S
WHERE   CITY = 'London'
```

```
SELECT  PNO
FROM    P
WHERE   CITY = 'London'
```

The meaning of the unqualified name CITY depends on the context—it is taken as S.CITY in the first of these examples and as P.CITY in the second. But now suppose the columns are renamed SCITY and PCITY respectively, so that now the names are globally unique, and consider the query "Find suppliers located in cities in which no parts are stored." The obvious formulation of this query is

```
SELECT  SNO
FROM    S
WHERE   NOT EXISTS
      ( SELECT *
        FROM    P
        WHERE   PCITY = SCITY )
```

However, this statement is invalid. SQL assumes that "SCITY" is shorthand for "P.SCITY," and then complains that no such field exists (I think—though I find the SQL definition rather obscure in this area). The following statement, by contrast, is perfectly valid:

```
SELECT  SNO
FROM    S
WHERE   NOT EXISTS
      ( SELECT *
        FROM    P
        WHERE   PCITY = S.SCITY )
```

So also is:

```
SELECT  SNO
FROM    S SX
WHERE   NOT EXISTS
      ( SELECT *
        FROM    P
        WHERE   PCITY = SX.SCITY )
```

Is the following legal? ("Suppliers who supply P1 and P2.")

```
SELECT  *
FROM    S
WHERE   EXISTS ( SELECT *
                 FROM    SP SPX
                 WHERE   SPX.SNO = S.SNO
                 AND     SPX.PNO = 'P1'
                 AND     EXISTS ( SELECT *
                                  FROM    SP SPX
                                  WHERE   SPX.SNO = S.SNO
                                  AND     SPX.PNO = 'P2' ) )
```

What if "FROM SP SPX" is replace by "FROM SP" (twice) and all other occurrences of "SPX" are replaced by "SP"? And is the following legal?

```
SELECT  *
FROM    S
WHERE   EXISTS ( SELECT  *
                 FROM    SP SPX
                 WHERE   SPX.SNO = S.SNO
                 AND     SPX.PNO = 'P1' )
AND     EXISTS ( SELECT  *
                 FROM    SP SPX
                 WHERE   SPX.SNO = S.SNO
                 AND     SPX.PNO = 'P2' )
```

(etc., etc.). In other words: What *are* the name scoping rules?

> *Comment:* The standard does define scoping rules, but (as already indicated) I do not find the definition particularly lucid. My own preferred rule is: When in doubt, qualify. *End of comment.*

There is another point to be made while on the subject of name resolution, incidentally. Consider the statement:

```
SELECT  S.SNO, P.PNO
FROM    S, P
WHERE   S.CITY = P.CITY
```

(reverting to the simple name CITY for each of the two tables). This statement is (conceptually) evaluated as follows:

- Form the product of S and P; call the result TEMP1
- Restrict TEMP1 according to the predicate S.CITY = P.CITY; call the result TEMP2
- Project TEMP2 over the columns S.SNO and P.PNO

But how can this be done? The predicate "S.CITY = P.CITY" does not refer to any columns of TEMP1 (it refers to columns of S and P, obviously). Similarly, S.SNO and P.PNO are not columns of TEMP2. In order for these references to be interpreted appropriately, it is necessary to introduce certain *name inheritance rules*, indicating how result tables inherit their column-names from their source tables (which may of course themselves also be [intermediate] result tables, with inherited column-names of their own). Such rules are currently defined only very informally, if at all. Such rules become even more important if SQL is to provide support for nested expressions, as suggested earlier in this paper.

> *Comment:* The standard does define a set of name inheritance rules. However, those rules are very incomplete. *End of comment.*

Base vs. Copy Data

When exactly does a cursor iterate over the real "base data" and when over a copy?

Binding of "SELECT *"

When exactly does "*" become bound to a specific set of field-names? [Answer: Implementation-defined—but this seems an unfortunate aspect to leave to the implementation, especially as the binding is likely to be different for different *uses* of the feature (e.g., it may depend on whether the "*" appears in a program or in a view definition).]

F.6   MISMATCH WITH HOST LANGUAGES

> *Comment:* Technically, the following criticisms do not apply to the standard, because embedded SQL is not truly part of the standard per se. In practice, however, many of the criticisms are still relevant. *End of comment.*

The general point here is that there are far too many frivolous distinctions between SQL and the host language in which it happens to be embedded; also that in some cases SQL has failed to benefit from lessons learned in the design of those host languages. Generally, orthogonality suggests that what is useful on one side of the interface in the way of data structuring and access for "permanent" (i.e., database) data is likely to be useful on the other side also for "temporary" (i.e., local) data; thus, a distinct sublanguage is the wrong approach, and a two-level store is wrong too (fundamentally so!). Some specific points:

- SQL does not exploit the exception-handling capabilities of the host (e.g., PL/I ON-conditions). This point and (even more so) the following one mean that SQL does not exactly encourage the production of well-structured, quality programs, and that in some respects SQL programming is at a lower level than that of the host.

- SQL does not exploit the control structures of the host (loop constructs in particular). See the previous point.

- SQL objects (tables, cursors, etc.) are not known and cannot be referenced in the host environment.

- Host objects can be referenced in the SQL environment only if:
  - They are specially declared (may not apply to all hosts)
  - They are scalars or certain limited types of structure (in particular, they are not arrays)
  - The references are marked with a colon prefix (admittedly only in some contexts—but in my opinion "some" is worse than "all")
  - The references are constrained to certain limited contexts (e.g., they can appear in a SELECT clause but not a FROM clause)

- The references are constrained to certain limited formats (e.g., no subscripting, only limited dot qualification, etc.)

Host procedures cannot be referenced in the SQL environment at all.

- SQL object names and host object names are independent and may clash. SQL names do not follow the scoping rules of the host.

- SQL keywords and host keywords are independent and may clash (e.g., PL/I SELECT vs. SQL SELECT).

- SQL and host may have different name qualification rules (e.g., T.F in SQL vs. F OF T in COBOL; and note that the SQL form must be used even for host object references in the SQL environment).

- SQL and host may have different data type conversion rules.

- SQL and host may have different expression evaluation rules (e.g., SQL division and varying string comparison differ from their PL/I analogs, at least in SQL/DS).

- SQL and host may have different Boolean operators (AND, OR, and NOT in SQL vs. &, |, and ~ in PL/I).

- SQL and host may have different comparison operators (e.g., COBOL has IS NUMERIC, SQL has BETWEEN [and several others]).

- SQL imposes statement ordering restrictions that may be alien to the host.

- SQL DECLARE cannot be abbreviated to DCL, unlike PL/I DECLARE.

- Null is handled differently on the two sides of the interface.

- Function references have different formats on the two sides of the interface.

- SQL name resolution rules are different from those of the host.

- Cursors are a clumsy way of bridging the gap between the database and the program. A much better method would be to associate a query with a conventional *sequential file* in the host program, and then let the program use conventional READ, REWRITE, and DELETE statements to access that file (maybe INSERT statements too).

Comment: Cursors are also not a good base on which to build distributed database systems. *End of comment.*

- The "structure declarations" in CREATE TABLE should use the standard COBOL or PL/I (etc.) syntax. As it is, it is doubtful whether they can be elegantly extended to deal with minor structures (composite fields) or arrays, should such extensions ever prove desirable (they will).

- The dynamic SQL parameter mechanism is regressive, clumsy, ad hoc, restrictive, and different from that of the host.

  Comment: This criticism does not apply to standard SQL, since the standard does not include any dynamic SQL facilities. However, it does apply to SQL2. *End of comment.*

F.7 MISSING FUNCTION

The "missing function" here refers primarily to the embedded (programming) version of SQL. Other missing function is discussed in Section F.9 later. In any case the list of desirable extensions for any given language is probably always endless. But the items listed below are particularly obvious omissions from a programmer's standpoint. *Note:* It is obviously possible to extend the existing language to incorporate most if not all of these features. I include them only for completeness.

- Ability to override WHENEVER NOT FOUND at the level of an individual statement.
- "Whole-record" UPDATE.
- Procedure call instead of GO TO on WHENEVER.
- Cursor stepping other than "next."
- Cursor comparison.
- Cursor assignment.
- Cursor constants.
- Cursor arrays.
- Dynamically created cursors and/or cursor stacks.
- Reusable cursors.
- Ability to access a unique record and keep a cursor on it without having to go through separate DECLARE, OPEN, and FETCH: e.g., "FETCH UNIQUE (EMP WHERE EMP.EMPNO = 'E2') SET (C) ;".
- Fine control over locking.

F.8 MISTAKES

Nulls

I have argued against SQL-style nulls at length elsewhere [6], and I will not repeat those arguments here. In my opinion the null concept is far more trouble than it is worth. Certainly it has never been properly thought through in the existing SQL implementations (see the discussion under "Lack of Orthogonality: Miscellaneous Items," earlier). For example, the fact that functions such as AVG simply ignore nulls in their argument violates what should surely be a fundamental principle, viz: *The system should never produce a (spuriously) precise answer to a query when the data involved in that query is itself imprecise.* At least the system should offer the user the explicit option either to ignore nulls or to treat their presence as an exception.

Unique Indexes

Field uniqueness is a logical property of the data, not a physical property of an access path. It should be specified on CREATE TABLE, not on CREATE INDEX. Specifying it on CREATE INDEX is an unfortunate bundling, and may lead to a loss of data independence (dropping the index puts the integrity of the database at risk).

Comment: The standard is better here. *End of comment.*

FROM Clause

The only function of the FROM clause that is not actually redundant is to allow the introduction of range variables, and that function would be better provided in some more elegant manner. (The normal use, as exemplified by the expression SELECT F FROM T, could better be handled by the expression SELECT T.F, especially since this latter expression—with an accompanying but redundant FROM clause—is already legal SQL.)

Punning

SQL does not make a clear distinction between tables, record types, and range variables. Instead, it allows a single symbol to stand for any one of those objects, and leaves the interpretation to depend on context. Conceptual clarity would dictate that it at least be *possible* always to distinguish among these different constructs (i.e., syntactically), even if there are rules that allow such punning games to be played when intuitively convenient. Otherwise it may be possible that—for example—extendability may suffer, though I have to admit that I cannot at the time of writing point to any concrete problems. (But it shouldn't be *necessary* to have to defend the principle of a one-to-one correspondence between names and objects!)

While on the subject of punning, I might also mention the point that SQL is ambivalent as to the meaning of the term "table." Sometimes "table" means, specifically, a *base* table (as in CREATE TABLE or LOCK); at other times it means "base table or view" (as in GRANT or COMMENT ON). Since the critical point about a view is that it *is* a table (just as the critical point about a subset is that it *is* a set), I would vote for the following changes:

(a) Replace the terms "base table" and "view" by "real table" and "virtual table," respectively;

(b) Use the term "table" generically to mean "real table or virtual table";

(c) In concrete syntax, use the expressions [REAL] TABLE and VIRTUAL TABLE (where it is necessary to distinguish them, as in CREATE), with REAL as the default.

"SELECT *"

This is a good example of a situation in which the needs of the end-user and those of the application programmer are at odds. "SELECT *" is fine for the interactive user (it saves keystrokes). I believe it is rather dangerous for the programmer (because the meaning of "*" may change at any time in the life of the program). The use of "ORDER BY n" (where n is an integer instead of a field-name) in conjunction with "SELECT *" could be particularly unfortunate. Similar remarks apply to the use of INSERT without a list of field-names.

Incidentally, I believe that the foregoing are the *only* situations in the entire SQL language in which the user is dependent on the left-to-right ordering of columns within a table. It would be nice to eliminate that dependence entirely (except possibly for "SELECT *" for interactive queries only).

=ANY (etc.)

The comparison operators =ANY, >ALL, etc., are totally redundant and in many cases actively misleading (error potential is high). The following example, which is taken from the IBM manual "IBM DATABASE 2 SQL Usage Guide" (IBM Form No. GG24–1583), illustrates the point very nicely: "Select employees who are younger than any member of department E21" (irrelevant details omitted).

```
SELECT EMPNO, LASTNAME, WORKDEPT
FROM    TEMPL
WHERE   BRTHDATE >ANY ( SELECT BRTHDATE
                        FROM    TEMPL
                        WHERE   WORKDEPT = 'E21' )
```

This SELECT does *not* find employees who are younger than any employee in E21!—at least in the sense that this requirement would normally be understood in colloquial English. Rather, it finds employees who are younger than *at least one* employee in E21.

To illustrate the redundancy, consider the query: "Find supplier names for suppliers who supply part P2." This is a very simple problem, yet it is not difficult to find no less than seven formulations for it, all of them at least superficially distinct (see below). Of course, the differences would not be important if all formulations worked equally well, but that is unlikely.

```
1. SELECT  S.SNAME
   FROM    S
   WHERE   S.SNO IN
           ( SELECT SP.SNO
             FROM    SP
             WHERE   SP.PNO = 'P2' )

2. SELECT  S.SNAME
   FROM    S
   WHERE   S.SNO =ANY
           ( SELECT SP.SNO
             FROM    SP
             WHERE   SP.PNO = 'P2' )

3. SELECT  S.SNAME
   FROM    S
   WHERE   EXISTS
           ( SELECT *
             FROM    SP
             WHERE   SP.SNO = S.SNO AND SP.PNO = 'P2' )

4. SELECT  S.SNAME
   FROM    S, SP
   WHERE   S.SNO = SP.SNO AND SP.PNO = 'P2'

5. SELECT  S.SNAME
   FROM    S
   WHERE   0 <
           ( SELECT  COUNT(*)
             FROM    SP
             WHERE   SP.SNO = S.SNO AND SP.PNO = 'P2' )

6. SELECT  S.SNAME
   FROM    S
   WHERE   'P2' IN
           ( SELECT SP.PNO
             FROM    SP
             WHERE   SP.SNO = S.SNO )

7. SELECT  S.SNAME
   FROM    S
   WHERE   'P2' =ANY
           ( SELECT SP.PNO
             FROM    SP
             WHERE   SP.SNO = S.SNO )
```

In general, the WHERE clause

```
WHERE x $ANY ( SELECT y FROM T WHERE p )
```

(where $ is any one of =, >, etc.) is equivalent to the WHERE clause

```
WHERE EXISTS ( SELECT * FROM T WHERE (p) AND x $ T.y )
```

Likewise, the WHERE clause

```
WHERE x $ALL ( SELECT y FROM T WHERE p )
```

is equivalent to the WHERE clause

```
WHERE NOT EXISTS ( SELECT * FROM T WHERE (p)
                                    AND NOT ( x $ T.y ) )
```

Note added in second edition: After the above was first written, I realized that the "equivalences" shown are not totally valid, owing to the anomalous behavior of EXISTS in SQL when nulls are present. Refer to Chapter 10 (Section 10.9) of this book for further discussion. *End of note.*

As a matter of fact, it is not just the comparison operators =ANY (etc.) that are redundant; the entire "IN subquery" construct could be removed from SQL with no loss of function at all! (Nested table- and column-expressions etc. would of course still be required, as argued earlier.) This is ironic, since it was the subquery notion that was the justification for the "Structured" in "Structured Query Language" in the first place.

Comment: In fact, subqueries per se were one of the worst mistakes of all! This point should have been called out explicitly as one of the "Mistakes" in this section. *End of comment.*

F.9 ASPECTS OF THE RELATIONAL MODEL NOT SUPPORTED

There are several aspects of the full relational model (as defined in, e.g., reference [2]) that SQL does not currently support. They are listed here in approximate order of importance. Again, of course, most of these features can be added to SQL at some later point—the sooner the better, in most cases. However, their omission now leads to a number of situations in current SQL that are extremely ad hoc and may be difficult to remedy later on, for compatibility reasons.

Comment: Primary and foreign key support, at least, has subsequently been added, but (as the foregoing suggests) it is indeed proving difficult to remedy some of the sins of the past. Furthermore, the primary and foreign key support is still not all that good (it suffers from a great deal of unnecessary complexity, as indicated earlier in this book). *End of comment.*

Primary Keys

Primary keys provide the sole record-level addressing mechanism within the relational model. That is, the *only* system-guaranteed method of identifying an individual record is via the combination (R,k), where R is the name of the containing relation and k is the primary key value for the record concerned. Every relation (to *be* a relation) is required to have a primary key. Primary keys are (of course) required to be unique; in the case of real (i.e., base) relations, they are also required to be wholly nonnull.

> *Comment:* In fact, of course, the relational model requires every relation to satisfy the requirement that there be *no duplicate rows* (this is implied by the primary key requirement). The fact that SQL does permit duplicate rows should be regarded as another grave mistake in the original design of the language. *End of comment.*

SQL currently provides mechanisms that allow users to apply the primary key discipline for themselves (if they so choose), but does not understand the semantics associated with that discipline. As a result, SQL support for certain other functions is either deficient or lacking entirely, as I now explain.

1. Consider the query

```
SELECT  P.PNO, P.WEIGHT, AVG ( SP.QTY )
FROM    P, SP
WHERE   P.PNO = SP.PNO
GROUP   BY P.PNO, P.WEIGHT
```

The "P.WEIGHT" in the GROUP BY clause is logically redundant, but must be included because SQL does not understand that P.WEIGHT is single-valued per part number (i.e., that parts have only one weight). This may be only a minor annoyance, but it could be puzzling to the user.

2. Primary key support is prerequisite to foreign key support (see the following subsection). This is probably the most significant justification for supporting primary keys in the first place, as a matter of fact.

> *Comment:* Primary key support is *not* prerequisite to foreign key support in the standard!—another mistake. *End of comment.*

3. An understanding of primary keys is required in order to support the updating of views correctly. SQL's rules for the updating of views are in fact disgracefully ad hoc. I consider projection, restriction, and join views in some detail here; further discussion of this topic can be found in reference [7]. *Note:* I assume in each case that the data underlying the view is itself updatable, of course.

(a) Projections are logically updatable if and only if they preserve the primary key of the underlying relation. However, SQL supports updates, not on projections per se, but on what might be called *column subsets*— where a "column subset" is any subset of the columns of the underlying table for which duplicate elimination is not requested (via DISTINCT)—with a "user beware" if that subset does not in fact include the underlying primary key. (Actually the situation is even worse than this. Even a column subset is not updatable if the FROM clause in the definition of that subset lists multiple tables. Moreover, updates are prohibited if duplicate elimination is requested, even if that request can have no effect because the column subset does include the underlying primary key.)

(b) Any restriction is logically updatable. SQL however does not permit such updates if duplicate elimination is requested (even though such a request can have no effect if the underlying table does have a primary key), nor if the FROM clause lists multiple tables. What is more, even when it does allow updates, SQL does not always check that updated records satisfy the restriction predicate; hence, an updated (or inserted) record may instantaneously vanish from the view, and moreover there are concomitant security exposures (e.g., a user who is restricted to accessing employees with salary less than $40K may nevertheless *create* a salary greater than that value via INSERT or UPDATE). [*Note:* The CHECK option, which is intended to prevent such abuses, cannot always be specified.] Also, the fact that SQL automatically supplies null values for missing fields in inserted records means that it is *impossible* for such records to satisfy the restriction predicate in some cases (consider, for example, the view "employees in department D3," if the view does not include the DEPTNO field). However, these latter deficiencies are nothing to do with SQL's lack of knowledge of primary keys per se.

(c) A join of two tables on their primary keys is logically updatable. So also is a join of one table on its primary key to another on a matching foreign key (though the details are not totally straightforward). However, SQL does not currently allow *any* join to be updated.

Foreign Keys

Foreign keys provide the principal referencing mechanism within the relational model. Loosely speaking, a foreign key is a field in one table whose values are required to match values of the primary key in another table. For example, field DEPTNO of the EMP table is a foreign key matching the primary key (DEPTNO) of the DEPT table.

SQL does not currently provide any kind of support for the foreign key concept at all. I regard lack of such support as the major deficiency in relational systems today (SQL is certainly not alone in this regard). One approach to providing such support is documented in some detail in reference [7].

Domains

SQL currently provides no support for domains at all, except inasmuch as the fundamental data types (INTEGER, FLOAT, etc.) can be regarded as a very primitive kind of domain.

Relation Assignment

A limited form of relation assignment is supported via INSERT . . . SELECT, but that operation does not overwrite the previous content of the target table, and the source of the assignment cannot be an arbitrary algebraic expression (or SQL equivalent).

Explicit JOIN

At present, SQL provides only rather circumlocutory support for the relational join operation (*very* circumlocutory, in the case of natural join). This observation is still more applicable to *outer* join. Reference [4] shows how awkward it is to extend the circumlocutory SELECT-style join to handle outer joins. Thus, support for an explicit JOIN operator is likely to become even more desirable in the future than it is already.

Explicit INTERSECT and DIFFERENCE

These omissions are not particularly serious (equivalent SELECT-expressions exist in each case); however, symmetry would suggest that, since UNION *is* explicitly supported, INTERSECT and DIFFERENCE ought to be explicitly supported too. Some problems are most "naturally" formulated in terms of explicit intersections and differences. On the other hand, as indicated earlier, it is usually not a good idea to provide a multiplicity of equivalent ways of formulating the same problem, unless it can be guaranteed that the implementation will recognize the equivalences and will treat all formulations in the same way, which is probably unlikely.

F.10 SUMMARY AND CONCLUSIONS

I have discussed a large number of deficiencies and shortcomings in the SQL language as currently defined. I have also suggested how matters might be improved in many cases. The primary purpose of the paper has been to identify certain problems, and thereby to try to contribute to the solution of those problems, before their influence becomes too irrevocably widespread. As mentioned earlier, many of the shortcomings have in fact already been addressed to some extent in the proposals of the ANSI Database Committee X3H2 [10]; the paper may thus also be seen as a rationale and justification for some of the decisions of that committee. I hasten to add, however, that the paper has no official status whatsoever—specifically, it carries no endorsement from ANSI or X3H2. Everything in it is entirely my own responsibility.

> *Comment:* Many of the X3H2 decisions referred to approvingly above were subsequently reversed. *End of comment.*

Of course, I realize that many of the deficiencies I have been discussing will very likely be dismissed as academic, trivial, or otherwise unimportant by many people, especially as SQL is so clearly superior to older languages such as the DML of DBTG. However, experience shows that "academic" considerations have a nasty habit of becoming horribly practical a few years further down the road. The mistakes we make now will come back to haunt us in the future. Indeed, the language in its present form is already proving difficult to extend in some (desirable) ways because of limitations in its present structure. A very trivial example is provided by the problems of adding support for composite fields or minor structures.

In conclusion, I should like to emphasize the point that most other database languages today suffer from deficiencies similar to those discussed in this paper; SQL is (as stated before) certainly not the sole offender. But the fact is that SQL is likely to be the most influential of those languages, for reasons adequately discussed earlier; and if it is adopted on a wide scale in its present form, then we will to some degree have missed the relational boat, or at least failed to capitalize to the fullest possible extent on the potential of the relational model. That would be a pity, because we had an opportunity to do it right, and with a little effort we could have done so. The question is whether it is now too late. I sincerely hope not.

F.11   ACKNOWLEDGMENTS

I am very pleased to acknowledge the helpful comments and criticisms I received on earlier drafts of this paper from my friends and colleagues Ted Codd, Phil Shaw, and Sharon Weinberg.

F.12   REFERENCES

1. M. M. Astrahan et al. "System R: Relational Approach to Database Management." *ACM TODS* 1, No. 2 (June 1976).

2. E. F. Codd. "Extending the Database Relational Model to Capture More Meaning." *ACM TODS* 4, No. 4 (December 1979).

3. C. J. Date. "Some Principles of Good Language Design." In *Relational Database: Selected Writings*, by C. J. Date (Addison-Wesley, 1986).

4. C. J. Date. "The Outer Join." In *Relational Database: Selected Writings*, by C. J. Date (Addison-Wesley, 1986).

5. C. J. Date. "An Introduction to the Unified Database Language (UDL)." In *Relational Database: Selected Writings*, by C. J. Date (Addison-Wesley, 1986).

6. C. J. Date. "Null Values in Database Management." In *Relational Database: Selected Writings*, by C. J. Date (Addison-Wesley, 1986).

7. C. J. Date and Colin J. White. *A Guide to DB2* (3rd edition, Addison-Wesley, 1989).

8. J. N. Gray. Private communication.

9. J. N. Gray et al. "Granularity of Locks in a Large Shared Data Base." *Proc. 1st International Conference on Very Large Data Bases,* Framingham, Mass. (September 1975).

10. X3H2 (American National Standards Database Committee). Draft Proposed Relational Database Language. Document X3H2–83–152 (August 1983).

Bibliography

1. American National Standards Institute: *Database Language SQL*, Document ANSI X3.135–1986. Also available as International Standards Organization Document ISO/TC97/SC21/WG3 N117.

   The original standard SQL definition (and the principal subject of the present book).

2. American National Standards Institute: *Database Language SQL Addendum-1*. Document ANSI X3.135.1–1989. Also available as International Standards Organization Document ISO/TC97/SC21/WG3 DBL AMS-10.

   Defines the Integrity Enhancement Feature.

3. American National Standards Institute/International Standards Organization: *ISO-ANSI (working draft) Database Language SQL2*. Document ANSI X3H2-88-259/ISO DBL SYD-2.

   The current officially proposed extensions to the standard ("SQL2"—see Chapter 12 of the present book).

4. X/OPEN: *Relational Database Language (SQL) Portability Guide* (January 1987).

   Defines the X/OPEN standard.

5. IBM Corp.: *Systems Application Architecture Common Programming Interface: Database Reference*. IBM Document No. SC26-4348.

   Defines IBM's SAA standard.

6. E. F. Codd: "A Relational Model of Data for Large Shared Data Banks." *Communications of the ACM*, Vol. 13, No. 6 (June 1970); reprinted in *Communications of the ACM*, Vol. 26, No. 1 (January 1983).

   The paper that (apart from some early internal IBM papers, also by Codd) first proposed the ideas of the relational model.

7. C. J. Date: *An Introduction to Database Systems: Volume I* (4th edition, Addison-Wesley, 1985); *Volume II* (1st edition, Addison-Wesley, 1983).

   These two volumes between them provide a basis for a comprehensive education in most aspects of database technology. In particular, they include a very detailed treatment of the relational approach.

8. D. D. Chamberlin and R. F. Boyce: "SEQUEL: A Structured English Query Language." *Proc. ACM SIGMOD Workshop on Data Description, Access, and Control,* Ann Arbor, Mich. (May 1974).

   The paper that first introduced the SQL language (or SEQUEL, as it was originally called).

9. M. M. Astrahan and R. A. Lorie: "SEQUEL-XRM: A Relational System." *Proc. ACM Pacific Regional Conference,* San Francisco, Calif. (April 1975).

   Describes the first prototype implementation of SEQUEL.

10. D. D. Chamberlin et al.: "SEQUEL 2: A Unified Approach to Data Definition, Manipulation, and Control." *IBM J. R&D*, Vol. 20, No. 6 (November 1976). See also errata in January 1977 issue.

    Describes the revised version of SEQUEL called SEQUEL/2.

11. M. M. Astrahan et al.: "System R: Relational Approach to Database Management." *ACM Transactions on Database Systems*, Vol. 1, No. 2 (June 1976).

    System R was intended as a major prototype implementation of the SEQUEL/2 (later SQL) language. This paper describes the architecture of System R as originally planned.

12. D. D. Chamberlin: "A Summary of User Experience with the SQL Data Sublanguage." *Proc. International Conference on Databases,* Aberdeen, Scotland (July 1980).

    Includes details of several enhancements and revisions to SQL (previously SEQUEL/2) that were made during the lifetime of the System R project.

13. D. D. Chamberlin et al.: "A History and Evaluation of System R." *Communications of the ACM*, Vol. 24, No. 10 (October 1981).

    Describes the pioneering work on relational implementation technology (specifically, on optimization technology) done as part of the System R project.

14. C. J. Date: *Relational Database: Selected Writings* (Addison-Wesley, 1986).

    A collection of papers on various aspects of relational database management, including several on the SQL language.

15. C. J. Date: *A Guide to INGRES* (Addison-Wesley, 1987); (with Colin J. White) *A Guide to SQL/DS* (Addison-Wesley, 1988); *A Guide to DB2* (3rd edition, Addison-Wesley, 1989). Colin J. White: *A Guide to ORACLE* (Addison-Wesley, to appear).

    Detailed descriptions of some commercially significant SQL implementations.

16. C. J. Date: "Where SQL Falls Short." *Datamation*, May 1, 1987.

    This brief paper shows why SQL is not the panacea it is sometimes claimed to be—not even as a basis for application portability.

17. E. F. Codd: "Fatal Flaws in SQL." Part I, *Datamation*, August 15, 1988; Part II, *Datamation*, August 31, 1988.

    Contains further criticisms of the standard.

Index